COMPUTER
BOOK SERIES
FROM IDG

Approac... For Windows F...

MW01241293

Browse Icons

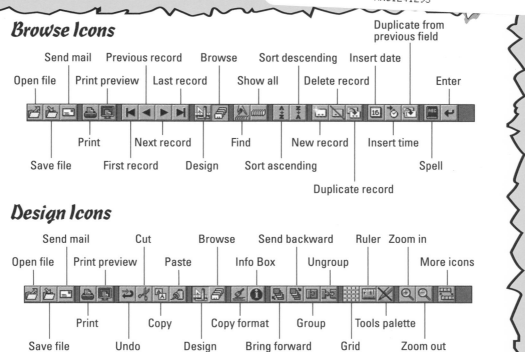

Duplicate from previous field

Send mail — Previous record — Browse — Sort descending — Insert date

Open file — Print preview — Last record — Show all — Delete record — Enter

Print — Next record — Find — New record — Insert time

Save file — First record — Design — Sort ascending — Spell

Duplicate record

Design Icons

Send mail — Cut — Browse — Send backward — Ruler — Zoom in

Open file — Print preview — Paste — Info Box — Ungroup — More icons

Print — Copy — Copy format — Group — Tools palette

Save file — Undo — Design — Bring forward — Grid — Zoom out

Data Entry

Function	Keys
Go to the first record	Ctrl+Home
Go to the last record	Ctrl+End
Go to a specific record	Ctrl+W
Create a new record	Ctrl+N
Hide the record	Ctrl+H
Delete the record	Ctrl+Delete
Print the current view	Ctrl+P

Design Commands

Function	Keys
InfoBox	Ctrl+E
Tools palette	Ctrl+L
Fast format	Ctrl+M
Ruler	Ctrl+J
Snap to grid	Ctrl+Y
Group	Ctrl+G
Ungroup	Ctrl+U
Align	Ctrl+I

. . . For Dummies: #1 Computer Book Series for Beginners

Approach 3 For Windows For Dummies

Cheat Sheet

The Approach Screen

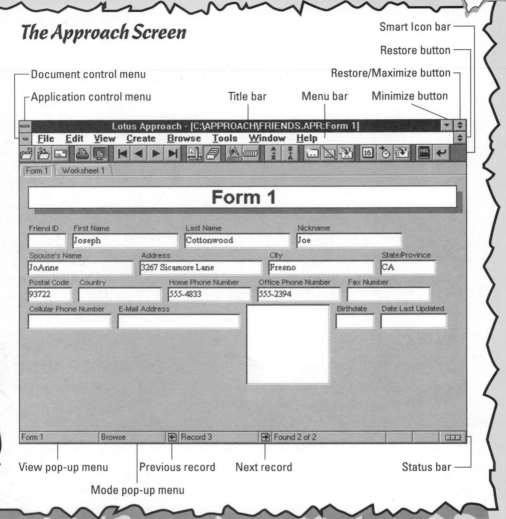

Smart Icon bar

Restore button

Restore/Maximize button

Document control menu

Application control menu

Title bar   Menu bar   Minimize button

View pop-up menu

Previous record   Next record

Mode pop-up menu

Status bar

Changing Modes

Mode	Keys
Design	Ctrl+D
Browse	Ctrl+B
Preview	Ctrl+Shift+B
Find	Ctrl+F

Tools Palette

Select objects — Text box
Rectangle — Ellipse
Rounded rectangle — Line
Field — Check box
Radio button — Macro button
Picture Plus field — Add fields

... For Dummies: #1 Computer Book Series for Beginners

TM

References for the Rest of Us

COMPUTER BOOK SERIES FROM IDG

Are you intimidated and confused by computers? Do you find that traditional manuals are overloaded with technical details you'll never use? Do your friends and family always call you to fix simple problems on their PCs? Then the ... *For Dummies*™ computer book series from IDG is for you.

... *For Dummies* books are written for those frustrated computer users who know they aren't really dumb but find that PC hardware, software, and indeed the unique vocabulary of computing make them feel helpless. ... *For Dummies* books use a lighthearted approach, a down-to-earth style, and even cartoons and humorous icons to diffuse computer novices' fears and build their confidence. Lighthearted but not lightweight, these books are a perfect survival guide to anyone forced to use a computer.

> *"I like my copy so much I told friends; now they bought copies."*
>
> **Irene C., Orwell, Ohio**

> *"Quick, concise, nontechnical, and humorous."*
>
> **Jay A., Elburn, IL**

> *"Thanks, I needed this book. Now I can sleep at night."*
>
> **Robin F., British Columbia, Canada**

Already, hundreds of thousands of satisfied readers agree. They have made ... *For Dummies* books the #1 introductory level computer book series and have written asking for more. So if you're looking for the most fun and easy way to learn about computers, look to ... *For Dummies* books to give you a helping hand.

IDG BOOKS

APPROACH 3
FOR WINDOWS
FOR DUMMIES™

APPROACH 3 FOR WINDOWS FOR DUMMIES™

by Doug Lowe

IDG BOOKS

IDG Books Worldwide, Inc.
An International Data Group Company

San Mateo, California ♦ Indianapolis, Indiana ♦ Boston, Massachusetts

Approach 3 For Windows For Dummies

Published by
IDG Books Worldwide, Inc.
An International Data Group Company
155 Bovet Road, Suite 310
San Mateo, CA 94402

Library of Congress Catalog Card No.: 94-79314

ISBN: 1-56884-233-3

Printed in the United States of America

10 9 8 7 6 5 4 3 2 1

1B/RQ/RQ/ZU

Distributed in the United States by IDG Books Worldwide, Inc.

Distributed in Canada by Macmillan of Canada, a Division of Canada Publishing Corporation; by Computer and Technical Books in Miami, Florida, for South America and the Caribbean; by Longman Singapore in Singapore, Malaysia, Thailand, and Korea; by Toppan Co. Ltd. in Japan; by Asia Computerworld in Hong Kong; by Woodslane Pty. Ltd. in Australia and New Zealand; and by Transworld Publishers Ltd. in the U.K. and Europe.

For general information on IDG Books in the U.S., including information on discounts and premiums, contact IDG Books at 800-434-3422 or 415-312-0650.

For information on where to purchase IDG Books outside the U.S., contact Christina Turner at 415-312-0633.

For information on translations, contact Marc Jeffrey Mikulich, Foreign Rights Manager, at IDG Books Worldwide; FAX NUMBER 415-286-2747.

For sales inquiries and special prices for bulk quantities, write to the address above or call IDG Books Worldwide at 415-312-0650.

For information on using IDG Books in the classroom, or for ordering examination copies, contact Jim Kelly at 800-434-2086.

About the Author

Doug Lowe

Doug Lowe has written 20 computer books or so (including *Networking For Dummies, PowerPoint 4 For Windows For Dummies,* and *MORE Word For Windows 6 For Dummies)* and knows how to present technobabble in a style that is both entertaining and enlightening. He is a contributing editor for the magazines *DOS Resource Guide* and *Maximize.*

ABOUT IDG BOOKS WORLDWIDE

Welcome to the world of IDG Books Worldwide.

IDG Books Worldwide, Inc., is a subsidiary of International Data Group, the world's largest publisher of business and computer-related information and the leading global provider of information services on information technology. IDG was founded more than 25 years ago and now employs more than 5,700 people worldwide. IDG publishes more than 200 computer publications in 63 countries (see listing below). Forty million people read one or more IDG publications each month.

Launched in 1990, IDG Books is today the fastest-growing publisher of computer and business books in the United States. We are proud to have received 3 awards from the Computer Press Association in recognition of editorial excellence, and our best-selling ...For Dummies series has more than 10 million copies in print with translations in more than 20 languages. IDG Books, through a recent joint venture with IDG's Hi-Tech Beijing, became the first U.S. publisher to publish a computer book in the People's Republic of China. In record time, IDG Books has become the first choice for millions of readers around the world who want to learn how to better manage their businesses.

Our mission is simple: Every IDG book is designed to bring extra value and skill-building instructions to the reader. Our books are written by experts who understand and care about our readers. The knowledge base of our editorial staff comes from years of experience in publishing, education, and journalism — experience which we use to produce books for the '90s. In short, we care about books, so we attract the best people. We devote special attention to details such as audience, interior design, use of icons, and illustrations. And because we use an efficient process of authoring, editing, and desktop publishing our books electronically, we can spend more time ensuring superior content and spend less time on the technicalities of making books.

You can count on our commitment to deliver high-quality books at competitive prices on topics customers want to read about. At IDG, we value quality, and we have been delivering quality for more than 25 years. You'll find no better book on a subject than an IDG book.

John J. Kilcullen

John Kilcullen
President and CEO
IDG Books Worldwide, Inc.

WINNER
Eighth Annual Computer Press Awards 1992

WINNER
Ninth Annual Computer Press Awards 1993

IDG BOOKS

IDG Books Worldwide, Inc., is a subsidiary of International Data Group. The officers are Patrick J. McGovern, Founder and Board Chairman; Walter Boyd, President. International Data Group's publications include: **ARGENTINA'S** Computerworld Argentina, Infoworld Argentina; **AUSTRALIA'S** Computerworld Australia, Australian PC World, Australian Macworld, Network World, Mobile Business Australia, Reseller, IDG Sources; **AUSTRIA'S** Computerwelt Oesterreich, PC Test; **BRAZIL'S** Computerworld, Gamepro, Game Power, Mundo IBM, Mundo Unix, PC World, Super Game; **BELGIUM'S** Data News (CW) **BULGARIA'S** Computerworld Bulgaria, Ediworld, PC & Mac World Bulgaria, Network World Bulgaria; **CANADA'S** CIO Canada, Computerworld Canada, Graduate Computerworld, InfoCanada, Network World Canada; **CHILE'S** Computerworld Chile, Informatica; **COLOMBIA'S** Computerworld Colombia, PC World; **CZECH REPUBLIC'S** Computerworld, Elektronika, PC World; **DENMARK'S** Communications World, Computerworld Danmark, Macintosh Produktkatalog, Macworld Danmark, PC World Danmark, PC World Produktguide, Tech World, Windows World; **ECUADOR'S** PC World Ecuador; **EGYPT'S** Computerworld (CW) Middle East, PC World Middle East; **FINLAND'S** MikroPC, Tietoviikko, Tietoverkko; **FRANCE'S** Distributique, GOLDEN MAC, InfoPC, Languages & Systems, Le Guide du Monde Informatique, Le Monde Informatique, Telecoms & Reseaux; **GERMANY'S** Computerwoche, Computerwoche Focus, Computerwoche Extra, Computerwoche Karriere, Information Management, Macwelt, Netzwelt, PC Welt, PC Woche, Publish, Unit; **GREECE'S** Infoworld, PC Games; **HUNGARY'S** Computerworld SZT, PC World; **HONG KONG'S** Computerworld Hong Kong, PC World Hong Kong; **INDIA'S** Computers & Communications; **IRELAND'S** ComputerScope; **ISRAEL'S** Computerworld Israel, PC World Israel; **ITALY'S** Computerworld Italia, Lotus Magazine, Macworld Italia, Networking Italia, PC Shopping, PC World Italia; **JAPAN'S** Computerworld Today, Information Systems World, Macworld Japan, Nikkei Personal Computing, SunWorld Japan, Windows World; **KENYA'S** East African Computer News; **KOREA'S** Computerworld Korea, Macworld Korea, PC World Korea; **MEXICO'S** Compu Edicion, Compu Manufactura, Computacion/Punto de Venta, Computerworld Mexico, MacWorld, Mundo Unix, PC World, Windows; **THE NETHERLANDS'** Computer! Totaal, Computable (CW), LAN Magazine, MacWorld, Totaal "Windows"; **NEW ZEALAND'S** Computer Listings, Computerworld New Zealand, New Zealand PC World, Network World; **NIGERIA'S** PC World Africa; **NORWAY'S** Computerworld Norge, C/World, Lotusworld Norge, Macworld Norge, Networld, PC World Ekspress, PC World Norge, PC World's Produktguide, Publish& Multimedia World, Student Data, Unix World, Windowsworld; IDG Direct Response; **PAKISTAN'S** PC World Pakistan; **PANAMA'S** PC World Panama; **PERU'S** Computerworld Peru, PC World; **PEOPLE'S REPUBLIC OF CHINA'S** China Computerworld, China Infoworld, Electronics Today/Multimedia World, Electronics International, Electronic Product World, China Network World, PC and Communications Magazine, PC World China, Software World Magazine, Telecom Product World; IDG HIGH TECH BEIJING'S New Product World; IDG SHENZHEN'S Computer News Digest; **PHILIPPINES'** Computerworld Philippines, PC Digest (PCW); **POLAND'S** Computerworld Poland, PC World/Komputer; **PORTUGAL'S** Cerebro/PC World, Correio Informatico/Computerworld, Informatica & Comunicacoes Catalogo, MacIn, Nacional de Produtos; **ROMANIA'S** Computerworld, PC World; **RUSSIA'S** Computerworld-Moscow, Mir - PC, Sety; **SINGAPORE'S** Computerworld Southeast Asia, PC World Singapore; **SLOVENIA'S** Monitor Magazine; **SOUTH AFRICA'S** Computer Mail (CIO), Computing S.A., Network World S.A., Software World; **SPAIN'S** Advanced Systems, Amiga World, Computerworld Espana, Communicacions World, Macworld Espana, NeXTWORLD, Super Juegos Magazine (GamePro), PC World Espana, Publish; **SWEDEN'S** Attack, ComputerSweden, Corporate Computing, Natverk & Kommunikation, Macworld, Mikrodatorn, PC World, Publishing & Design (CAP), Datalngenjoren, Maxi Data, Windows World; **SWITZERLAND'S** Computerworld Schweiz, Macworld Schweiz, PC Tip; **TAIWAN'S** Computerworld Taiwan, PC World Taiwan; **THAILAND'S** Thai Computerworld; **TURKEY'S** Computerworld Monitor, Macworld Turkiye, PC World Turkiye; **UKRAINE'S** Computerworld; **UNITED KINGDOM'S** Computing /Computerworld, Connexion/Network World, Lotus Magazine, Macworld, Open Computing/Sunworld; **UNITED STATES'** Advanced Systems, AmigaWorld, Cable in the Classroom, CD Review, CIO, Computerworld, Digital Video, DOS Resource Guide, Electronic Entertainment Magazine, Federal Computer Week, Federal Integrator, GamePro, IDG Books, Infoworld, Infoworld Direct, Laser Event, Macworld, Multimedia World, Network World, PC Letter, PC World, PlayRight, Power PC World, Publish, SWATPro, Video Event; **VENEZUELA'S** Computerworld Venezuela, PC World; **VIETNAM'S** PC World Vietnam

Acknowledgments

Thanks to Pat Seiler for wrestling with my prose and transforming it into a readable form, for keeping track of all those figures, icons, and buttons that threatened to fall through the cracks, and for not interpreting the meaning of the word *deadline* too literally (whew!). Thanks also to Kristin Cocks for keeping things moving along and helping in myriad other ways and to Megg Bonar and Janna Custer here on the Left Coast for signing me up to do this book in the first place.

Thanks also to Lotus's own Paul Santinelli for an excellent technical review, especially in light of his carefully-timed wedding. Good luck, Paul....

Oh, and thanks to all those people who are listed in the Help⇨About box for creating a great product.

(The publisher would like to give special thanks to Patrick J. McGovern, without whom this book would not have been possible.)

Credits

Publisher
David Solomon

Managing Editor
Mary Bednarek

Acquisitions Editor
Megg Bonar

Production Director
Beth Jenkins

Senior Editors
Tracy L. Barr
Sandra Blackthorn
Diane Graves Steele

Associate Production Coordinator
Valery Bourke

Pre-Press Coordinator
Steve Peake

Editorial Assistants
Suki Gear
Laura Schaible

Project Editors
Pat Seiler
Kristin A. Cocks

Technical Reviewer
Paul A. Santinelli, Jr.

Production Staff
Paul Belcastro
Linda M. Boyer
Sherry Dickinson Gomoll
Drew R. Moore
Carla Radzikinas
Dwight Ramsey
Patricia R. Reynolds
Gina Scott

Cover Design
Kavish+Kavish

Proofreader
Sandra Profant

Indexer
Steve Rath

Book Design
University Graphics

Contents at a Glance

Cartoons at a Glance

By Rich Tennant

Page 249

Page 201

Page 96

Page 189

Page 83

Page 109

Page 7

Page 315

Page 220

Page 287

Table of Contents

Introduction

. . . .

*W*elcome to *Approach 3 For Windows For Dummies,* the book written especially for those of you who are forced to use Approach at gunpoint and want to learn just enough to save your neck.

Has your boss just dumped a shoe box full of customer receipts and ordered you to organize them into a database by Tuesday or find a new job? You need Approach! Are you frustrated because your seven-year-old version of PC-CheaperBase can't create the reports you need? You need Approach! Have you all but given up on figuring out how to send out 400 letters to the parents at your kid's school to beg for donations to the PTA? You *really* need Approach!

Or maybe you're one of those hapless chaps who bought Lotus SmartSuite because it was such a bargain and you needed a Windows word processor and a spreadsheet anyway and, hey, you're not even sure what Approach is, but it was practically free and you love things that are free. What now?

Good news! You've found the right book. Help is here, within these humble pages.

This book talks about Approach in everyday — and often irreverent — terms. No lofty prose here; the whole thing checks in at about the fifth-grade reading level. I have no Pulitzer expectations for this book (maybe one of these days I'll write a novel about the Civil War). My goal is to make an otherwise dull and lifeless subject at least tolerable, if not kind of fun.

About This Book

This book isn't the kind of book you pick up and read from start to finish, as if it were a cheap novel. If I ever see you reading it at the beach, I'll kick sand in your face. This book is more like a reference, the kind of book you can pick up, turn to just about any page, and start reading. It has 28 chapters, each one covering a specific aspect of using Approach — such as printing reports, using macros, or joining databases. Just turn to the chapter you're interested in and start reading.

Each chapter is divided into self-contained chunks, all related to the major theme of the chapter.

For example, the chapter on drawing pictures on database forms contains nuggets such as these:

- Drawing simple lines and shapes
- Drawing text objects
- Creating drop shadows, embossed effects, and other fancy looks
- Understanding layers and groups
- Lining things up
- Stealing pictures from other programs

You don't have to memorize anything in this book. It's a "need-to-know" book: you pick it up when you need to know something. Need to know how to create a new form? Pick up the book. Need to know how to add a picture to your database? Pick up the book. Otherwise, put it down and get on with your life.

How to Use This Book

This book works like a reference. Start with the topic that you want to learn about and look for it in the table of contents or in the index to get going. The table of contents is detailed enough that you should be able to find most of the topics you'll look for. If not, turn to the index, where you'll find even more detail.

After you find your topic in the table of contents or the index, turn to the area of interest and read as much or as little as you need or want. Then close the book and get to it.

On occasion, this book directs you to use specific keyboard shortcuts to get things done. When you see something like this

```
Ctrl+Z
```

it means to hold down the Ctrl key while you press the Z key and then release both keys at the same time. Don't type the plus sign.

Sometimes I tell you to use a menu command, such as this one:

```
File⇨Open
```

This line means to use the keyboard or mouse to open the File menu, and then select the Open command. (The underlined letters are the keyboard hot-letters for the command. To use them, first press the Alt key. In the preceding example, you would press and release the Alt key, press and release the F key, and then press and release the O key.)

Whenever I describe a message or information that you'll see on the screen, it looks like this:

```
Are we having fun yet?
```

Anything you are instructed to type appears in boldface type, like so: Type **B:SETUP** in the Run dialog box. You type exactly what you see, with or without spaces.

Another little nicety about this book is that when you are directed to click one of those little icon buttons that litter Approach's screen, a picture of the button appears in the margin. It's there so that you know what the button looks like when you need to find it on the screen.

This book rarely directs you elsewhere for information — just about everything you need to know about using Approach is right here. On occasion, I'll suggest that you turn to *DOS For Dummies* (by Dan Gookin) or *Windows For Dummies* (by Andy Rathbone) for more specific information about ancient Egypt and the etymology of certain Klingon words — oops — I mean DOS and Windows. Both books are published by IDG Books Worldwide.

What You Don't Need to Read

Much of this book is skippable. I've carefully placed extra-technical information in self-contained sidebars and clearly marked them so you can give them a wide berth. Don't read this stuff unless you just *have* to know and you feel really lucky. Don't worry; I won't be offended if you don't read every word.

Foolish Assumptions

I'm making only three assumptions about you:

- ✔ You use a computer.
- ✔ You use Windows.
- ✔ You use or are thinking about using Approach 3.0.

Nothing else. I don't assume that you're a computer guru who knows how to change a controller card or configure memory for optimal usage. Such computer chores are best handled by people who *like* computers. I hope that you are on speaking terms with such a person. Do your best to keep it that way.

How This Book Is Organized

Inside this book, chapters are arranged into five parts. Each chapter is divided into sections that cover various aspects of the chapter's main subject. The chapters are in a logical sequence, so reading them in order makes sense if you want to read the book that way. But you don't have to read them in order. You can flip the book open to any page and start reading.

Here's the low down on what's in each of the five parts:

Part I: Basic Approach Stuff

In this part, you learn the basics of using Approach. This is a good place to start if you're clueless about what Approach is, let alone about how to use it.

Part II: Polishing Your Database

The six chapters in this part show you how to create top-quality Approach databases that not only work, but also look good. You learn how to make spiffy forms and reports that help you get all the right information into and out of your database, plus how to embellish databases with pictures, sounds, and other fancy stuff.

Part III: Getting Real Work Done

The chapters in this part show you how to create form letters, mailing labels, worksheets, crosstabs, and charts.

Part IV: Definitely Database Grad School Stuff

The four chapters in this part are for those adventurous souls who want to go a bit beyond the basics. These chapters show you how to create and use macros, how to run Approach on a network, how to customize Approach's preferences, and how to convert data to and from other file formats.

Part V: The Part of Tens

This wouldn't be a... *For Dummies* book without lists of interesting snippets: Ten Database Commandments, Ten Things That Often Go Wrong, Ten Approach Shortcuts, Ten New Features of Approach 3.0, and so on.

Part VI: The Appendixes

A free bonus appendix shows you how to install Approach, and another one explains how to survive the dreaded File Manager. Sorry, no Ginsu knives. Also, you'll find a glossary that takes the mystery out of all those esoteric database terms computer gurus tend to bandy about.

Icons Used in This Book

As you are reading all this wonderful prose, you'll occasionally see the following icons. They appear in the margins to draw your attention to important information.

Did I tell you about the memory course I took?

Watch out! Some technical drivel is just around the corner. Read only if you have your pocket protector firmly attached.

Pay special attention to this icon — it lets you know that some particularly useful tidbit is at hand, perhaps a shortcut or a way of using a command you might not have considered.

Danger! Danger! Danger! Stand back, Will Robinson!

Where to Go from Here

Yes, you can get there from here. With this book in hand, you're ready to charge full speed ahead into the strange and wonderful world of Approach. Browse through the table of contents and decide where you want to start. Be bold! Be courageous! Be adventurous! Above all else, have fun!

Part I
Basic Approach Stuff

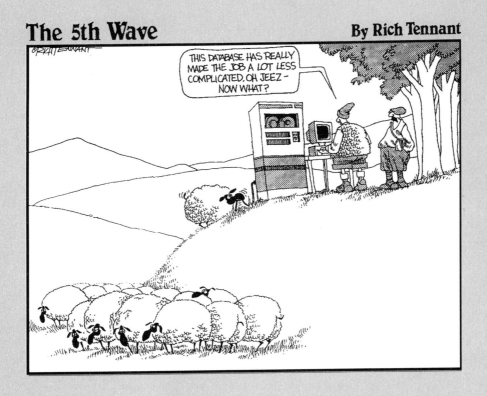

In this part ...

Just a few short years ago, database programs were so complicated that only true computer gurus, brandishing pocket-protectors and taped-together glasses, would dare to use them. Now Lotus Approach brings the power of relational database management (whatever that means) to the average user. Oh boy.

The chapters in this part comprise a bare-bones introduction to Approach. You learn what Approach is and how to use it to create simple databases. More advanced stuff, such as database joins, mail-merge, and incorporating graphics into a database, is covered in later chapters. This part is just the beginning. As a great king once advised, begin at the beginning and go on 'til you come to the end; then stop.

Chapter 1

Database 101

● ●

In This Chapter

▶ Introducing databases in general and Approach in particular

▶ Looking at database data

▶ Starting Approach and creating a new database

▶ Filling out a form

▶ Using a worksheet

▶ Printing a database

▶ Saving, retrieving, and closing a database

▶ Exiting Approach

● ●

*T*his chapter is sort of the kindergarten of Approach. It takes your hand and walks you around, telling you what a database program is and what you can do with one, explaining why Approach is such a great database program, and showing you how to start Approach and deal with its moods. If you get tired midway through this chapter, feel free to have some milk and graham crackers and maybe even take a nap.

What the Hex Is a Database?

It's time to put on your pointy cap, sharpen your Number 2 pencil, and prepare yourself for a definition. Here it is: a *database* is a collection of information. Here are some examples of databases from everyday life:

✔ Your personal address book

✔ The shoe box that contains your tax records for the year

✔ Your baseball card collection

✔ All those parking tickets conveniently stuffed into your car's glove compartment

- ✔ The phone book
- ✔ That pile of score cards that has been accumulating in the bottom of your golf bag for 15 years
- ✔ For you compulsive types, your Rolodex file and your Day Timer

You can think of each of these databases as a collection of records. In the database *lingua franca* (that's not a type of pasta), a *record* consists of all the useful information you can gather about a particular thing. In your address book, each record represents one of your friends or enemies. For your tax records database, each receipt in the shoe box is a record. Each baseball card in your card collection is a record, as is each parking ticket stuffed into the glove box.

Each little snippet of information that makes up a record is called a *field*. Using the address book as an example once again, each person's record — that is, each entry in the address book — consists of several fields: name, street address, city, state, zip code, and phone number. It also may include other information, such as the person's birthday, whether you received a Christmas card from that person last year, and how much money that person owes you.

An Approach database is much like these noncomputerized databases. Like your address book or shoe box full of tax records, an Approach database is a collection of records, and each record is a collection of fields. The biggest difference is that when you use Approach, your database is recorded on the computer's hard disk rather than on paper. Using the hard disk gives Approach several distinct advantages over address books and shoe boxes. For example, searching an Approach database for a particular receipt is much easier than riffling through an overstuffed shoe box.

Approach automatically keeps records organized and enables you to conduct a search for particular records that is based on any field in the record. For example, if you kept your address book as an Approach database, you could quickly print a list of all your friends who live in Iowa and owe you more than $10. Try that trick with your noncomputerized address book.

As the old saying goes, there's no such thing as a free lunch; and Approach is no exception. Approach does have some disadvantages when compared with an old-fashioned address book or a shoe box. For starters, Approach (and any other computerized database program, for that matter) forces you to think ahead before you start saving data in a database. Before you can add information to an Approach database, you have to *design* the database. Yuck. Fortunately, Approach comes with a bevy of already-designed databases for such common uses as address books, business contacts, inventories, and even a wine list. But you still have to look at the fields provided by these database templates, add fields you want that are missing, and remove fields that you don't need. Fortunately, you can easily add fields later if you forget some important detail that you just have to keep track of. So designing a database isn't something to lose sleep over.

TECHNICAL STUFF

Relational nonsense you should skip

One of the most used and abused buzzwords in the computer business is *relational database*. The term *relational database* has at least four common meanings:

✔ A type of database in which data is stored in tables made up of rows and columns, and relationships are established among the various tables. These relationships are based on common information that is stored in both fields — for example, a customer table and an invoice table may both have a customer number field that enables you to establish a relationship between the tables. Hence the name, *relational database*.

This definition sounds kind of like a Tim Allen routine. "Say Al, do you think they call it a *relational database* because it's good at dealing with relationships?"

"I don't think so, Tim."

Actually, Al's response is correct. Relational databases do not get their name from the fact that you can create relationships among tables. See the second definition to find out why.

✔ A database model that is based upon a Conehead branch of mathematics called Set Theory.

In mathematics, a *relation* is an unordered set of n-tuples. Never mind what an n-tuple is, because I'm not about to tell you and it doesn't matter anyway. I wouldn't even mention the term, except that I'd like to point out that the term *relational database* is derived from an esoteric mathematical concept that has nothing to do with the way normal people ordinarily use the word *relational*. The term *rela-*

tion refers to the way data is arranged into tables of rows and columns, not to relationships between tables.

(It is a little-known fact that relational database theory was invented at about the same time that the Coneheads from the planet Remulak first came to earth, back in the 1970s. I have always suspected that these two developments are — dare I say it? — *related*.)

On to the third definition.

✔ A religion whose followers believe that the world can be saved only by strict adherence to the essential tenets of the Relational Creed.

A relational database is more than a database model; it is a religion. There was a time when relational database fanatics could be seen passing out tracts at airports. The Great High Priest of the relational faith, E. J. Codd, even made up a list of rules that one must follow to be considered truly relational.

It got so bad that the ACLU tried to stop public schools from teaching about relational databases. The fervor has died down a bit, but there are still many devoted followers.

✔ Any database system developed since 1980, with the exception of a few cutting-edge, object-oriented databases that have recently appeared.

Marketers quickly figured out that the way to sell database programs was to advertise them as relational. Relational zealots had fits when programs such as dBase claimed to be relational, although they clearly violated some aspect of the Relational Catechism. But the marketers prevailed, and just about every database program ever made has claimed to be relational.

(continued)

(continued)
It wasn't until recently, when the new *Object Oriented* religion began to emerge, that database companies started to let go of the relational label. We're now starting to see object-oriented databases. But that's another book. . . .

Where does Approach fit into all of this? It may not qualify as a truly relational database according to all the criteria of the relational creed, but it's pretty darn close. It certainly is as "relational" as other popular database programs, including Access, FoxPro, dBase, and Paradox.

An even bigger drawback of using Approach is that it forces you to use your computer. Double-yuck. You have to deal with such unpleasantries as DOS, Windows, the Program Manager, filenames, directories, mouse clicks and double-clicks, an occasional drag, backing up, and all of the other routine chores of using a computer. Not to mention the simple fact that dropping an address book into your handbag is much easier than dropping a typical desktop computer into it.

If you're uneasy with the basic aspects of using your computer, check out *PCs For Dummies* by Dan Gookin and Andy Rathbone. For more specific information about working with Windows, see *Windows For Dummies* by Andy Rathbone. Both books are published by IDG Books Worldwide.

What's So Hot about Approach?

Approach is different from most database programs. For years, full-fledged database programs have been considered too complicated for typical computer users. Only computer gurus were expected to do any reasonable work with programs such as dBase IV or Paradox. The less knowledgeable were expected to use watered-down database programs that were easier to use but too limited in function to be useful for anything more complicated than simple address lists. (These watered-down programs are often called *flat-file* databases by relational database snobs.)

Approach is one of the first database programs that is as powerful as dBase IV or Paradox but is easy enough for mere mortals to use. You don't have to have a Ph.D. in computer science or seven years of programming experience to use Approach to set up even a sophisticated database.

Here are a few of the nifty features that make Approach one of the best database programs available:

- ✔ Approach comes with a truckload of predefined database templates that you can use out of the box or modify to suit your needs. Many of these templates are designed to work together for complete business applications.

- ✔ A feature called SmartMasters enables you to create great-looking database entry forms and reports without the hassle of setting dozens of formatting options individually.

- ✔ Approach can work with existing databases that have been created with dBase III or dBase IV, Paradox 3.5 or 4.0 (including Paradox for Windows), FoxPro 2.1, Lotus Notes, and other file formats that you've probably never heard of, such as Microsoft/Sybase SQL Server Oracle SQL, or IBM's DB2. It works directly with these file formats, sparing you the drudgery of a complicated conversion process.

- ✔ Approach enables you to join data from two or more databases. For example, suppose that you own a video rental store and you have two databases: one containing customer information and the other containing information about the video tapes. By joining these databases, you can easily display a list of all the video tapes that are currently rented to a particular customer. The customer's name and address would come from the customer database, and the video tape information would be obtained from the video tape database. (This important feature is standard fare for muscle-bound database programs such as dBase or Paradox, but it is a rarity in more down-to-earth database programs such as Approach.)

- ✔ Approach is automatically set up to work on a network. No fancy network twiddling is required.

- ✔ Approach looks and works like 1-2-3 for Windows and Ami Pro. If you know how to use either of those programs, you already know how to use many of Approach's basic features.

- ✔ The best thing about Approach is that you can get it practically free. Lotus bundles it with 1-2-3, Ami Pro, Freelance Graphics, and Organizer for a ridiculously low price in a package called SmartSuite. The whole SmartSuite package costs about what 1-2-3 and Ami Pro would cost if purchased separately, so everything else is essentially free.

Version diversion

Way back in March of 1992, a small software company called Approach released Version 1.0 of Approach for Windows. In October of 1992, it released Version 2.0 of Approach. The following summer, a funny thing happened: the giant software company, Lotus, looking for a database program to add to its SmartSuite collection, purchased Approach. In September of 1993, Lotus released Approach Version 2.1, which provided essentially the same features as Approach 2.0 but had new menus and buttons and whatnot to make it look more like a Lotus program. In fact, Lotus referred to this version as the "Lotus-ized" version of Approach.

At the same time, Lotus set the Approach programmers to work on a totally new version of Approach that would offer major improvements over the earlier versions. Thus was born Approach 3.0, with more than 200 new features.

This book is written specifically for Approach 3.0. If you're still using Approach 2.1, consider upgrading to 3.0. The new features are well worth the small upgrade cost.

Forms, Reports, and Other Database Portals

One of the most important features of Approach is that it does not confine you to a single way of viewing the information in a database. For example, even though a database of customer information may contain detailed sales and credit information, you may not want to see all of that information every time you look at the customer's record. Approach enables you to extract just the fields that you want to see at any time and arrange them neatly on the screen however you want them. You also can embellish the screen layout with fancy text or drawings. (This feature sometimes makes Approach almost fun to use.)

Here is the low down on the various types of views that you can create to get information into and out of a database:

Form: A layout of the way information from each database record is presented on the screen. You can design several forms for a database, thereby giving yourself several ways to peek at the data. Sometimes you may want to see every bit of detail on record for a customer, but other times you may want only the name and address. When you work in a form view, you work with database records one at a time.

When you create a new database, Approach automatically creates a form view that includes all of the fields in the database, lined up neatly. You can easily modify this default form to make it more attractive and functional.

Report: A layout of the way information from a database is printed on the printer. You can design as many reports for a particular database as you need. Reports can include information summarized from several database records (such as a total of all sales for a particular customer) or values that are calculated from fields in the record (such as a customer's total sales minus the customer's total returns).

Worksheets: If you're familiar with spreadsheet programs such as Lotus 1-2-3, you'll understand the worksheet view right away. It presents the data in a database in a worksheet format — arranged as a grid of rows and columns. Each row in the worksheet represents one record in the database, and each column represents one field. An advantage of using a worksheet view, rather than a form view, is that the worksheet view enables you to display more than one record at a time on the screen.

Approach automatically creates a default worksheet view when you create a new database.

Crosstabs: A crosstab is like a worksheet, except that each row does not correspond to a single database record. Instead, each cell contains information that is summarized for several related database records. For example, if you have a sales database that has one record for every invoice, you can create a crosstab that contains one row for each sales rep that summarizes the rep's total sales.

Charts: This view would be Ross Perot's favorite part of Approach. If Ross had had an Approach database that listed all the poultry sales from Arkansas during the 1980s, he could have used this feature to quickly prepare a pie chart for one of his infomercials. It might have changed history.

Form letters: You can use Approach to create your own junk mail by creating a form letter view. The form letter can include fields extracted from database records, such as a name and address, a salutation, and perhaps other information. For sophisticated mail merge operations, you'll probably want to use a full-fledged word processing program, such as Ami Pro, WordPerfect for Windows, or Word for Windows. But simple one-page merge letters are much easier to do correctly by using Approach's form letter view.

Mailing labels: For a database that contains names and addresses, you can use a mailing label view to print labels quickly. Approach automatically works with Avery label formats, but you can create your own custom formats if you prefer a different brand of labels.

Approach lingo you can't escape

I hate to be the bearer of bad news, but if you expect to have a satisfying relationship with Approach, you have to learn to speak its language. Here are a few of the most important terms, detechnicalized for your reading enjoyment:

Database: A collection of related information. For example, a customer database would contain information about your valued customers; a parts database would contain information about the various parts stocked at your shop; a wine list database would contain information about your favorite wines.

Record: A database is a collection of records. Each record contains the information about a particular customer, part, wine, or whatever.

Field: A record is a collection of fields. Each field contains one snippet of information, such as the name of a customer, the number of a part, or the price of a wine.

Database file: A disk file that contains the information for a database. Approach can work with database files in any of several popular disk formats—dBase, Paradox, and FoxPro—and a few other esoteric file formats such as IBM DB2, Oracle SQL, or SQL Server. In fact, Approach has no database format to call its own. When you create a new database, Approach uses the popular dBase IV format unless you tell it to use one of the other formats. (There's little reason to change formats unless you want to be able to access the database using another database program such as Paradox or FoxPro.)

View: A way of looking at the data in a database file. Suppose that a database file contains customer records that have 50 different fields of information for each customer. You may not want to look at all 50 fields every time you display a customer record. By creating a view, you can select just the fields that you're interested in — perhaps the customer's name and address information and credit status. Approach enables you to create several different types of views: forms, reports, worksheets, crosstabs, charts, merge letters, and mailing labels.

Join: A way of combining information from two or more database files. For example, if you have a customer database and a sales database, you can join the two databases to access information about the sales for a particular customer. The sales information would come from the sales database, but the customer's name and address information would come from the customer database.

Approach file: An Approach file (.APR) is the file that enables you to access a database file through Approach. The Approach file contains information about the layout of the data stored in the database file, plus all of the views used to get at the data that is stored in the database file. If you've joined several database files, information about the join is stored in the Approach file as well.

Starting Approach

Enough of the preliminaries; it's time to get to work. The first step in learning how to use Approach is learning how to get it started. Here's the procedure:

1. **Get ready.**

   Light some votive candles. Take two Tylenol. Sit in the Lotus Position facing Redmond, WA, and recite the Windows creed three times:

   Windows is my friend. Windows loves me, and I love Windows.
   Windows is my friend. Windows loves me, and I love Windows.
   Windows is my friend. Windows loves me, and I love Windows.

2. **Start your engines.**

   Turn on your computer. You may need to flip only one switch, but if the computer, monitor, and printer are plugged in separately, you have to turn on each one separately.

3. **Start Windows.**

   If you're lucky, Windows starts right up when you start your computer. If it doesn't, you are greeted with the warm and friendly DOS prompt, which usually looks like C:> or C:\>. Close your eyes; don't look at it, lest you turn into a pillar of salt. Instead, type **WIN** and press the Enter key:

   ```
       C:\> WIN
   ```

   This command blasts you into the world of Windows, wherein Approach is surely to be found.

4. **Find the Approach icon.**

   Lotus
   Approach 3.0

   Next, you need to find the little picture, called an *icon,* that represents Approach. If you can't find the Approach icon, it's probably nestled safely in a group window labeled Lotus Applications. Find the Lotus Applications icon, double-click it, and pray that the Approach icon appears. (If you're not sure what *double-click* means, read the sidebar, "The mouse is your friend.")

5. **Start Approach.**

   Having found the Approach icon, double-click it. Stare at the screen for a few seconds while the hard disk whirs and gyrates. In a few moments, Approach pops to life. (Approach actually starts up pretty fast, especially compared with certain other database programs that shall not be named here for fear of litigation. If you're lucky enough to have the new Binford 200MHz Tri-Pentium Deluxe with 128MB of RAM and alloy trim, Approach sometimes appears 2 to 3 seconds before you double-click the icon.)

The mouse is your friend

Remember that scene in *Star Trek IV* when Scotty, having been zapped back into the 1980s and forced to use a primitive computer (it was a Macintosh), picked up the mouse and talked into it as if it were a microphone? "Computer! Hello computer! Humph. How quaint."

You don't get very far with Approach (or any other Windows program) until you learn how to use the mouse. You can try picking it up and talking to it if you want, but you won't get any better results than Scotty did.

Most mice have two or three buttons on top and a ball underneath. When you move the mouse, the ball rolls. The rolling motion is detected by little wheels inside the mouse and sent to the computer, which responds to the mouse movements by moving the mouse pointer on-screen. What will they think of next?

A mouse works best when you use it with a *mouse pad*, a small (7-inch by 9-inch or so) rubbery pad that gives better traction for the rolling ball on the mouse's rump. You can use the mouse directly on a desk surface, but it doesn't roll as smoothly.

Here's the lowdown on the various acts of mouse dexterity that you are asked to perform as you use Approach:

✔ To *move* or *point* the mouse means to move it, without pressing any mouse buttons, so that the mouse pointer moves to a desired screen location. Remember to leave the mouse on the mouse pad as you move it; if

you pick it up, the ball doesn't roll, and your movement doesn't register.

✔ To *click* means to press and release the left mouse button. Usually, you are asked to click something, which means to point to the something and then click the left button.

✔ To *double-click* means to press and release the left mouse button twice, as quickly as you can.

✔ To *triple-click* means to press and release the left mouse button three times, as quickly as you can.

✔ To *right-click* means to click the right mouse button instead of the left one.

✔ To *drag* something with the mouse means to point at it, press the left button (or right button, depending on the task), and move the mouse while holding down the button. When you arrive at your destination, you release the mouse button.

✔ To *stay* the mouse means to let go of the mouse and give it the command "Stay!" You do not need to raise your voice. Speak in a normal but confident and firm voice. If the mouse obeys, give it a treat. (They are especially fond of Chee-tos crumbs.) But if the mouse starts to walk away, say, "No," put it back in its original position, and repeat the command "Stay!" Under no circumstances should you strike the mouse. Remember, there are no bad mice.

6. Take off your shoes and sit a spell.

Other than the logo screen, which displays for a few moments while Approach starts up, the first thing you'll notice about Approach is the welcome screen shown in Figure 1-1. (This welcome screen is more formally known as the Welcome to Approach dialog box, but I like to call it the *welcome mat*.) The welcome mat cordially invites you to pick whether you want to work with an existing database or create a new one based on one of its many templates. It also lists the five Approach files you've worked with most recently so you can quickly get back to work. You can skip the welcome mat for now, but don't worry: it's covered in the next chapter, where you learn how to create database files. I just wanted you to see it here so you'd get an idea of how friendly Approach is, for a database program.

If you don't like the welcome mat (maybe you're from New York), check the Don't show this screen again check box.

Figure 1-1:
The
Approach
welcome
mat.

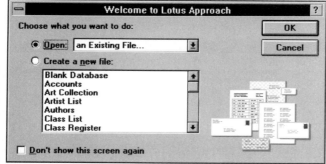

What Is All This Stuff?

After you get past the superficial simplicity of the welcome mat, Approach greets you with a screen that's so cluttered that you'll soon be considering a shoe box as a reasonable alternative to computerizing your database. Just about every nook and cranny has been filled with a menu, button, field, status indicator, or some other barely recognizable gizmo or doohickey. What is all this stuff?

Figure 1-2 provides a road map to the Approach screen. Look this map over briefly to get your bearings. North is up.

Five items on the Approach screen are worthy of your attention:

✔ Across the top of the screen, just below the Lotus Approach title, is the *menu bar*. Approach's deepest and darkest secrets are hidden within the menu bar. Wear eye protection when exploring it.

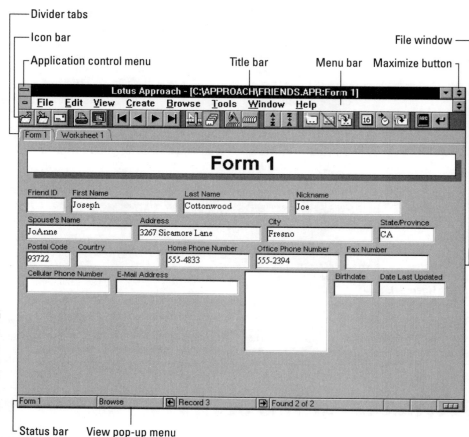

Divider tabs
Icon bar
Application control menu
Title bar
Menu bar
Maximize button
File window

Figure 1-2:
A road map
to the
Approach
screen.

Status bar   View pop-up menu

✔ Just below the menu bar is the *icon bar,* which contains a useful collection of little buttons that Lotus calls *SmartIcons.* Each of the SmartIcons on the icon bar is equivalent to a commonly used command that you would ordinarily have to rummage through the menu bar to find. As you work with Approach, you'll notice that the SmartIcons that appear in the icon bar occasionally rearrange themselves according to the task at hand.

✔ Right smack in the middle of the screen is the *file window,* where the file that you're working on is displayed. The appearance of the file window depends on the view in which you're working. In Figure 1-2, the view is the default form (Form 1), so the file window contains the fields for a single database record. If you switch to other views, such as a worksheet, report, or form letter view, the file window changes accordingly.

✔ At the bottom of the screen is the *status bar,* which tells you which view is currently displayed, what record is displayed, the number of records in the database, and other useful information. The status bar contains helpful pop-up menus for carrying out common tasks. Also, the status bar occasionally morphs itself to reveal information that's pertinent to the task at hand.

✔ The *salad bar* is located... well, actually, there is no salad bar. I lied. Figure 1-2 has only four things that are worth noticing.

Here are a few points to ponder as you meditate on the complexity of the Approach screen:

✔ You'll never get anything done if you feel that you have to understand every pixel of the Approach screen before you can do anything. Don't worry about the stuff you don't understand; just concentrate on what you need to know to get the job done.

✔ A great deal of stuff is crammed into the Approach screen, enough stuff that the program works best if you run it in *full screen* mode. If Approach doesn't take over the entire screen, click the upward-pointing arrowhead (the maximize button) in the upper-right corner of the Approach window. This action *maximizes* the window, enabling Approach to take over the entire screen. (When the window is maximized, the maximize button changes to the double-headed arrow that is visible in Figure 1-2.)

✔ The status bar contains a most useful pop-up menu that is called the *view menu.* This menu enables you to switch among Approach's working environments, which I call *moods.* Click the view menu to reveal a list of the mood choices; then click on the mood that you want to switch to. Table 1-1 summarizes the various Approach moods.

Table 1-1	Approach Moods
Mood	*What It Does*
Browse	Displays information from the database and enables you to add or update individual records. This mood is the one you work in most.
Design	Enables you to design the layout of views, such as forms, reports, form letters, and so on.
Find	Enables you to search for records that match a search criteria that you set up. For example, you work in Find mood to search for all friends who live in Iowa and owe you more than $10.
Preview	Shows what the current view will look like when printed, thus helping to preserve the rain forest.

> ✔ If you're not sure about the function of any of the SmartIcons that appear in the icon bar, point to the SmartIcon with the mouse, let the mouse hover over the button for a moment, and a brightly colored cartoon balloon will appear, containing a brief description of the SmartIcon's function. Very ingenious.

Creating a New Database

If you want to set up a brand new database file, follow these steps:

1. **Start Approach by double-clicking its icon in the Lotus Applications Program Manager group.**

   Approach starts up and displays the Welcome to Lotus Approach dialog box, which is illustrated in Figure 1-1.

2. **Select the Create a new file option by clicking it.**

3. **Pick a database from the list box to use as a model for your new database.**

   The list in the box contains 51 different database templates. Select the one that most closely resembles the type of database that you want to create.

4. **Click OK.**

   Approach displays the New dialog box that is shown in Figure 1-3.

Figure 1-3:
The New
dialog box.

```
┌─────────────────────────────── New ──────────────────────────── ? ──┐
│  File name:                    Directories:              ┌──────────┐ │
│  ┌──────────────┐              c:\approach               │    OK    │ │
│  │ *.dbf        │                                        └──────────┘ │
│  ├──────────────┤┬             ┌ c:\          ┬          ┌──────────┐ │
│  │ art.dbf      ││             📂 approach     │          │  Cancel  │ │
│  │ artist.dbf   ││             🗀 cust          │          └──────────┘ │
│  │ authors.dbf  ││             🗀 examples      │          ┌──────────┐ │
│  │ chess.dbf    ││             🗀 icons         │          │ Connect..│ │
│  │ contname.dbf ││             🗀 sales         │          └──────────┘ │
│  │ contract.dbf ││             🗀 samples       │          ┌──────────┐ │
│  │ cust.dbf     ││                              │          │Disconnect│ │
│  │ dinner.dbf   │┴                              ┴          └──────────┘ │
│  └──────────────┘                                                      │
│  List files of type:           Drives:                                │
│  ┌──────────────┬┐             ┌────────────────┬┐                    │
│  │ dBASE IV (*.DBF)│           │ 🖳 c: ms-dos_6  │                    │
│  └──────────────┴┘             └────────────────┴┘                    │
└────────────────────────────────────────────────────────────────────┘
```

Approach suggests a filename for the new database file. You can use the filename proposed by Approach or supply your own filename.

5. **If the filename proposed by Approach is acceptable, click OK; otherwise, type a filename that you like better and then click OK.**

   Make sure that you don't use the name of an already existing database.

6. Approach creates the file.

Approach displays a blank form that you can use to add records to the new database. Glance back at Figure 1-2 to see what such forms look like.

Here are some things to consider when you are creating a new database file:

✔ The new database file created by Approach is empty. You have to add records to it by typing in the data for each record. See the following section, "Filling Out a Form," for the procedure.

✔ Unfortunately, Approach does not provide a way to preview the database template before you create a database. As a result, you can easily make all kinds of silly mistakes, such as using the Wine List template when you want to compile a database of your favorite complaints. If you choose the wrong template, close the database and then use the Windows File Manager to delete the files that you inadvertently created.

✔ Refer to Chapter 2 for more information about creating databases, especially for adding or removing database fields and changing the layout of the database form.

✔ If you try to create a database that uses a filename that you have already used for a database in the same directory, Approach displays the message, "This file already exists. Replace existing file?" Be careful! If you click Yes, the existing file, along with all of its records, will be irretrievably lost. If you see this message, click No and type a different filename to avoid destroying an existing database.

✔ *Note:* If the Welcome to Lotus Approach dialog box has disappeared, you can get it back again by opening a database (any database will do) and then closing it. In the absence of the Welcome dialog box, you can create a new database by using the File⇨New command. However, because this procedure is more complicated (trust me), I won't describe it in detail until Chapter 2.

Filling Out a Form

After you create a database, you have to type in the information for each database record. The details of entering and editing this data are in Chapter 4. Here are enough basics to get you going:

✔ An *insertion point* marks the spot where text you type will be inserted on the screen. The insertion point is a special type of cursor that appears on-screen as a flashing vertical line. You can move the insertion point from field to field by pressing the Tab key, or you can click the mouse in any field to move the insertion point directly to the field.

✔ When you have typed in all of the information for one record and you want to start a new record, click the New Record SmartIcon in the icon bar or press Ctrl+N. Approach will record the information you just typed and then create a new, blank record.

✔ If Approach just beeps at you when you try to type into a field, you're probably trying to type some illegal characters or you've typed more characters than will fit in the field. For example, you can type only numbers into a date field. If you try to type anything other than numbers, Approach just beeps. (Be thankful that the penalty for illegal typing is a mere beep. Some less civilized programs cart you off and flog you with a cane for typing illegal characters or too many characters.)

✔ There's no rule that says that you have to type something into every field on the form. If you don't have anything to type into a field, press Tab to skip the field.

✔ New database records are automatically inserted at the end of the database, but you can tell Approach to store database records in a sorting sequence. In that case, new records are inserted into their proper location so that the sorting sequence is preserved. You can find all the information that's worth knowing about sorting database records in Chapter 6.

✔ If you want to review the records that you have entered into a database, you can click the left and right arrows that appear in the status bar at the bottom of the screen and on the SmartIcon bar. The left arrow moves back through the database one record at a time; the right arrow moves forward one record at a time.

Looking at the Worksheet

A worksheet view enables you to access the fields and records in an Approach database in an arrangement that is similar to a spreadsheet in a program such as Lotus 1-2-3. A row in the worksheet represents each database record, and a column represents each field.

When you create an Approach database, a default worksheet view named Worksheet 1 is automatically created for you. To switch to this worksheet view, click the tab labeled Worksheet 1 at the top of the file window. Figure 1-4 shows a worksheet view of a database.

Unlike forms, which show one database record at a time, worksheets show as many database records as will fit on the screen, and each record is in a separate worksheet row.

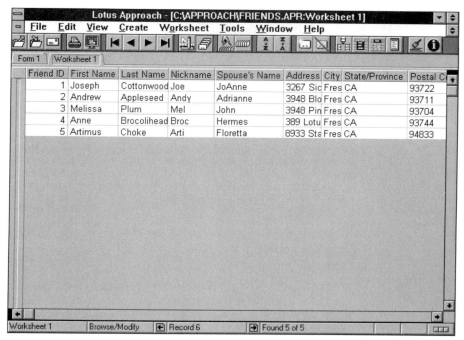

Figure 1-4:
Worksheet
view.

Chapter 17 covers the details of using worksheet views. For now, here are some basics to get you going:

- ✔ Your Lotus 1-2-3 instincts should serve you well in worksheet view. The basics of navigating around the worksheet — such as using the arrow keys to move from cell to cell — are the same.

- ✔ Inserting a new record in worksheet view is the same as inserting a new record in a form. You click the New Record SmartIcon or press Ctrl+N.

- ✔ If a worksheet column is not wide enough to display all of the data it contains, you can increase the column's width by positioning the mouse pointer at the right edge of the column's header and dragging the header to the right.

- ✔ You can freely rearrange the order of columns in the worksheet, and you can even remove entire columns to hide fields that you're not interested in. For details, see Chapter 17.

Printing a Database

After you have gone to the trouble of entering thousands of database records into your computer, you will probably want to print them. For premium printouts, you'll want to create a custom report, following the procedures outlined in Chapter 10. For quick-and-dirty printouts, follow these steps:

1. **Make sure that the printer is turned on and ready to print.**

   Make sure that the select or on-line light is turned on. If it isn't, press the select or on-line button to turn on the light. Check the paper while you're at it.

2. **Switch to the view that you want to print.**

   To print a single record, switch to a form view (such as Form 1) and call up the record that you want to print. To print all of the records in a database, switch to a worksheet view (such as Worksheet 1).

3. **Click the Print button on the icon bar.**

    Or if you prefer, choose the File➪Print command or press Ctrl+P. However you do it, the Print dialog box appears. It has myriad options that you can fiddle with to print your database just so, but you can leave them alone to print the current view.

4. **Click the OK button or press Enter.**

   Make sure that you say, "Engage," in a knowing manner and point at your printer as you do so. The main idea is to fool your printer into thinking that you're the boss.

Printed pages should soon appear on your printer. In all likelihood, you won't be completely satisfied with the layout of the printed output. To print a proper database listing, you need to design a custom report. Fortunately, the procedure is simple, and you can find everything you need to know in Chapter 10.

Save Your Work

Any good Windows user knows about the importance of using the File➪Save command to save work. Approach works a little differently from most other Windows programs, though. Whenever you make a change to a database by adding a new record or deleting or changing an existing record, the change is immediately recorded in the database file. As a result, you don't have to bother with saving the file after making database changes.

But wait . . . Approach has a File⇨Save command, and a Save SmartIcon appears on the icon bar. What gives?

Here's the story: Approach automatically saves any changes that you make to the data in a database, but it does not save any changes that you make to database views, such as forms, worksheets, or reports. When you create a database, you have to save any new views that you have created for it. And any time you change the design of a view or create a new view, you have to save the views again.

At least two files are stored on disk for each Approach database. The *database file* contains the actual records of the database. Database files usually have a DBF or DB filename extension, depending on the database file format you choose; the default is DBF. The *Approach file* contains the views that are used to access the data in the database file. Approach files have APR as their filename extension. Whenever you change the contents of a database, the changes are automatically recorded in the database file. However, you have to manually save changes to the Approach file.

You can save an Approach file in any of the following four ways:

- ✔ Use the File⇨Save command.
- ✔ Click the Save Approach File icon in the icon bar.
- ✔ Press Ctrl+S.
- ✔ Close the file by using the File⇨Close command or exit Approach by using the File⇨Exit command. If you have made changes to any views, Approach asks whether you want to save the Approach file.

If you are saving the Approach file for the first time, the Save Approach File dialog box appears so that you can type a filename for the Approach file. Use the same name that you used for the database file and click OK to save the file. After you have saved the file once, subsequent saves update the Approach file with any changes that you made to the database views since the last time you saved it.

Here are some notes to keep in mind when you are saving Approach files:

- ✔ If you decide to opt for a name other than the name proposed by Approach, use your noggin. You will use the filename to recognize the file later on, so pick a meaningful name that suggests the file's contents.
- ✔ Database changes are automatically recorded in the database file. Use the File⇨Save command only to save changes that you make to database views.

> ✔ If you're not sure about how to make up a filename, consult the sidebar, "I wish I didn't have to tell you about DOS filenames." If you try to use a filename that doesn't conform to the rules listed in the sidebar, you will receive an electrical jolt of approximately 3 gazillion volts through the mouse. (Just kidding.)

I wish I didn't have to tell you about DOS filenames

DOS is very strict about the names that you can use for files. Obey the following restrictions, and you will be a happy Approach user all the days of your life:

✔ No more than eight characters per filename, please.

✔ You can use letters and numbers. Avoid special characters such as *#*, *$*, and *%;* some of them are legal, but others are considered contraband. I never can remember which is which, so I just avoid them all.

✔ Did you know that the use by cartoonists of a bunch of those special characters in place of swearing is called a *maladictory?* DOS considers these characters profane. That's why you can't use them in filenames.

✔ DOS enables you to add a three-character *extension* to the end of the filename. The extension is separated from the rest of the filename by a period, but the period isn't part of the filename itself . . . it's just a separator. Approach automatically adds appropriate extensions to database files and Approach files, so you needn't mess with extensions or periods.

Here are some acceptable filenames for files used by Approach:

CUSTOMER.APR	A perfectly acceptable filename, and slightly descriptive too.
27.APR	DOS will allow it, but how will you ever know what is contained in a file that has such a name?

Here are some unacceptable filenames:

MY FILE.APR	Nope. No spaces are allowed in the middle of a filename.
W+E.APR	Nope. The plus sign is off limits. A hyphen would work, but avoiding all special characters is best.
WESTREGION.APR	Nope. Way too many characters. Sorry.
W.REGION.APR	Nope. Too many periods.
@#$%&*!	Nope. Profane filename. Makes DOS blush.

Retrieving a Database from Disk

Having entered thousands upon thousands of records into a database, you'll probably long for some method of retrieving those records later, either to print a report, to change records that have become out of date, or just to gloat.

You can open a database in any of three ways:

- ✔ Choose the File⇨Open command.
- ✔ Click on the Open a File icon in the icon bar.
- ✔ Press Ctrl+O.

All three methods pop up the Open dialog box, which gives you a list of files to choose from. Click the file you want and then click the OK button or press Enter.

Here are a few points to ruminate on when you are opening files:

- ✔ The Open dialog box has controls that enable you to rummage through the various directories on the hard disk to search for files. If you know how to open a file in any Windows application, you know how to do it in Approach, because the Open dialog box is pretty much the same as other Open dialog boxes.

- ✔ You can quickly open a file from the Open dialog box by double-clicking the file that you want to open. This method spares you from having to click the file and then click the OK button. It also exercises the fast-twitch muscles in your index finger.

- ✔ Approach keeps track of the last five files that you opened and displays them on the File menu. To open a file that you've recently opened, click the File menu and inspect the list at the bottom of the menu. If the file you want is on the list, click it to open it.

- ✔ You also can open a file from the Welcome to Lotus Approach dialog box that's displayed when you start Approach or when you close a database. Refer to Figure 1-1 if you've forgotten what the dialog box looks like.

Closing a Database

After you finish working on a database, you will want to close it. Closing a database is kind of like stuffing your important papers back into the shoe box and shoving the shoe box back onto the top shelf in the closet. Out of sight, out of mind. The database disappears from the computer screen, but don't worry. It's tucked safely away on the hard disk where you can get to it later if you need to. To close a file, use the File⇨Close command.

Here are some closing arguments to consider:

- ✔ Closing a file closes both the database file and the Approach file that contains the views used to access the database. You cannot close one of these files without simultaneously closing the other.

- ✔ Yet another way to close a file is to double-click the control box that appears on the far left edge of the menu bar.

- ✔ You don't have to close a file before you exit Approach. If you exit Approach without closing a file, Approach graciously closes the file for you. The only time that you may want to close a file is when you want to work on a different file and you don't want to keep both files open at the same time.

- ✔ If you have made changes to the views that are in the Approach file, Approach offers to save the file before closing it. Click Yes to save the file or click No to abandon the changes.

- ✔ *Note:* When you close a file, Approach politely offers up the Welcome to Lotus Approach dialog box so that you can easily create a new database or open an existing database. Presenting the dialog box is a deliberate attempt to discourage you from playing Solitaire instead of continuing with your work.

Exiting Approach

Had enough excitement for one day? Use any of the following techniques to shut Approach down:

- ✔ Choose the File⇨Exit command.
- ✔ Double-click the control box in the upper-left corner of the Approach window.
- ✔ Press Alt+F4.

Bammo! Approach is outta here.

You should know a few things about exiting Approach:

✔ Approach doesn't let you exit without first considering whether you want to save changes that you made to a view stored in an Approach file. If you made any design changes, Approach offers to save the changes for you. Accept its generous offer with thanksgiving.

✔ Never, never, never ever, never, no never turn off the computer while Approach or any other Windows program is running. You may as well pour acid into the keyboard or drop the system unit from the top of the Chrysler Building. Always exit Approach and any other program that's running before you turn off your computer.

✔ In fact, you'd best get clean out of Windows before you shut down the computer. Exit all of the programs the same way you exited Approach. Then, when Windows is the only thing left, exit it the same way. Only when you see the happy DOS prompt (C:\>) can you safely turn off the computer.

Chapter 2
Creating Database Fields

· ·

In This Chapter

▶ The lowdown on database fields

▶ Adding database fields

▶ Updating database field definitions

▶ Setting field defaults

▶ Validating database fields

▶ Using calculated fields

· ·

*T*his chapter is a good news/bad news chapter.

The bad news is that you have to design and create a database before you can get any useful work done with Approach. This task involves figuring out what fields to include in each database record, what to name the fields, how to format each field, and so on. If you're incredibly lucky, someone else has done this work for you — or will if you bribe them sufficiently. If not, you're on your own.

The good news is that Approach is very flexible when it comes to designing and creating databases. When you use Approach, you can create a database by copying fields from one of the supplied templates, or you can start with a blank template and add your own fields. But the database layout is never fixed in stone. You can easily revisit your design at any time to add fields that you forgot, delete fields that you no longer need, and change fields that you originally defined as too small, too large, or otherwise inappropriate.

All about Fields

A field is a field is a field, right? Wrong. Approach enables you to create nine different types of database fields. Table 2-1 summarizes the nine field types, and the following sections describe them in excruciating detail.

Table 2-1	Approach Field Types
Field Type	*Characteristics*
Text	Holds text values such as names, addresses, titles, and so on; can be up to 255 characters in length.
Numeric	Holds numbers such as sales amounts, prices, quantities, and so on.
Memo	Holds extra-long text information.
Boolean	Holds a yes or no value.
Date	Holds a date.
Time	Holds a time.
PicturePlus	Holds a graphic picture or an OLE object.
Calculated	Holds the result of a calculation derived from other fields.
Variable	Used by Approach gurus to hold temporary results in macros.

Text fields

A *text field* is a database field that holds text information. Text can be any combination of characters that you can type on the keyboard, including letters, numerals, and special symbols. Text fields are used for names, addresses, titles, descriptions, and other similar information.

Here are a few points to ponder concerning text fields:

- ✔ When you define a text field, you have to specify a maximum length for the field. Approach doesn't let you type more characters than the maximum number into the field.

- ✔ Most database file types allow up to 255 characters per text field. If you need to store more text than that, use a memo field instead.

- ✔ A text field can sometimes look like a numeric field. For example, a zip code or phone number field may look like a number. However, you can't use such a field in a numeric calculation.

- ✔ You can search a database for records that contain specific text in a text field. See Chapter 5 for more information about searching text fields.

- ✔ You can sort a database into sequence by basing the sort on a text field. For example, you can sort a Customer database into alphabetical order by basing the sort on each customer's last name. Sorting is covered in Chapter 6.

Numeric fields

Numeric fields contain — you guessed it — numeric values. Use numeric fields for information such as sales amounts, prices, quantities, and so on.

Keep the following in mind when you are using numeric fields:

- ✔ Approach ignores any nonnumeric characters that you type into a numeric field. For example, if you type $123.45, Approach ignores the dollar sign and treats the number as 123.45. You also can enter terribly mutilated numbers, such as #123k$.G45D; Approach removes all the junk and once again treats the number as 123.45.

- ✔ You can specify the size of the numeric data that can be stored in a numeric field by telling Approach how many digits to allow on the left and the right of the decimal point. For example, if you specify 10.2, Approach will allow ten digits to the left of the decimal point and two to the right. The largest value that you can store in such a number is 9,999,999,999.99. Such a field is just large enough to store Bill Gates's net worth.

- ✔ You can use numeric fields in calculations. In an invoicing database, for example, you can use a subtotal field to calculate a sales tax field and then add both fields together to calculate a total field.

- ✔ You can base a search for specific database records on the value stored in numeric fields. For example, in an invoice database, you can search for all invoices whose Invoice Total field is $100.00 or more. Chapter 5 explains how to conduct such a search.

- ✔ You can base a sort on numeric fields to sort a database into sequence. For example, you can base a sort on a Year-To-Date Sales field to sort a customer database into sequence. Chapter 6 covers sorting.

Memo fields

Memo fields are used for text information that doesn't fit into a normal text field. Memo fields are usually used as a place to store extra information or "notes" about a database record. For example, you can use a memo field in a client database to jot down notes about the client's family or hobbies. Then you can review these notes before you meet with the client, and the client will think you care.

Here are some thoughts to mull over when you use memo fields:

- ✔ The maximum length of a memo field is typically 64K, but it may be less for certain database file types. Unless you're remarkably prolific, you can think of memo fields as providing practically unlimited text storage.

✔ Memo fields are stored in a separate memo file rather than in the main database file. The memo file extension depends on the type of database file being used:

dBase	DBT
FoxPro	FPT
Paradox	DBQ

✔ You can search for text in a memo field, but you can't sort a database in sequence based on a memo field. See Chapter 5 for instructions on searching memo fields.

Boolean fields

Boolean fields hold Yes/No values. Or, if you prefer, True/False values. A boolean field is usually shown on forms as a check box. Use boolean fields to record information such as, Did we send this customer junk mail last month? or Does this person like jazz?

Here are some thoughts to consider when using boolean fields:

✔ Boolean fields have only two values: Yes or No. To enter a Yes value into a field, type **Yes**, **Y**, **yes**, **y**, or **1** into the field. To enter a No value, type **No**, **N**, **no**, **n**, or **0**.

✔ As a tribute to propeller heads and IBM engineers, Approach allows 0 or 1 as values for boolean fields.

✔ The easiest way to work with boolean fields is to set them up in your forms as check boxes. Then the user simply clicks the check box to select a Yes or No value for the field. Instructions for setting up check box form fields are found in Chapter 9.

✔ Boolean fields are very useful when you are setting up conditional calculations. For example, a customer database can have a boolean field to indicate whether a customer is tax exempt. This tax-exempt field can be used in a conditional sales tax calculation to make sure that tax-exempt customers are not charged sales tax.

Date fields

Date fields store dates. For example: Invoice Date, Last Order Date, Due Date, Birth Date, Date Joined, and so on. You get the idea.

✔ You can display dates in several formats, such as the following:

```
09/30/94
Feb 12, 1994
Monday, May 16, 1994
```

Chapter 14 explains how to set the appropriate date format when you design a form, report, or other view.

✔ Date fields are usually set up so that you enter the date into a field that's preformatted with separator characters, like this

```
_ _ / _ _ / _ _
```

Then you just type numbers for the month, day, and year. When you move out of the field by pressing the Tab key, Approach redisplays the date according to the date format that you selected for the field. Once again, see Chapter 14 for details.

✔ You can enter two or four digits for the year. If you enter two digits, the twentieth century is assumed. If you omit the year altogether, the current year is assumed.

✔ You can press Ctrl+Shift+D to enter the current date into a date field.

✔ You can use dates in calculations. For example, to calculate the number of days between two date fields, just subtract one date field from the other. Such calculations are explained in Chapter 14.

Time fields

Time fields store — hold your breath — times, as in 8:00 PM or 3:42:23 AM. Time fields are fairly easy to understand, as long as you keep the following points in mind:

✔ You can enter a time value that uses 12-hour or 24-hour notation. For example, 13:35 and 1:35 PM represent the same time. If you enter an hour that's less than 12, Approach assumes the time is AM unless you type PM following the time.

✔ Most of the time, you'll enter just the hours and minutes; for example, 5:56 PM. For more precise times, enter the seconds as well; for example, 5:56:32 PM. You can even enter hundredths of seconds, as in 5:56:32.58 PM, but by the time you finish typing, the time you enter will be inaccurate anyway.

✔ To enter the current time, press Ctrl+Shift+T. This command pastes the current time into the field as text.

PicturePlus fields

A *PicturePlus field* is a field that can store a picture or an embedded object that was created by another Windows program. You can, for example, store a sound file, a chart, or a range of cells from a spreadsheet program such as 1-2-3 in a PicturePlus field. PicturePlus fields are most often used to store pictures of customers or products in a customer or inventory database.

PicturePlus fields are complicated enough that I've devoted an entire chapter to them (Chapter 12). Until you get to that chapter, the following snippets of information should satisfy your curiosity:

- ✔ You can place a picture into a PicturePlus field by opening the picture in a drawing program (such as Paintbrush), copying the picture to the Clipboard, switching to Approach, and pasting the picture from the Clipboard into the PicturePlus field. Or you can use the Edit⇨Paste from File command to copy a picture directly from a file into a record.

- ✔ If you want to, you can create an OLE link to a graphic or any other type of OLE object, such as a sound, chart, or spreadsheet range. Then, when you double-click the object, the program that created the object is opened so you can edit the object.

- ✔ OLE stands for *Object Linking and Embedding*, but that doesn't matter now. In fact, the whole subject of OLE and PicturePlus fields is too far out for a chapter like this one, so early in the book. If you really have to know about these things, jump ahead to Chapter 12.

Calculated fields

A *calculated field* is a field whose value Approach calculates automatically, basing the calculations on other fields in the record. For example, an Invoice database can represent sales tax by using a calculated field. Then Approach can calculate the sales tax by basing it on the invoice subtotal.

If you think of a calculated field as being like a formula in a spreadsheet cell, you have the right idea. The concept is the same. The advantage of using calculated fields is that they eliminate the possibility that a lowly human will make a dumb mistake, such as charging $70 sales tax on a $10 order.

- ✔ When you define a calculated field, you type in a formula that is used to calculate the field's value. Here are some typical formulas for calculated fields:

```
Subtotal * 0.0725
Subtotal + Tax
IF(Taxable,Subtotal*0.0725,0)
PMT(Prin,Rate,48)
```

- ✔ An entire chapter of this book, Chapter 13, is devoted to devising formulas such as these. Refer to that chapter for more information.

- ✔ You cannot type a value into a calculated field. Instead, Approach calculates the field's value each time you display a record. The calculated field's value is recalculated whenever you change a field that is mentioned in the calculated field's formula. For example, if a Sales Tax field multiplies a Subtotal field by a fixed tax rate, the Sales Tax field is automatically updated whenever you change the value of the Subtotal field.

- ✔ The value of a calculated field is not stored in the database file. Instead, the value is recalculated each time a record is retrieved from the database file. This method saves space in the database file and assures that calculated fields always have up-to-date values.

Variable fields

A variable field is not really a database field, at least not in the same sense that the other fields are. Variable fields are used in macros to temporarily store calculated results. Variable fields are best used by computer gurus who don't realize that life consists of more than writing macros.

Adding Fields to a Database

When you create a blank database, you have to add fields before you can store data in the database. To add fields to a new database, follow these steps:

1. **From the Welcome to Lotus Approach dialog box, choose Create a new file, select Blank Database as the template, and click OK.**

   Or, if the Welcome to Lotus Approach dialog box isn't visible, use the File⇨New command.

2. **When the New dialog box appears, type a filename for the new database and click OK.**

   An empty database file will be created, with no fields. Then the Creating New Database dialog box will appear, as shown in Figure 2-1.

3. **Type the name of the first field that you want to create in the Field Name column and then press Tab.**

   The number of characters that you can use to make up the field name depends on the type of database file that you created. For the default dBase file format and for FoxPro files, you can use up to 32 characters for each field name. For Paradox files, the limit is 25 characters. Either way, the name can include embedded spaces, so names such as Customer Number and Risk Factor are allowable field names.

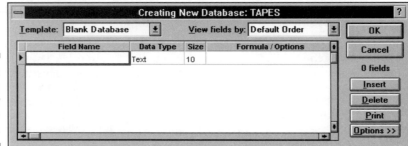

When you press Tab, the insertion point jumps to the Data Type column.

4. Select the field's data type from the drop-down list that appears in the Data Type column for the field. Then press Tab to move to the Size field.

When the insertion point moves into the Data Type column, a drop-down list appears. Click the down arrow to reveal the drop-down list, as shown in Figure 2-2. Scroll through this list to find the data type that you want to use, click the data type to select it, and then press Tab.

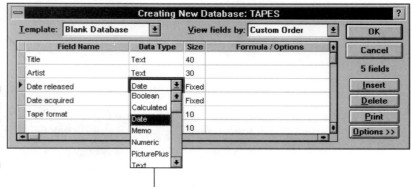

Data Type drop-down list

5. For text or numeric fields, type the field length for the field in the Size column.

For text fields, type the maximum number of characters that you want to allow for the field. The default size, 10, is adequate for short fields, but not for longer fields such as names and addresses.

For numeric fields, type the number of digits to allow to the left of the decimal point, type a decimal point, and then type the number of digits to allow on the right of the decimal point. For example, type **7.2** to allow numbers ranging up to 9,999,999.99.

6. **Repeat Steps 3 – 5 for other fields you want to add to the database.**

7. **When you have added all the fields that you want to use, click OK to dismiss the Creating New Database dialog box.**

When you're finished, all the fields of the database will be lined up neatly, as shown in Figure 2-3. If the database contains more fields than can be displayed at once in the Creating New Database dialog box, you can see additional fields by using the scroll bar to scroll the list of fields. (You can work the scroll bar by dragging the slider box that starts out at the top of the scroll bar or by clicking either of the arrow buttons that appear at the top and bottom of the scroll bar.)

Figure 2-3:
The list of fields after you finish creating them in the Creating New Database dialog box.

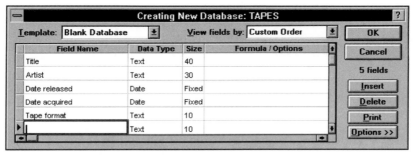

Here are some field-definition tidbits that are worthy of your consideration:

✔ If you want to copy fields from one of the database templates supplied with Approach, select the template that you want to use from the Template drop-down list. Be warned, however, that if you apply a template to a database, any fields that you have already defined for the database will be lost.

✔ You can use the drop-down list in the View fields box to change the order in which database fields are displayed in the dialog box. The sort options are Default Order, Field Name, Data Type, and Custom Order. This setting affects only how fields are displayed in the Creating New Database dialog box; it doesn't affect how fields are displayed in forms or how records are sorted in the database.

✔ New fields are normally added to the end of the list of database fields. If you want to insert a field in the middle of the list, click the field immediately after the location where you want the new field inserted and click Insert. Approach will insert a new row so you can define a new field.

- ✔ Notice that just below the Cancel button Approach displays the total number of fields that you have defined for the database. See? Computers can count!

- ✔ You can print a listing of the fields in your database by clicking the Print button.

- ✔ After you have created a database, you can return to this dialog box at any time by using the Create⇨Field Definition command. Then you can add new fields, delete fields you don't need, or change the format of database fields. When you choose the Create⇨Field Definition command, the dialog box title changes from Creating New Database to Field Definition. Otherwise, it is the same. For more information, see the next section, "Adding, Changing, or Deleting Fields.".

Adding, Changing, or Deleting Fields

If you decide that you need to add more fields to a database, remove a database field you don't need, or change a field's name, data type, size, or options, follow this painless procedure:

1. **Open the database by using the File⇨Open command or the Open an Existing File option from the Welcome to Lotus Approach dialog box.**

2. **Choose the Create⇨Field Definition command.**

   The Field Definition dialog box appears.

3. **To add a field, scroll to the end of the field list, type the field name in the first available Field Name cell, and then select the data type and size for the field.**

   If you prefer to insert the field somewhere in the middle of the list, click the field immediately after the location where you want the new field inserted and click Insert. Then type the name, field type, and length for the new field.

4. **To delete a field, select the field that you want to delete by clicking it, click Delete, and when Approach asks whether you're sure you want to delete the field, click OK.**

   The field will be deleted. Any data stored in the field in any records in the database will be lost.

5. **To change a field, select the Field Name, Data Type, or Size settings for the field by clicking them and then enter new values.**

   The field will be adjusted according to the new specifications.

6. To change a field's options, select the field by clicking it and then click the Options button and change the options.

The field will be adjusted according to your new specifications.

Be sure to consider the following points before changing or deleting database fields:

✔ Any data contained in a field will be lost when you delete the field. Make sure that you don't need the data in a field before you delete the field. (Approach will ask for confirmation with a message that goes something like, "Are you out of your mind?")

✔ If the field is used in a join, you have to unjoin the field before you can delete it. Refer to Chapter 8 for more information about joins.

✔ Think twice before deleting a field that is used in a calculated field. You'll probably have to change the calculated field's formula. For example, if a Sales Tax field is calculated with a formula such as Subtotal * 0.0725, you'll get bogus results in the Sales Tax field if you delete the Subtotal field.

✔ If you reduce a field's size, Approach may be forced to whack off data that won't fit in the reduced field. Be careful!

Creating Fields That Fill Themselves In

A *default value* is a value that is applied to a field unless the user changes the value. Default values are useful for fields whose values are predictable. For example, in a personal address book database, you can use the name of your hometown as the default value for the City field. Then you only have to type the city for friends who don't live in your hometown.

Default value options

Approach provides several different kinds of default options for database fields:

Nothing: This default is used for most fields. A field whose default option is set to Nothing is not given a value until the user types a value for the field.

Previous record: The field takes on the same value as the database record that was most recently added or modified. This type of default setting is useful for fields whose values usually run in spurts. For example, in an Orders database, you can set the Sales Person field's default to Previous record to make entering a batch of orders for a particular sales person easier.

<u>C</u>reation date: The field's value is set to the current date when the record is created. Use this option only for date or text fields.

<u>M</u>odification date: The field's value is set to the current date when the record is created and is updated whenever the record is modified. Use this option only for date or text fields.

<u>C</u>reation time: The field's value is set to the current time when the record is created. Use this option only for time or text fields.

<u>M</u>odification time: The field's value is set to the current time when the record is created and is updated whenever the record is modified. Use this value only for time or text fields.

<u>D</u>ata: A specific value is used as the default for the field. For example, for a Payroll Check database, you could set the default for the Pay To field to Doug Lowe.

<u>S</u>erial number: A sequence number that is used to uniquely identify each record in the database. Approach automatically assigns the correct value to serial number fields whenever you create a record that contains one.

<u>C</u>reation formu<u>l</u>a: A formula that is used to calculate a value for the field. The calculation is made when the record is created. Using this option is different from making the field a calculated field. The user cannot change the value of a calculated field. But the user can type a new value to replace the value calculated by a default formula.

<u>M</u>odification formu<u>l</u>a: A formula that is used to calculate a value for the field. The calculation is made when the record is created and is updated whenever the record is modified.

Setting a default value

Here is the procedure for setting a field's default value:

1. **In the Field Definition or Creating New Database dialog box, select the field for which you want to provide a default.**

   If the Field Definition or Creating New Database dialog box isn't visible, make sure that the database is open and then use the <u>C</u>reate⇨Field <u>D</u>efinition command to summon the Field Definition dialog box.

2. **Click the <u>O</u>ptions button.**

   The dialog box will be expanded to reveal the options settings, as shown in Figure 2-4. Notice that the bottom portion of the dialog box contains two tabbed sections — Default Value and Validation. If the Validation options are shown, click the Default Value tab to switch to the default value options.

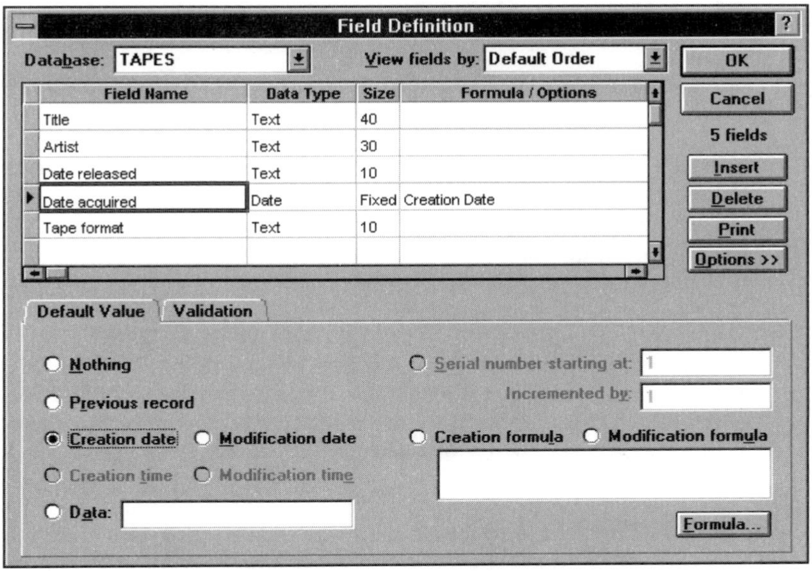

Figure 2-4:
Setting a
default
value for a
field.

3. **Select the Default Value option that you want for the field by clicking the option.**

   Only one of the options listed on the Default Value tab can be in effect for a field. Note that for some field types, inappropriate option settings will be disabled. In Figure 2-4, for example, the Creation time, Modification time, and Serial number options are disabled because you can't use those default options for a date field.

4. **If you select the Data default option, you type the default value in the text box that is adjacent to the Data button.**

   For example, type **Doug Lowe.**

5. **Select another database field to set its default value or click OK to dismiss the Field Definition dialog box.**

Keeping Out the Bad Data

Garbage In, Garbage Out, so the old saying goes. If only you could prevent bad data from getting into your database. When you use Approach, you can — sort of. When you define the database fields, you can set up Validation options that help prevent bad data from getting into the database. Validation options can't eliminate all bad data, but they can eliminate many common data entry mistakes.

Validation options

In Approach, you can set any of the following Validation options for database fields:

Unique: The field must have a different value for every record in the database. Be careful how you use this option. For example, if you specify Unique for a Last Name field, the database doesn't allow for two records that have the same last name. Use Unique only for fields that have to have unique values, such as Customer Number or Social Security Number.

From/to: The field must have a value that falls within a range of values. This option is most useful for numeric fields or date fields. For example, you can specify that a Quantity Ordered field must be From 0 to 99999. This setting eliminates unreasonably large orders (of course, exactly what constitutes an unreasonably large order depends on the kind of business you're in) and rejects negative numbers.

Filled in: The field must be given a value by the user. Use this option for fields that are not optional, such as a customer's Last Name, an employee's Social Security Number, or a video tape's Title field.

One of: This option is my personal favorite. You use it to restrict a field to certain preset values. For example, suppose that you have a Territory field in a customer database and you have four territories: North, South, East, and West. By using the One of validation option, you can prevent the user from entering anything other than North, South, East, or West for the field. If the user tries to enter only W, instead of West, Approach slaps the user's hands. (When you use One of validation, the best thing to do is to create a drop-down list for the field on the form. Chapter 9 explains how to create such a list.)

Formula is true: This option specifies a condition that must be true for the value of the field to be accepted. For example, you can use the formula >0 to ensure that only positive numbers are entered into the field.

In field: This option is the trickiest validation option. It says that the value typed into a field must match a value stored in a different database field. The field can be in the same database, but it is more likely to be in a different database. For example, an Invoice database can contain a Customer Number field that always has to correspond to a Customer Number in the Customers database. In order to use this type of validation, the two databases must be joined. See Chapter 8 for information about joining databases.

Setting the validation options

Here is the procedure for setting a field's validation options:

1. **In the Field Definition (or Creating New Database) dialog box, select the field for which you want to set the validation options.**

   If the Field Definition or Creating New Database dialog box isn't visible, make sure that the database is open and then use the Create⇨Field Definition command to summon the Field Definition dialog box.

2. **Click the Options button if you haven't already done so to reveal the field options. Then click the Validation tab to reveal the validation options.**

   Figure 2-5 shows the Field Definition dialog box with the validation options visible.

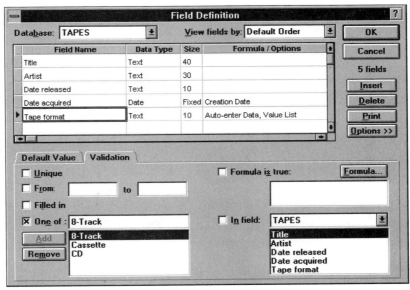

Figure 2-5:
The validation options in the Field Definition dialog box.

3. **Select the validation options that you want to use by clicking the appropriate check boxes.**

   Unlike the default value options, you can check more than one validation option.

4. **If you select the One of option, add all of the allowable field values to the list by typing each value in the text box immediately to the right of the One of caption and then clicking the Add button.**

In Figure 2-5, I created three allowable values for the Tape format field: 8-Track, Cassette, and CD. If you make a mistake, select the incorrect value by clicking it and then click Remove. Then retype the value (this time paying more attention) and click Add to add the corrected value.

5. **Select another database field to set its validation options or click OK to dismiss the Field Definition dialog box.**

Setting the Formula for a Calculated Field

When you create a calculated field, you have to supply the formula that you want Approach to use to calculate the field's value. When you set a field's Data Type to Calculated, Approach expands the Creating New Database (or Define Fields) dialog box to show the formula options, as shown in Figure 2-6.

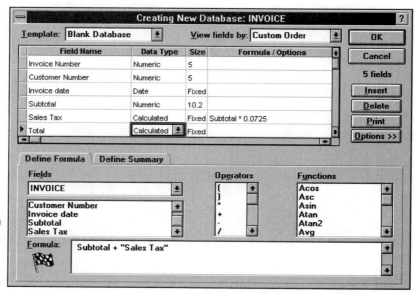

Figure 2-6:
Defining a
formula.

You can use two methods to construct the formula: either type the formula in the Formula box or construct the formula piece by piece by clicking fields, operators, and functions that you want to include in the formula. For example, to construct the formula shown in Figure 2-6, I first clicked the Subtotal field in the Fields list, then I clicked the plus sign, and then I clicked the Sales Tax field. Each time you click an element, Approach adds it to the Formula box.

- ✔ Approach formulas are similar to the formulas used in 1-2-3 or other spreadsheet programs. For all the gory details on creating formulas, see Chapter 13.

- ✔ If a field name consists of two or more words, such as Sales Tax, it must be enclosed in quotation marks in a formula. If you copy the field name into the formula by clicking it in the Fields list, Approach supplies the quotes for you. If you type the formula yourself, don't forget the quotes.

- ✔ The checkered flag next to the formula indicates whether the formula is acceptable. When the checkered flag has a red X through it, the formula isn't acceptable. Usually, a red X just means that you're in the process of building an acceptable formula and haven't finished adding all the pieces. After you complete the formula, the red X will disappear, indicating that the formula is finished.

- ✔ See the Define Summary tab? Try to ignore it for now. Resist the temptation to click it until you have read Chapter 13.

- ✔ Remember that the user cannot type a value into a calculated field. If you want to use a formula to provide a default field value that the user can override, use a default formula instead. See the section, "Creating Fields That Fill Themselves In," earlier in the chapter, for details.

Chapter 3

Self-Help for Lonely Approach Users

• •

In This Chapter

▶ Don't panic! Help is on the way!

▶ Using Help

▶ Getting Help that doesn't go away

▶ Searching for specific Help topics

• •

*T*he ideal way to use Approach would be to have an Approach expert sitting patiently at your side, answering your every question with a straightforward answer, gently correcting you when you make silly mistakes, and otherwise minding his or her own business. All you'd have to do is occasionally toss the expert a Twinkie and let him or her outside once a day.

Short of that, the next best thing is to learn how to use Approach's built-in help system. No matter how deeply you're lost in the Approach jungle, help is never more than a few keystrokes or mouse clicks away.

Approach's Help system is similar to the Help system found in other Windows programs, so if you know how to use another program's Help, you'll have no trouble figuring out Approach's.

Several Ways to Get Help

As with everything else in Windows, more than one method is available for calling up help when you need it. The easiest thing to do would be to simply yell, "Skipper!!!!!!" in your best Gilligan voice. Otherwise, you have the following options:

✔ Press F1 at any time and help is on its way. If you press F1 when you're in the middle of something, odds are Approach will come through with help on doing just the task you are trying to accomplish. This slick little bit of wizardry is called *context-sensitive help.*

✔ If you click <u>H</u>elp on the menu bar, you get a whole menu of help stuff, most of which is only moderately helpful. <u>H</u>elp⇨<u>C</u>ontents shows a list of broad Help categories that you can pick from. It's useful when you're not sure what you're looking for. <u>H</u>elp⇨Help <u>S</u>earch enables you to search for help on a specific topic by typing a word to look up, such as **field** or **sort**. Other <u>H</u>elp menu items give you additional Help information that is worth perusing on a rainy day. Details on finding your way around the <u>H</u>elp commands are found in later sections in this chapter.

✔ Whenever a dialog box is displayed, you can click the question mark in the upper-right corner of the dialog box to call up specific help for that dialog box.

✔ If you're baffled by an icon on the icon bar, try pointing at it. After a second, a cartoon balloon appears, explaining the function of the button. This balloon Help works the same as in other Lotus programs.

✔ With a sound card, a microphone, and the right voice recognition software, you probably could teach your computer to call up Help when you yell, "Skipper!" That would be kind of silly, though, don't you think?

Finding Your Way Around in Help

If you click <u>H</u>elp in the Approach menu bar or press Alt+H, you see the menu shown in Figure 3-1. The <u>H</u>elp menu is similar to the Help menus found in most other Windows programs, except that it contains a few commands that are specific to Approach, just to complicate your life. If you know how to use Help in any other Windows program, you already have a head start.

Figure 3-1:
The <u>H</u>elp
menu.

Help
<u>C</u>ontents
Help <u>S</u>earch...
<u>U</u>sing Help
<u>F</u>or Upgraders
<u>H</u>ow Do I?
<u>K</u>eyboard
F<u>u</u>nctions
<u>W</u>orking Together
Customer Su<u>p</u>port
<u>T</u>utorial
<u>A</u>bout Approach...

To get started with Help, choose the Help⇨Contents command. You'll be greeted with the colorful display that Figure 3-2 shows in black and white. This dialog box is the contents page, in which the entire contents of Approach's on-line Help is divided into 12 neat categories — Basics, How Do I?, Approach Work Area, and so on.

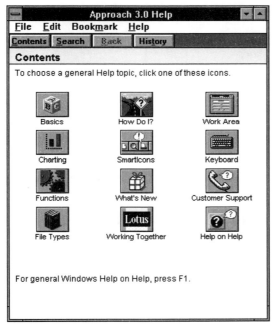

Figure 3-2:
Help
contents.

To display help on one of these subjects, just click the appropriate icon. A detailed contents list for the subject will appear. For example, Figure 3-3 shows the Contents list that is displayed when you click the How Do I? icon. Click any of the items in the Contents list to see a submenu that lists the Help topics related to the item. In Figure 3-3, the submenu for "Find and sort records" is visible.

To display a particular Help topic, click the topic title in the Contents list. For example, Figure 3-4 shows the Help topic for the About joining and unjoining topic.

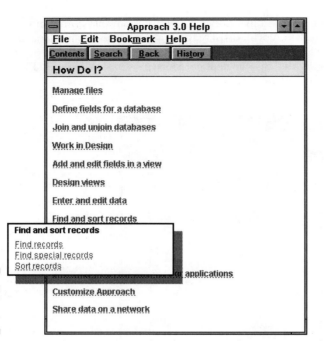

Figure 3-3:
How Do I?
Help topics.

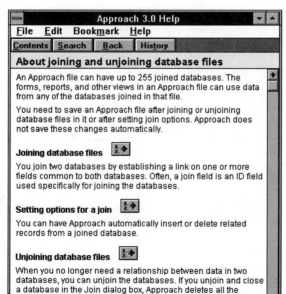

Figure 3-4:
The Help
topic for
joining and
unjoining
databases.

After you get yourself this deep into the Help system, you need to heed the following advice to find your way around and get out when you find out what you want to know:

- ✔ You can retrace your steps by clicking the Help window's Back button. You can use Back over and over again, retracing all your steps if necessary.

- ✔ Click the Contents button to return directly to the Contents screen.

- ✔ If you find a Help topic that you consider uncommonly useful, choose File➪Print to print a copy of it.

- ✔ If you see a word or phrase that is underlined, you can click it to zip to a Help page that describes that word or phrase. By following these underlined words, you can bounce your way around from Help page to Help page until you eventually find the help you need.

- ✔ If you find a Help topic that you like, choose the Bookmark➪Define command and click the OK button in the dialog box that appears. Then, when you want to call up the same Help topic quickly, click the Bookmark menu item. Lo and behold, the topic you defined as a bookmark will appear right there in the Bookmark menu. Click it, and — Presto! — the topic will appear.

- ✔ Help operates as a separate program in its own window, and you can resize the Help window to your taste. As you resize it, Windows automatically adjusts the text displayed in the window to fit the margins dictated by the new window size. You also can use the Alt-Tab key combination to switch back and forth between Approach and Help.

- ✔ When you've had enough of Help, you can dismiss it by pressing the Esc key, choosing File➪Exit, or double-clicking Help's control box in the upper-left corner of the Help window.

Using Stay-on-Top Help Procedures

Approach has an unusual Help feature that enables you to display step-by-step procedures in Help topics while you work. For example, if you're not sure how to join databases, you can call up the procedure for joining databases and keep it on the screen while you follow the steps. This method is considerably more convenient than pasting yellow sticky-notes all over the computer screen.

Lotus calls these procedures *Steps topics* because they contain step-by-step instructions. I prefer to call them *stay-on-top Help procedures* to emphasize that these windows always stay visible, even while you work in Approach.

To call up a stay-on-top Help procedure, follow these steps:

1. **Choose Help⇨How Do I?**

   You can find the stay-on-top Help procedures elsewhere in Help, but the easiest way to find them is through the How Do I? Contents list.

2. **Click the How Do I? item that relates the closest to the topic you're looking for.**

   The topic's submenu appears.

3. **Click the submenu item that describes the procedure you want to display.**

4. **If another submenu appears, find the specific procedure you want and click it.**

5. **The stay-on-top procedure is displayed.**

   The procedure is displayed in its own Help window, which stays on top of the screen while you work. See Figure 3-5.

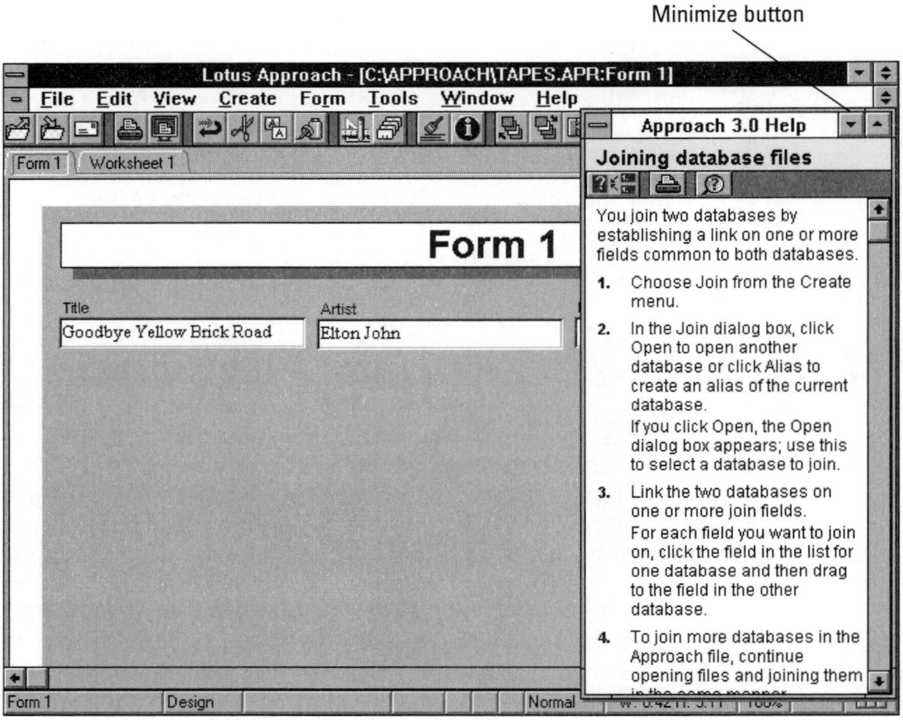

Minimize button

Figure 3-5:
A stay-on-top Help window.

6. Follow the steps listed in the Help window.

The Help window stays visible, even while you work in Approach. That way, you can easily follow the steps listed in the procedure.

7. If the Help window gets in the way, move it by dragging its title bar or minimize it to an icon by clicking the minimize button in the upper-right corner of the Help window.

Sometimes, the Help window just gets in the way. You can move it temporarily by dragging it to a new location or dropping it down to an icon. Double-click the icon to restore the Help window.

8. When you're done, click in the Help window and then press Esc.

This action dismisses the Help window.

Here are a few ponderables concerning stay-on-top windows:

 ✔ Some of the How Do I? topics begin with the word *About;* for example, About joining and unjoining. When you select one of these topics, you see an overview of the procedures that are available for the topic, along with a special icon that enables you to call up the stay-on-top window to display the procedure. If you click this icon, the procedure will appear in its own stay-on-top window.

 ✔ To display the About topic for a procedure, click the About icon.

 ✔ To display additional details about a procedure, click the Details icon.

 ✔ To print the procedure, click the Print icon.

Searching for Lost Help Topics

If you can't find help for a nasty problem by browsing through Help⇨Contents, try using Help⇨Help Search instead. It enables you to whittle your way through an alphabetical listing of all of the Help topics that are available. With luck, you can quickly find the help you're looking for.

When you choose the Help⇨Help Search command, the dialog box shown in Figure 3-6 is displayed. In this box, you can type the text that you want to search for to zip quickly through the list to the words you want to find. If you see a match that looks as if it may be helpful, click the Show Topics button. A list of all related topics will appear in the bottom part of the window. Then double-click the topic that you want to display.

Instead of typing a word, you can just scroll through the entire listing of Help topics. This method is sometimes the only way to find the help you need.

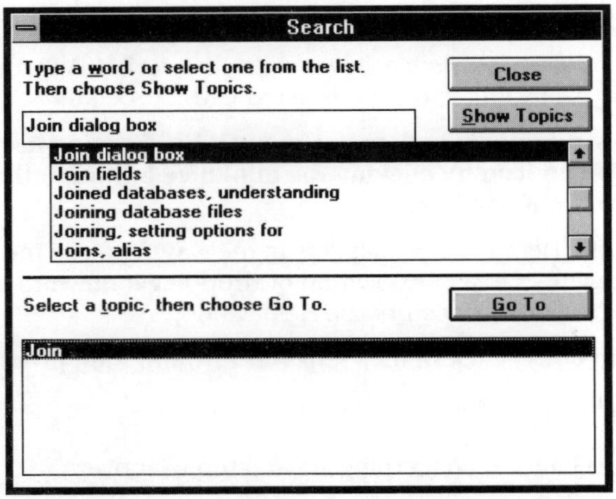

Figure 3-6: Searching for help.

Chapter 4
Entering and Updating Data

● ●

In This Chapter
▶ Using Browse mode
▶ Adding records
▶ Duplicating records
▶ Deleting database records
▶ Locating records
▶ Entering and changing data

● ●

*T*he fun part of working with Approach is designing databases, forms, reports, and other glitzy stuff. The not-so-fun part is doing real work: typing in the names of 600 customers and prospects, updating records when people have the gall to move without first considering how much work the address changes will cause you, and deleting records for customers you haven't heard from in umpteen years.

The best way to deal with this chapter is to delegate the responsibility of entering and updating data to someone else. Then you can hand this book to the person who is doing data entry and say, "Read Chapter 4! You'll love it!" If you haven't been able to find someone gullible enough to take the work off your hands, all I can say is, "Read Chapter 4! You'll love it!"

Working in Browse Mood

As I pointed out in Chapter 1, Approach is a moody program. Altogether, Approach has four moods:

✔ *Design mood* is where you create new database files, lay out forms and reports, and so on.
✔ *Browse mood* is where you enter information into the database.

✔ *Find mood* is where you tell Approach that you want to find all of the database records that meet some criteria, such as "everyone who owes you more than $20" or "all brown-eyed, left-handed Republicans who live within two miles of a WalMart."

✔ *Preview mood* is where you check the final appearance of a report, mailing label, form letter, or anything else you want to print before you print it.

This chapter explains how to work in Browse mode to add new database records, update existing records, and delete records that you no longer need.

You can tell what mood Approach is in by looking at the status bar on the bottom of the Approach window.

When you open an existing database, you are automatically placed in Browse mood so you can begin entering data. When you create a new database, you're placed in Design mood so you can lay out the database. You have to switch to Browse mood before you can enter data.

You can switch to Browse mood by using any of the following techniques:

✔ Press Ctrl+B.

 ✔ Click the Browse icon.

✔ Choose the View⇨Browse command.

✔ Select Browse mood from the View pop-up menu on the status bar.

Note: When you work in Browse mood, any changes that you make to the database file are immediately written to the file. You do not need to use the File⇨Save command to save changes. You use the File⇨Save command for saving changes that you make to the *design* of the database while you are working in Design mood.

Adding a New Record

To add a new record to a database, use one of the following techniques:

✔ Press Ctrl+N.

 ✔ Click the New Record icon.

✔ Choose the Browse⇨New Record command.

A new record will be added at the end of the database. The new record will be blank, except for fields that are given a default value. If you have assigned a sort order for the database, the record will be relocated to its proper location in the database after you have entered the record's data.

Duplicating a Database Record

You'll often find yourself entering a sequence of records that are similar, with data that varies in only a few of each record's fields. In this case, duplicating an existing record and changing a few of the fields is easier than entering the entire record from scratch.

To duplicate a database record, follow this procedure:

1. **Select the record that you want to duplicate.**

   For information about moving to a specific record, see the section, "Moving Around in a Database," later in this chapter.

 2. **Click the Duplicate Record icon or choose the Browse⇨Duplicate Record command.**

   Approach will insert a new record containing data copied from the existing record that you selected in Step 1.

3. **Make whatever changes you want to make to the duplicate record.**

Here are some points to ponder when you are duplicating database records:

✔ Database purists who need to get a life throw their arms up in disgust and emit vile sounds when told that Approach enables you to create duplicate database records. According to their religious beliefs (that is, according to Relational Database Theory), duplicate records in a relational database are strictly anathema.

✔ If a default value is specified for a field, the default value is used rather than the value of the existing record's field. For example, a record that has a serial number field won't be an identical duplicate of the original record.

✔ To duplicate the value of a single field rather than an entire record, see the section "Duplicating a field's value" later in this chapter.

✔ Too bad there's no keyboard shortcut for duplicating records.

Deleting a Record

To delete a database record, follow this procedure:

1. **Select the record that you want to delete.**

   For information about moving to a specific record, see the section "Moving Around in a Database" later in this chapter.

 2. **Click the Delete icon, use the Browse⇨Delete command, or press Ctrl+Delete.**

   Approach will display a gentle reminder that what you are about to do could be foolish.

3. **Click Yes.**

   The record is deleted.

Don't you dare forget the following important safety tips:

✔ Double-check that you have selected the correct record before you delete it. You cannot recover a deleted record; you can only create a new record and retype the deleted record's information.

✔ You can quickly delete all of the records that match a search criteria by first choosing the Find command to find all of the records that you want to delete and then choosing the Browse⇨Delete Found Set command. The Find command is discussed in Chapter 5.

Moving Around in a Database

When you work with data in Browse mood, you work with one record at a time in forms. To get any work done, you need to know how to move forward and backward through the database to work with different records, unless you're content to work with the same record every time you use Approach!

Moving forward one record

To move forward to the next record in the database, do any of the following:

 ✔ Click the Next Record icon in the icon bar at the top of the screen.

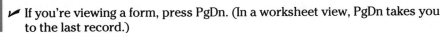 ✔ Click the Next Record button in the status bar at the bottom of the screen.

✔ If you're viewing a form, press PgDn. (In a worksheet view, PgDn takes you to the last record.)

Moving backwards one record

To move backwards to the previous record in the database, do any of the following:

 ✔ Click the Previous Record icon in the icon bar at the top of the screen.

 ✔ Click the Previous Record button in the status bar at the bottom of the screen.

✔ If you're viewing a form, press PgUp. (In a worksheet view, pressing PgUp takes you to the first database record.)

Moving to the first record

To move directly to the first record in the database, do any of the following:

 ✔ Click the First Record icon in the icon bar at the top of the screen.

✔ Press Ctrl+Home.

✔ In a worksheet view, press PgUp.

Moving to the last record

To move directly to the last record in the database, do any of the following:

✔ Click the Last Record icon in the icon bar at the top of the screen.

✔ Press Ctrl+End.

✔ In a worksheet view, press PgDn.

Moving to a specific record

To move directly to a specific record in the database, follow this procedure:

1. Click the record number in the status bar or press Ctrl+W.

Either way, the Go To Record dialog box shown in Figure 4-1 appears.

Figure 4-1:
The Go To
Record
dialog box.

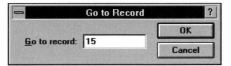

2. **Type the number of the record that you want to go to.**

3. **Click OK.**

Entering and Editing Data

To enter data into a form field, all you have to do is move the insertion point to the field and start typing. You need to know several techniques, such as how to move from field to field, how to select text, and so on. Although most of these techniques are similar to the techniques that you use to perform the same functions in other Windows programs, you need to be aware of a few variations.

Moving from field to field

You can move the insertion point from field to field in several ways:

- ✔ Click the field to which you want to move the insertion point.

- ✔ Press the Tab key to move forward from field to field until the insertion point moves to the field you want.

- ✔ Press Shift+Tab to move backwards from field to field until you arrive at the field you want.

  You can change the tabbing order for form fields if you choose. See Chapter 9 for details.

- ✔ If the Preferences are set up properly, you also can press Enter to move forward from field to field or press Shift+Enter to move backwards. See Chapter 21 for information about setting the Preferences to work this way.

The normal way to enter values for a database record is to type the value for the first field and then press Tab (or Enter, if the Preferences are set to enable you to do so) to move to the next field. Type the value for the next field and then press Tab or Enter again, until you have entered all of the field values.

To skip a field, simply press Tab twice so the insertion point jumps over that field to the next field in sequence. If the field you want to skip is defined with the Filled In validation option, you cannot use this method. In that case, after the insertion point enters the field, Approach doesn't let it escape until you enter a value for the field.

You also may notice that some fields are given default values. You can change the default values if you want, or you can tab over the field to let the default value stand.

If you cannot select a field by clicking in it or by tabbing to it, the field is probably a calculated field. Approach doesn't let you type anything into calculated fields because Approach automatically computes the value of a calculated field by using a formula.

Moving the insertion point

As in other Windows programs, you can use the arrow keys alone or in combination with other keys to move the insertion point around and to select text. To move the insertion point around, use the keyboard keys listed in Table 4-1.

Table 4-1	Keyboard Tricks for Moving the Insertion Point
Keystroke	*What It Does*
→	Moves the insertion point one character to the right
←	Moves the insertion point one character to the left
↑	Moves the insertion point up one line (memo fields only)
↓	Moves the insertion point down one line (memo fields only)
End	Moves the insertion point to the end of the field value
Home	Moves the insertion point to the first character of the field
Ctrl+→	Moves the insertion point one word to the right
Ctrl+←	Moves the insertion point one word to the left
Tab	Moves the insertion point to the next field on the form
Shift+Tab	Moves the insertion point to the preceding field on the form

You also can move the insertion point to any location by moving the mouse pointer to the new location and clicking the left mouse button.

To select text so you can delete it or copy it, hold down the Shift key while you move the insertion point by using the appropriate keys. Or drag the mouse over the text that you want to select. Two text-selecting shortcuts require a modest bit of mouse dexterity:

✔ To select an entire word, double-click anywhere in the word.

✔ To select all of the text in a field, hold down Ctrl and click anywhere in the field.

Some commonly used keyboard combinations do unexpected things when you use them in Approach:

- ✔ Ctrl+Delete deletes the current record. In most other Windows programs, Ctrl+Delete deletes the current word. Fortunately, Approach asks for confirmation before it deletes the record.

- ✔ Ctrl+Backspace doesn't delete the preceding word as it does in most other Windows programs. Actually, it doesn't do anything worthwhile, so don't use it.

- ✔ Approach always operates in Insert mode, in which characters you type at the keyboard are inserted at the location of the insertion point. In many other Windows programs, the Insert key switches between Insert mode and Overtype mode, in which characters you type at the keyboard replace existing text in the field.

Cutting, copying, and pasting

You can use the standard Windows commands to cut, copy, and paste text from one field to another. When you cut a block of text, the text is removed from the field and placed on the Clipboard, where you can retrieve it later if you want. Copying text stores the text in the Clipboard but doesn't remove it from the field.

To cut text, first mark the block of text that you want to cut by using the keyboard or the mouse. Then conjure up the Cut command by using either of these methods:

- ✔ Choose the Edit⇨Cut command from the menu bar.
- ✔ Press Ctrl+X.

The text will vanish from the screen, but don't worry. The text is safely nestled away in the Clipboard.

To copy text, mark the block and invoke the Copy command by using one of these methods:

- ✔ Choose the Edit⇨Copy command from the menu bar.
- ✔ Press Ctrl+C.

The text is copied to the Clipboard, but this time it doesn't vanish from the screen.

To paste text from the Clipboard, move the insertion point to the field where you want the text pasted. Then invoke the Paste command by using one of these techniques:

- ✔ Use the Edit⇨Paste command from the menu bar.
- ✔ Press Ctrl+V.

You can paste text into a different field within the same record, or you can paste text into a different record or even into a different database.

Duplicating a field's value

You can quickly duplicate a field value from another record by moving the insertion point to the field and using one of the following techniques:

- ✔ Click the Previous Value icon.
- ✔ Press Ctrl+Shift+P.
- ✔ Choose the Browse⇨Insert⇨Previous Value command.

The value from the corresponding field in the most recently modified database record will be copied into the field. Copying a value is useful when you're entering in succession several records that have the same value for certain fields.

Setting every field to the same value

Approach provides a simple way to enter the same value into a field in every record in a database or in a set of records that match some criteria you specify. This feature is best used in conjunction with the Find command, which enables you to select a set of records to be modified based on any criteria you want.

Follow these steps to set every field to the same value:

1. **Use the Find command to select the records that you want to modify.**

   Skip this step if you want to set the field value for every record in the database. For details on using the Find command, see Chapter 5.

2. **Select the field that you want to modify.**

   It doesn't matter which record is displayed when you set the field.

3. **Choose Browse⇨Fill Field.**

   The Fill Field dialog box appears, as shown in Figure 4-2.

Fill Field

For each record in the found set, set field "TAPES.Tape format" to:

OK

Cancel

8-Track

Figure 4-2:
The Fill Field
dialog box.

4. **Type the value that you want to enter into every record in the dialog box and then click OK.**

   The fill value is copied into the selected field in every record.

The Fill Field command replaces any values that are currently in the selected field. You are not prompted before such replacements are made, so be sure to read carefully the message in the Fill Field dialog box to make sure that you have selected the correct field.

Entering Field Values

Entering a value into a field is as simple as selecting the field and typing the value. Well, almost. You need to be aware of a few details for certain field types.

Text fields

You can type any value that you want into a text field. The only restriction is that you cannot type more characters than you specified as the field length when you defined the field. In other words, if the field length is 30, you cannot type more than 30 characters into the field.

Note that you can't always judge the maximum length of a field by its size on a form. When you lay out a form, you can make the form field as large or as small as you want. If the form field is not large enough to display the entire text of the field, the text will automatically be scrolled within the field.

Also, some text fields allow only certain values to be entered into the field. If you're lucky, such fields are set up in the entry form as a drop-down list that includes the allowable values. To select a value, you click the down-arrow next to the field to reveal the list and then click the value that you want to use for the field.

Numeric fields

Approach ignores any nonnumeric characters that you type into a numeric field. Thus, if you type $49.95, Approach ignores the dollar sign and treats the number as 49.95.

If a numeric form field has the Use as Data Entry Format option setting, underlines appear in the field to show how many digits you can enter.

Memo fields

You can type an almost unlimited amount of text into a memo field. If you type more text than will fit in the form field, a scroll bar appears so that you can scroll the text.

Boolean fields

To enter data into a boolean field, type **Yes**, **Y**, **yes**, **y**, or **1** for a yes value or **No**, **N**, **no**, **n**, or **0** for a no value. If the boolean field is a check box field, just click the check box to switch between Yes and No values.

Date fields

To enter a date field, type the month, day, and year by using numbers separated by nonnumeric characters, such as 05/16/94 or 12/31/95.

To enter the current date in a date field, use one of the following techniques:

  ✔ Click the Insert Today's Date icon.

  ✔ Press Ctrl+Shift+D.

  ✔ Choose the Browse⇨Insert⇨Today's Date command.

If date fields are set up with the Use as Data Entry Format option, separator characters and underlines will appear to indicate how to type the date. In this case, you don't have to type the separator characters yourself; just type the month, day, and year values, and Approach will format the date accordingly.

Time fields

To enter a time value, you can use a 12-hour clock or a 24-hour clock to type the hours and minutes. Type the hour and minutes as numbers separated by colons, as in **11:30** or **7:15**. If you use a 12-hour clock, you have to type **PM** to indicate a PM time; otherwise, AM is assumed. If you want to, you can type seconds and even hundredths of seconds. For example, you can type 11:30:45 or 11:30:45.99.

To enter the current time in a time field, use one of the following techniques:

- ✔ Click the Insert Current Time icon.
- ✔ Press Ctrl+Shift+T.
- ✔ Choose the Browse➪Insert➪Current Time command.

As with date fields, you can use the Use as Data Entry Format option when you set up time fields. Separator characters and underlines will appear to indicate how to type the time. Then you just type the hours and minutes (and seconds if indicated), and Approach will format the time accordingly.

PicturePlus fields

PicturePlus fields can hold graphics or embedded OLE objects such as sound files, charts, spreadsheet ranges, or Lord knows what. For details on working with PicturePlus fields, turn ahead to Chapter 12.

Chapter 5
Finders Keepers

● ●

In This Chapter
▶ Working in Find mood
▶ Using the all-powerful Find
▶ Using advanced search criteria
▶ Using multiple find requests
▶ Dealing with duplicates

● ●

*T*he Find feature has many uses. For example, it can help you find that elusive record that you know is in the database somewhere when you're too busy to examine 5,000 records, one at a time, to locate it. Or it can enable you to restrict reports to records that meet certain criteria, such as everyone who owes you more than $20 or all left-handed bald customers. Or it can enable you to ask silly questions, such as, "I wonder how many of my customers live in California?" or, better yet, "I wonder how many of my customers live in California, are left handed, bald, and owe me more than $20?"

Archimedes (287 – 212 B.C.), the ancient mathematician of Syracuse on whom you can blame much of high school geometry, would have loved Find. You can almost hear him shouting, "Eureka! I found it!" as the Find command completes a painstaking search of a database.

Understanding Find Mood

In Chapter 1, I pointed out that Approach is a moody program. Find is one of Approach's four basic modes (which I like to refer to as *moods*). Besides Find mood, the other three moods are Browse, Design, and Preview. To search a database for certain records, you first need to enter Find mood. Entering Find mood brings up the views (forms, reports, worksheets, and so on) that you have created for the database so that you can type search values into database fields. For example, to find all of your customers who are unlucky enough to live in Los Angeles, type **Los Angeles** in the City field.

You can switch to Find mood by using any of the following techniques:

- ✔ Click the Find icon.
- ✔ Choose Find from the pop-up View menu in the status bar at the bottom of the screen.
- ✔ Choose the Browse⊃Find command.
- ✔ Press Ctrl+F.

Each of these methods displays the current database form so that you can type the search values that you want to look for.

After you finish typing the search criteria, Approach searches the database and selects the records that match the search criteria. Approach then automatically puts you back in Browse mood, but this time it displays only the records found in the search. Approach calls these records the *found set.*

The status bar at the bottom of the screen indicates how many records are included in the found set. For example, if Find selects 75 records from a database that contains a total of 300 records, the status bar indicates Found 75 of 300. (The only way to tell that you are working with the entire database, rather than with a found set, is that both numbers in the status bar are the same; for example, Found 300 of 300.)

Here are some important facts to keep in mind when you are using Find:

- ✔ The values you type into database fields for a Find are called *search criteria.* Each form you fill in with search criteria is called a *find request.* You can use several find requests together for elaborate searches.

- ✔ Although you usually work with forms when you are setting up a find request, you also can work with worksheets or reports. The database view that is active when you choose the Find command is the one that's used to create the find request.

- ✔ You can search for a specific value in a field by typing the value in the field, or you can use special symbols to search for a range of values. For example, type >**100** in a numeric field to find all records that have a value greater than 100 in the field.

- ✔ You can search for values in more than one database field at a time. For example, you may want to find all customers who live in Los Angeles and owe you more than $100. To perform that task, type **Los Angeles** in the City field and >**100** in Amount Owed field.

- ✔ In general, the more fields you type search criteria into, the fewer records will be included in the found set. That's just common sense. All of your Los

Angeles customers probably don't owe you $100 or more; just as not all of the customers who owe you $100 live in L.A.

✔ To cancel a Find and redisplay all of the records in the database, choose the Browse⇨Show All command, click the Show All icon, or type Ctrl+A.

Using Find

The simplest way to use Find is to look for records that have specific values in one or more database fields. Follow this procedure:

1. Open the database that you want to search if it is not already open.

Choose the File⇨Open command, click the Open icon, or open the file from the Welcome to Lotus Approach dialog box.

2. Click the Find icon to switch to Find Mood.

Or choose Find from the pop-up View menu in the status bar at the bottom of the screen, choose the Browse⇨Find command, or press Ctrl+F. Either way, the current form will be displayed in Find Mood, as shown in Figure 5-1.

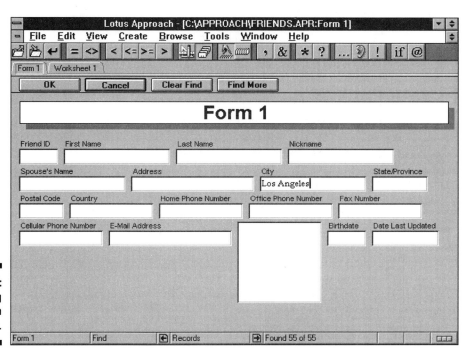

Figure 5-1: Entering search criteria.

3. **Type the search criteria into each field that you want searched.**

In Figure 5-1, I typed Los Angeles into the City field but left all the other fields blank. The Find will select all records that have Los Angeles in the City field.

4. **Click OK.**

Alternatively, press the Enter key or click the Enter icon.

5. **Marvel at the results.**

Approach puts you back into Browse mood, displaying just the records that match the search criteria, as Figure 5-2 shows. Notice how the status bar indicates how many records are in the found set — in this case, by displaying Found 5 of 55.

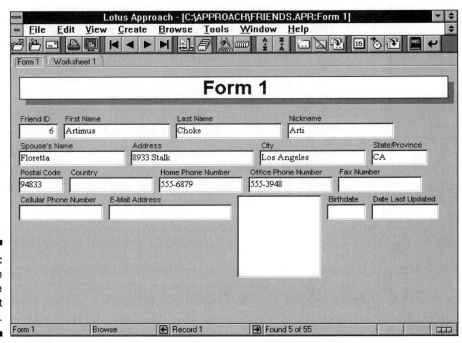

Figure 5-2: Approach displays the records it finds.

Here are a few deep thoughts concerning Find:

- ✔ If the database has a large number of records and you realize mid-way through a Find that you made a boo-boo, you can halt Approach in the middle of the Find by pressing Esc.

- ✔ To "unfind" records and redisplay all of the records in the database, click the Show All icon, choose the Browse⇨Show All command, or press Ctrl+A.

- ✔ To delete all records that match a criteria, first use Find to find the records you want to delete. Then choose the Browse⇨Delete Found Set command to delete the duplicates that were found.

- ✔ Each time you use Find, the previous found set is discarded, and the entire database is searched again. For example, if you first use Find to display all Los Angeles customers and then use Find again to display all customers who owe you more than $100, every customer who owes you more than $100 will be displayed, regardless of where they live. If you want to display all L.A. customers who owe you more than $100, you have to do so in a single Find by entering the search criteria for both fields at once.

Fiendishly Advanced Finds

If you could search only for records that contained specific values in specific fields, Find would be useful only in limited situations. For example, you could find customers who live in Los Angeles; but what if you wanted to find customers who live in Los Angeles or in San Francisco? Or what if you wanted to find customers who live in California but not in Los Angeles?

Fortunately, Approach enables you to search for just about every oddball combination of field values by using special *operators* in the search criteria. Table 5-1 summarizes these operators, and the following sections describe them in detail. Note that you can type the operators directly into a field or you can click on the operator's icon to insert it into a field.

Table 5-1		Search Operators
Operator	*Icon*	*What It Means*
<	<	Less than
<=	<=	Less than or equal to
>=	>=	Greater than or equal to
>	>	Greater than
=	=	Equal to
<>	<>	Not equal to
,	,	Or (within a field)
&	&	And (within a field)
...	...	Range of values (for example, 500...1000)
*	*	Wild card for zero or more characters
?	?	Wild card for a single character
@	@	Formula
!	!	Case sensitive
~	~	Sounds like
If	if	Advanced comparisons for database geeks

Greater Than, Less Than, and so on

The comparison operators are used mostly with numbers to search for field values that are greater than or less than a particular value. Here are some examples:

>0	Any value greater than zero
>=0	Any value greater than or equal to zero
<1000	Any value less than 1000
<=10	Any value less than or equal to 10

These operators also can be used with dates and times:

>=1/1/94	January 1, 1994, or later
<12:00	Before 12:00 noon

You also can use the equal sign as an operator, but doing so is not usually necessary. For example, to match the number *100,* you can type **100** or **=100**. The result is the same.

Not Equal To

Use the Not Equal To operator to find all records in which a particular field's value is anything but the value you specify. For example, to find all customers who do not live in Los Angeles, type **<>Los Angeles** as the search criteria for the City field.

Blank and nonblank fields

To find all records in which a particular field is blank, type an equal sign (=) by itself as the search criteria for the field.

To find all records in which a particular field is not blank, but has a value typed into it, type **<>** by itself as the search criteria for the field.

Ranges

To search for a range of values in a field, use the ellipses (...) operator. For example, type **0...100** as a search criteria to search for all values from 0 to 100.

You can use ranges in text fields, too. For example, typing **A...M** finds all strings that begin with A through M. This operator is perfect for assigning main dishes or desserts for a potluck.

Ranges also can be used with dates. For example, to find any date in the 1960s, use the range **1/1/60...12/31/69**.

And/Or

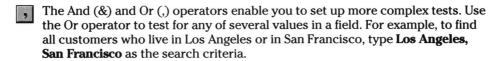

The And (&) and Or (,) operators enable you to set up more complex tests. Use the Or operator to test for any of several values in a field. For example, to find all customers who live in Los Angeles or in San Francisco, type **Los Angeles, San Francisco** as the search criteria.

The And operator is a bit confusing. You use it when you want to find all records in which a field's value meets two distinct conditions. For example, to find customers who owe you $100 or more, but not more than $1000, type **>=100 & <=1000**. (However, you can more easily express this condition as a range: **100...1000**.)

You have to be careful how you use &; you can all too easily concoct conditions that can never be met. For example, if you type **Los Angeles & San Francisco**, no records will be selected, except for those few customers who have figured out how to make some sort of cross-dimensional leap such that they are able to be in two places at the same time.

One way to use & is in conjunction with wild card characters, which are described next. For example, suppose that a database contains a text field named Hobbies. To find anyone who enjoys both hiking and fishing, you type ***hiking*&*fishing*** as the search criteria.

Wild cards

Approach enables you to use wild cards when you are searching text fields. These wild cards stand for unknown characters in the field's value.

 You can use an asterisk (*) wild card to search for any combination of characters, including no characters at all. For example:

John*	Finds John, Johnson, Johnny, and John Smith
*son	Finds Johnson, Olson, Carlson, and Son
*s*on	Finds Johnson, Olson, Carlson, Son, Johnston, and Stallion
son	Finds Johnson, Olson, Carlson, Son, Sonny, and Arsonist

The question mark stands in for a single character:

jo?n	Finds John and Join
??join	Finds Enjoin or Rejoin
????	Finds all four-letter words

Formulas

You can incorporate a formula or function into a search criteria by using the @ operator. This operator is most often used in conjunction with the Today function, which provides the current date. For example:

@today( )	Finds all date values that match today's date
<@today( )	Finds all date values that precede today's date
>=@today( ) + 30	Finds all date values that are 30 or more days from today's date

Case-sensitive searches

 Approach usually doesn't care whether you type text in uppercase or lower-case letters. Thus, if you type **Los Angeles** as a search value, Approach matches values such *as Los Angeles, LOS ANGELES, los angeles,* or *LoS AnGEleS.*

If the text needs to be in uppercase or lowercase, use the ! operator and then type the text exactly as you want Approach to match it. For example, if you specify **!Los Angeles** as the search value, Approach matches only fields in which both the L and the A are capitalized and all the other letters are lower-case.

Sounds like . . .

 The Sounds Like operator (~) lets you fudge a bit on the spelling. For example, if you search for *~Jeff,* Approach finds *Jeff, Jeph, Jaf,* and even *Geoff.* Sounds Like is great for catching simple misspellings, but it's also good for words that may have several alternative spellings.

The Sounds Like operator freely substitutes vowels, ignores doubled letters, and accounts for consonants that sometimes sound similar, such as *G* and *J* or *C* and *S.* It is also aware of like-sounding letter combinations such as *ck* and *k* and can properly ignore the silent *e* that frequently shows up at the end of words.

Sounds Like doesn't catch every possible phonetic misspelling. I tried it on George Bernard Shaw's famous alternative spelling of the word *fish: ghoti.* (That's *gh* as in *enough, o* as in *women,* and *ti* as in *fictitious.*) It didn't work, so be careful how you spell *fish.*

Find It Again, Sam

One way to search fields for several values is to use the Or operator (,) to separate the values in the search criteria. For example, typing **Los Angeles, San Francisco** in the City field finds everyone who lives in L.A. or Frisco. But what if you want to find everyone who lives in L.A. *or* owes you more than $100? Your first instinct would be to type **Los Angeles** in the City field and **>100** in the Amount Owed field, but that method doesn't work. It finds only those people in Los Angeles who owe you more than $100.

TECHNICAL STUFF

Skip this iffy stuff about if statements

Real database geeks don't mess around with fill-in-the-blanks search criteria. Instead, they scrape the Cheetos gunk out of their teeth and get straight to work typing If statements. If statements do the same thing as regular search criteria, but they look more like stuff Scotty would type when recalibrating the warp core or inventing transparent aluminum.

An If statement enables you to lay out the search criteria as a conditional expression, such as the following:

```
if(City = 'Los Angeles')
```

This If statement has the same effect as simply typing Los Angeles in the City field. A more useful way to use the If statement is to compare two different fields on the form. For example, if you type the following, the record will be included in the found set if the OnHand field is less than the Usage field:

```
if(OnHand < Usage)
```

You can gang conditions up on one another, too:

```
if(OnHand < Usage) And (Usage >
   10)
```

In this case, the record will be selected if the OnHand field is less than the Usage field and the Usage field is greater than 10.

The weird thing about If statements is that you can type them into any field you want; you don't have to type them into the field they test. If I were to use If statements (I don't if I can avoid it, but just in case I did), I'd type them into the first available text field on the form.

Another weird thing about If statements is the way that you use quotation marks and apostrophes. Quotation marks are required whenever you use a field *name* that includes a space or a special character that Approach may otherwise think is a math symbol, such as +, -, /, and so on (for example, "State/province" and "Customer Name"). Apostrophes are used to mark text field *values*).

To find everyone who either lives in L.A. or owes you more than $100, you have to set up two separate find requests: one that specifies Los Angeles in the City field and another that specifies >100 in the Amount Owed field. Then, when Approach searches the database, it selects all records that match either of the find requests.

Here is the procedure for setting up multiple find requests:

1. **Call up Find mood by clicking the Find icon.**

   Or choose the Browse⇨Find command, select the Find command from the pop-up menu in the status bar, or press Ctrl+F.

2. **Fill in the search criteria for the first find request.**

   For the example, type **Los Angeles** in the City field.

3. **Click the Find More button.**

   You see a blank form into which you can type additional search criteria.

4. **Fill in the search criteria for the second find request.**

   Once again using the example, type **>100** in the Amount Owed field.

5. **If you want to create even more find requests, repeat Steps 3 and 4.**

6. **When you have completed all the find requests you can tolerate, click OK to initiate the search.**

   Approach searches the database, selecting all records that match any of the find requests you create.

Here are a few titillating details regarding multiple finds:

- ✓ If you realize that you made a mistake in one of the find requests, you can cycle through the various find requests by clicking the arrows that appear in the status bar at the bottom of the screen or pressing PgUp or PgDn.

- ✓ You can think of each find request as being connected by one giant Or operator. In other words, Approach searches for all records that meet the search criteria on the first find request, or the second find request, or the third find request, and so on.

- ✓ To search for records that have one of several values in a single field, simply type the values in a single find request, separated by commas. The only time that you need to use multiple find requests is when the Or operation involves two or more fields.

- ✓ Don't press Enter or click the OK button until you have created all of the find requests.

Finding Duplicate Records

Approach provides a special Find command that helps you weed out duplicate records in a database. You can use it in three ways:

- ✓ You can search for all records that have duplicate values for certain fields. The found set includes all the duplicate records.

- ✓ You can search for all records that have duplicate values for certain fields, but then exclude the first occurrence of each set of duplicates. This option is most useful when you plan on deleting the duplicates; it leaves one copy of each duplicated record intact.

- ✓ You can search for all records that have duplicate values for certain fields, but then exclude all but the first occurrence of each set of duplicates. The found set then consists of all distinct records in the database.

Here is the procedure for finding duplicate records:

1. Choose the Browse⇨Find Special command.

The Find Special dialog box appears, as shown in Figure 5-3.

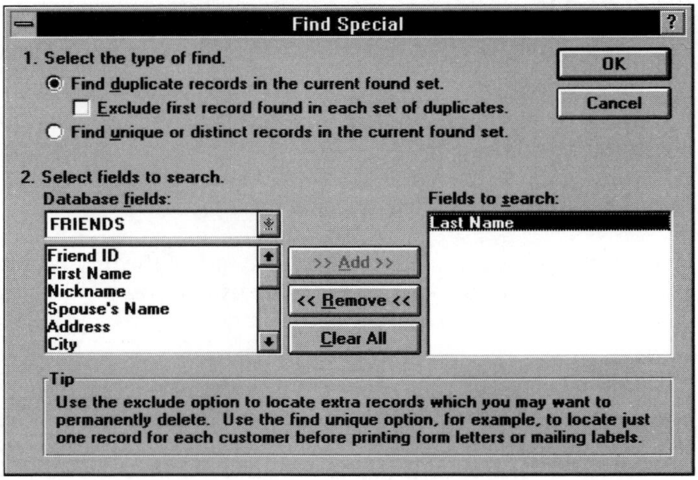

Figure 5-3:
The Find
Special
dialog box.

Inside the dialog box:

Find Special

1. Select the type of find.
   ⦿ Find duplicate records in the current found set.
     ☐ Exclude first record found in each set of duplicates.
   ◯ Find unique or distinct records in the current found set.

2. Select fields to search.
   Database fields:
   FRIENDS

   Friend ID
   First Name
   Nickname
   Spouse's Name
   Address
   City

   >> Add >>
   << Remove <<
   Clear All

   Fields to search:
   Last Name

   OK
   Cancel

   Tip
   Use the exclude option to locate extra records which you may want to
   permanently delete. Use the find unique option, for example, to locate just
   one record for each customer before printing form letters or mailing labels.

2. Select which Find Special option you want to use.

To find all duplicate values, select the Find duplicate option.

To find all duplicate values but exclude the first record of each set, select the Find duplicate option and check the Exclude check box.

To find distinct records, select the Find unique option.

3. Select the fields that you want Approach to use for comparing records.

To select a field, click it in the Database fields list and then click the Add button.

4. Click OK.

Approach searches the entire database and finds duplicate or unique records according to the Find Special option you picked in Step 2.

5. You're done!

Unlike other Find requests, you can apply the Find Special command to an existing found set. For example, you can use the Find command to find all your friends who live in Los Angeles and then use the Find Special command to weed out duplicate Los Angeles records.

To delete duplicate records, first use the <u>B</u>rowse⇨Find Spe<u>c</u>ial command to isolate the duplicates. Be sure to check the <u>E</u>xclude check box. Then use the <u>B</u>rowse⇨Delete Fo<u>u</u>nd Set command to delete the duplicates that were found.

Chapter 6

Putting Your Affairs in Order (or Sorting Database Records)

In This Chapter

▶ Sorting a database the easy way

▶ Sorting a database the hard way

▶ Creating a default sort sequence

*O*rdinarily, Approach stores database records in the order in which you enter them. For some databases, that sequence is the most practical one in which to store records. More often than not, however, another sequence is more helpful. For example, you may want to list customers by last name, inventory parts by item description, or employees by social security number.

Sort to the rescue! By using the Sort command, you can change the order in which database records are displayed. This change affects the order in which records are retrieved when you are using a form, viewing a worksheet, printing a report, or using any other database view.

The Easy Way to Sort a Database

You can sort the records in a database the easy way or the hard way. Here's the easy way:

 1. **Open the database that you want to sort.**

Use the File⇨Open command, click the Open icon, or select Open an Existing File from the Welcome to Lotus Approach dialog box.

2. **Click the field that you want the database sorted by.**

For example, to sort customer records into last name sequence, click the Last Name field.

3. Click the Sort field in ascending order icon in the icon bar.

Or choose Browse⊏>Sort⊏>Ascending. Either way, the database is sorted into *ascending* sequence according to the values in the field. In other words, ABC. . . .

If you want to sort records into *descending* sequence (ZYX . . .), click the Sort field in descending order icon or choose Browse⊏>Sort⊏>Descending.

4. Wait while Approach sorts the database.

The sort will probably take only a few seconds unless the database is really huge, such as a list of all the observable stars in the galaxy or, even worse, a list of all the line items in the federal budget.

5. Gasp in amazement when Approach displays the record in the new, hopefully more useful, sequence.

An utterance such as "Isn't that amazing?" would be appropriate here. However, your irrational sense of euphoria over what is really nothing more than a mundane computer task will soon pass. Computers have been good at sorting since about 1950, so it's really nothing to get excited about.

Here are a few sorting pointers, in no particular order:

✔ If you sort a database by clicking one of the sort icons and then select a different field and click a sort icon again, the file will be re-sorted according to the new sort field. The only way to create a two-level sort that has primary and secondary sort fields is to use the Sort command, which is described in the next section.

✔ To redisplay records in the default sequence, click the Show All icon.

✔ When you sort the database into ascending sequence, numerals come before the letters of the alphabet. When you sort it into descending sequence, numerals come after letters.

✔ Approach sorts letters without regard to case, color, or creed. Thus, field values that begin with *A* appear along with values that begin with *a,* which is as it should be.

✔ If the database is under the influence of a Find command, only the records in the found set are sorted.

Sorting terminology you can't avoid

Sorting is fairly straightforward as far as computer chores go, but a few special words have been coined by computer propellerheads in an effort to make sorting sound more complicated than it really is. Here are the more important terms demystified:

Sort field: The database field or fields that are used to sort the database records. If you sort a database into alphabetical order by using a field called Last Name, Last Name is the sort field.

Primary sort field: The main field that is used to sort the database. Most sorts use only a primary sort field. However, if more than one record in the database is likely to have the same value in the primary sort field, you can specify additional sort fields, called *secondary sort fields,* to further refine the sort.

Secondary sort field: An additional sort field that is used to sort records that have the same value for the primary sort field. For example, if you use

Last Name as the field by which to sort a database, you'll probably want to specify First Name as the secondary sort field. Then any records that have the same last name will be further sorted by first name.

Ascending sequence:
0123456789ABCDEFGHIJKLMNOPQRSTUVWXYZ, not counting special characters such as #$%^& and *.

Descending sequence:
ZYXWVUTSRQPONMLKJIHGFEDCBA9876543210, not counting special characters such as *&^%$ and #.

Default sequence: The sequence in which records are stored in the database and normally displayed. This sequence is usually the order in which you added records to the database, but you can change the default sort sequence for a database by using the Tools⇨Preferences command.

The Hard Way to Sort a Database

The easiest way to sort a database is to click the field by which you want to sort the records and then click one of the sorting icons in the icon bar. This method limits you to sorting records by only one field, however. If you want to draw several sort fields into the fray, you have no alternative but to use the intimidating Sort command.

Follow this step-by-step procedure:

1. **Choose Browse⇨Sort⇨Define.**

   Or use the handy keyboard shortcut Ctrl+T. Either way, the Sort dialog box appears, as shown in Figure 6-1.

Figure 6-1:
The Sort
dialog box.

2. **Scroll through the Database fields list until you find the field you want to use as the primary sort field, click it, and then click the Add button.**

   The field name is copied to the Fields to sort on list.

3. **Click Ascending or Descending to specify whether you want the records to be sorted on the field in ascending or descending sequence.**

4. **Repeat Steps 2 and 3 for any additional sort fields that you want to use.**

   In Figure 6-1, I selected two sort fields: Last Name and First Name.

5. **Click OK to sort the database.**

6. **Wait.**

   You probably won't have to wait more than a few seconds unless the database contains a huge amount of data, such as a detailed listing of your favorite politician's broken campaign promises.

7. **Behold your data, sorted!**

Here are a few consoling thoughts concerning the Sort dialog box:

- ✔ If you make a mistake and want to remove a field from the Fields to sort on list, click the field you want to remove in the Fields to sort on list and then click the Remove button.

- ✔ To remove all sort fields from the Fields to sort on list, click the Clear All button.

 ✔ To restore the default sort order, click the Show All icon.

- ✔ Wouldn't it be great if you could attach a sort sequence to a form, report, or other view? You can, but only by using a macro. See Chapter 19 if you're brave and have nothing better to do.

 ✔ Don't include sort fields that you don't really need. For example, I could have included City as a third sort field in Figure 6-1. That way, any friends who have the same first and last name would be further sorted by City. But is it really necessary to make sure that Joseph McGillicudy in Detroit comes before Joseph McGillicudy in Sioux City? Really?

Creating a Default Sort Sequence

Approach normally keeps records sorted in the order in which you entered them. That is, whenever you add a record to a database, that record is stored at the end of the database. If you find that you're frequently sorting the database into some other sequence, consider changing the default sort sequence for the field. Here's the procedure:

1. **Open the database that you want to sort.**

   Choose File➪Open, click the Open icon, or select Open an Existing File from the Welcome to Lotus Approach dialog box.

2. **Choose Tools➪Preferences.**

   The Preferences dialog box appears, as shown in Figure 6-2.

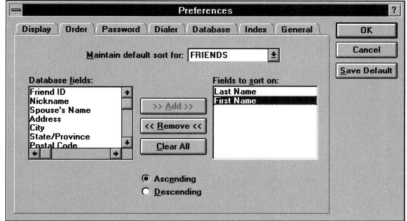

Figure 6-2:
The Preferences dialog box.

3. **Click the Order tab if the sort order options are not shown.**

4. **Scroll through the Database fields list until you find the field that you want to use as the primary sort field, click it, and then click the Add button.**

   The field name is copied to the Fields to sort on list.

5. **Click Ascending or Descending to specify whether the records should be sorted on the field in ascending or descending sequence.**

6. **Repeat Steps 4 and 5 for any additional sort fields that you want to use.**

7. Click OK.

8. You're done!

The Order options in the Preferences dialog box are similar to the Sort dialog box options, so you won't have any trouble using one if you know how to use the other.

Chapter 7
Checking Your Speling

● ●

● ●

I was voted Worst Speller in the Sixth Grade. Not that that qualifies me to run for vice president or anything, but it shows how much I appreciate computer spell checkers. Spelling makes no sense to me. I feel a little better after watching "The Story of English" on public television. Now at least I know who to blame for all the peculiarities of English spelling — the Angels, the Norms (including the guy from "Cheers"), and the Saxophones.

Once was the day that only word processors had spell checkers. Now, just about every program imaginable has a spell checker. Not wanting to be left out, Lotus vested Approach with an excellent spell checker. The same spell checker, in fact, is used by other Lotus programs such as Ami Pro and 1-2-3 for Windows.

Checking Your Spelling

Thank goodness for Approach's spell checker. It works its way through your database, looking up every word in its massive list of correctly spelled words and bringing any misspelled words to your attention. It performs this task without giggling or snickering. It gives you the opportunity, in fact, to tell it that you are right and it is wrong and that it should learn how to spell words the way you do.

Approach enables you to check the spelling in a single field of a single database record, all fields in the current record, all records in the database or in a found set, or the same field in every database record.

The following steps show the procedure for checking spelling in an Approach database:

1. **If the database is not already open, open it.**

   The view that you are in doesn't matter. You can spell check from a form, worksheet, report, or other view.

2. **If you want to check the spelling in only one record, go to that record.**

   If you plan to spell check an entire database, you can start in any record.

3. **If you want to check the spelling in only one field, click that field to select it.**

   To spell check all of the fields in the view, make sure that no field is selected. Click anywhere on the view's background to unselect any fields.

   If you want to spell check a range of text in a text or memo, drag the mouse over the text to highlight it.

 4. **Fire up the spell checker.**

   Click the Check Spelling icon in the icon bar, choose Tools⇨Spell Check, or press Ctrl+K. Whichever way you choose, the Spell Check dialog box appears, as shown in Figure 7-1.

Figure 7-1:
The Spell
Check
dialog box.

Spell Check

Check
- ◉ Selection
- ○ Current record
- ○ Found set
- ○ Selection across found set

OK
Cancel

Language Options...   Options...

Edit Dictionary...   ☒ Memo fields only

5. **Tell Spell Check what data you want it to check.**

   Click one of these four buttons:

   Selection: spell checks a single field or a range of text that is highlighted.

   Current record: spell checks all fields in the current record.

   Found set: spell checks all fields in all records in the current found set. If you haven't used the Find command, Found Set checks all records in the database.

Selection across found set: spell checks a single field in all records in the current found set or in the entire database if you haven't used the Find command.

6. **Click OK.**

7. **Tap your fingers.**

   Approach is searching your database for misspelled words. Be patient.

8. **Don't be startled if Approach finds a spelling error.**

   If Approach finds a spelling error, it uses the dialog box shown in Figure 7-2 to display the misspelled word along with suggested alternatives.

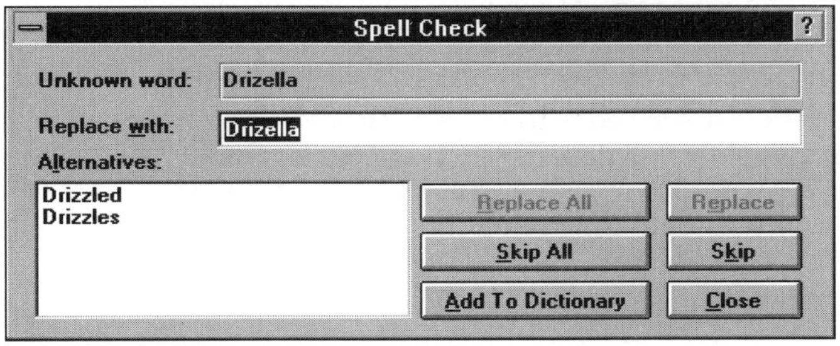

Figure 7-2:
Approach
gloats over
a spelling
error it has
found.

9. **Choose the correct spelling or laugh in Approach's face.**

   If you agree that the word is misspelled, scan the list of alternatives that Approach offers and click the one you like. Then click the Replace button. If you like the way you spelled the word in the first place (maybe it's an unusual word that isn't in Approach's dictionary, or maybe you like to spell the way that Chaucer did), click the Skip button. Watch as Approach turns red in the face.

10. **Repeat Steps 8 and 9 until Approach gives up.**

    When you see the dialog box shown in Figure 7-3, you know that you've won.

Figure 7-3:
Approach
says
"Uncle."

The remainder of this section presents some random thoughts to ponder as you spell check a database.

- ✔ Approach's dictionary is surprisingly complete when it comes to names. It didn't find Drizella in Figure 7-2, nor does it find Anastasia or Clementine. But it does find common names such as John, Judy, Johnson, and Williams.

- ✔ If Approach cannot come up with a suggestion or if none of its alternatives is correct, you can type your own correction in the Replace with field and click the Replace button. If the word you type isn't in the dictionary, Approach will flag it as an error. Click Replace again to tell Approach you really mean it.

- ✔ If you want Approach to ignore all occurrences of a particular misspelling, click the Skip All button. Likewise, if you want Approach to correct all occurrences of a particular misspelling, click Replace All.

- ✔ If you become bored with having Approach always complain about a word that's not in its dictionary (such as *Drizella*), click Add To Dictionary to add the word to the user dictionary. If you cannot sleep at night until you know more about the user dictionary, read the following section, "Using the User Dictionary."

Using the User Dictionary

Approach's spell checker uses two spelling dictionaries: a *standard dictionary*, which contains untold thousands of words all reviewed for correctness by George Bernard Shaw himself (just kidding!), and a *user dictionary,* which contains words you have added by clicking the Add To Dictionary button when the spell checker found a spelling "error."

You can edit the user dictionary directly by calling up the Spell Checker and clicking the Edit Dictionary button. Doing so brings up the Edit Dictionary dialog box that is shown in Figure 7-4.

To add a new word to the dictionary, type the word in the New word field and click Add. Words are automatically added in alphabetical order.

To delete a word from the user dictionary, scroll through the list of words in the Current word list until you find the word. Then select the word and click Delete.

Here are a couple of things to note when you are using the user dictionary:

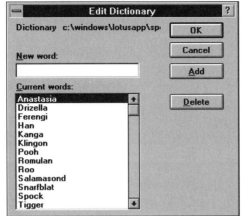

Figure 7-4:
The Edit
Dictionary
dialog box.

✔ You usually use the user dictionary for proper nouns and specialized jargon that aren't in the main dictionary. When you first begin to use the spell checker, you can expect to spend a bit of time adding entries to the user dictionary. This task will require less time, however, as the user dictionary becomes saturated with the oddball words you use most often.

✔ Approach shares the user dictionary with other Lotus applications. Thus, words that you have added in Ami Pro or 1-2-3 will be included when you are spell checking Approach files.

Setting the Spelling Options

If you call up the spell checker and click the Options button, the Speller Options dialog box shown in Figure 7-5 is displayed. This dialog box enables you to control four speller options:

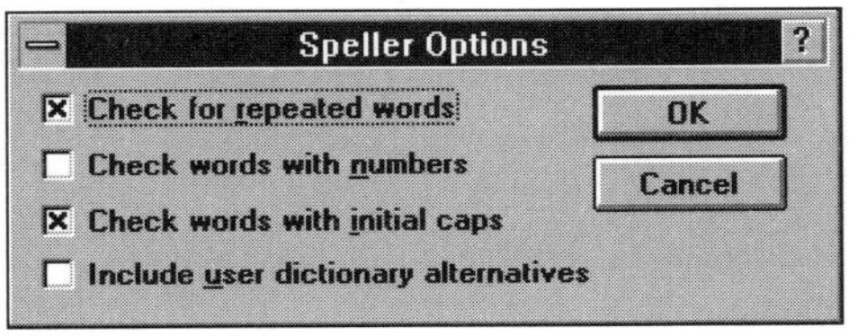

Figure 7-5:
The Speller
Options
dialog box.

Speller Options

- ☒ Check for repeated words
- ☐ Check words with numbers
- ☒ Check words with initial caps
- ☐ Include user dictionary alternatives

OK Cancel

✔ The Check for repeated words option tells Approach to to check for for repeated words in your your database. This option should usually be enabled.

✔ The Check words with numbers option tells Approach to check words that include numerals, such as T1000. If the databases include values that often mix letters and numerals (for example, B10 or I24 — Bingo!), you may want to disable this option.

✔ The Check words with initial caps option tells Approach to check words that begin with capital letters. If you deactivate this option, Approach skips most proper nouns, so you won't have to worry about adding them in a user dictionary.

✔ The Include user dictionary alternatives option tells Approach to use the user dictionary as well as the main dictionary when it suggests words as alternatives to a misspelled word.

To change the speller options, call up the Spell Checker, click the Options button, check the options you want to use, and click OK.

The 5th Wave   By Rich Tennant

Chapter 8

Joining Databases

● ●

● ●

*M*etaphor alert! The following paragraphs contain a sincere yet futile attempt on the part of the author to draw an analogy between the dry and lifeless database concept of *joins* and the real-life concept of human relationships. Computer book authors often lie awake at night, pondering the eternal significance of their writing and feeling guilty about the fact that, while they spend their lives hammering out meaningless computer books and actually make a decent living at it, their old college buddies who are actually far better writers are happy to sell their beautifully crafted short stories to obscure literary journals for $100.

When they finally drift off to sleep, computer book authors frequently have nightmares about meeting their college English professors and being asked to justify their life's work. This is why they so often attempt to use metaphors and other literary devices such as alliteration and allegory.

Relationships add spice to database life. Without relationships, databases would be empty and unsatisfied, without substance or meaning. For just as no man is an island, neither is any database an island; but rather all datakind is linked in an ever-expanding web of relationships, a vast computerized tapestry of databases joined to databases joined to databases in the never-ending circle of data.

And so it came to pass that the customer database knew the sales database, and the sales database knew the products database, and thus did they beget still more databases, all related, each after its kind.

Or something like that.

This chapter is a gentle introduction to *joins,* the amazing Approach feature that enables you to connect one database to another. If you manage to stay awake through this entire chapter, you'll discover that joins are one of Approach's most useful features, useful enough that they are worth the mental and emotional struggle that are necessary to figure out how they work.

Understanding Joins

Suppose that you own a small video rental store and you have decided to use Approach to computerize your business. You immediately create a database of all your video tapes. The records in the VIDEOS database contains information about each of the video tapes, as well as information about the customers who rent them:

- ✔ Video number (an otherwise meaningless number assigned to each tape so you can keep track of it)
- ✔ Title
- ✔ Status (IN or OUT)
- ✔ Due date
- ✔ Customer number (usually the customer's phone number)
- ✔ Customer's last and first names
- ✔ Customer's street address, city, state, and zip code
- ✔ Customer's credit card number (in case the customer skips town)

Before long, you realize that every time a customer rents a video tape, you have to type in the customer's name, address, and credit card number. To make matters worse, if the customer rents all six Star Trek movies on the same day, you have to type in this information six times. (Odds are that a customer who wants all six Star Trek movies will immediately point out how illogical such a database design is.)

Being the wise database user that you are, you decide to divide the video database into two smaller databases, one for video tapes and the other for customers. The VIDEOS database includes the following information:

- ✔ Video number (an otherwise meaningless number assigned to each tape so you can keep track of it)
- ✔ Title
- ✔ Status (IN or OUT)
- ✔ Due date
- ✔ Customer number

The VIDCUST database includes:

- ✔ Customer number
- ✔ Customer's last and first names
- ✔ Customer's street address, city, state, and zip code
- ✔ Customer's credit card number (in case the customer skips town)

Now, whenever a customer rents a video tape, all you have to do is call up the VIDEO record for the tape and type in the customer number and due date. You have to type in the customer's name, address, and credit card information only one time, in the VIDCUST database. Plus, your database design wastes disk space by needlessly duplicating this information.

That's all well and good, but what a bother to have to look up information in both databases constantly. Wouldn't it be great if you could combine these two databases onto the same form so that they appear to be a single database? I thought you'd never ask. That capability is exactly what joins are all about.

Join types

Just as there are different types of relationships in real life — for example, husbands and wives, parents and children, aunts and uncles and nieces and nephews, and of course, in-laws — there are different types of database relationships that you can create with joins. Four, to be exact. These four types of relationships are illustrated in textbook fashion in Figure 8-1.

One-to-one relationships: In a one-to-one relationship, each record in one database is related to one and only one record in another database. One-to-one joins aren't used too often because you may as well combine the two databases into a single database.

Note that one-to-one relationships are useful in situations in which databases weren't planned very well from the start. For example, perhaps the credit department sets up a customer database to track each customer's credit history, and the marketing department sets up a customer database to track each customer's sales history. A one-to-one join would enable you to combine these databases as if they were a single database, which maybe they should have been in the first place.

One-to-one relationship

One-to-many relationship

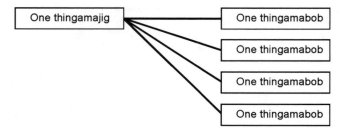

Many-to-one relationship

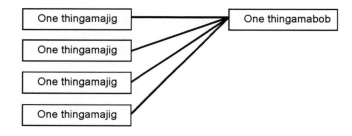

Many-to-many relationship

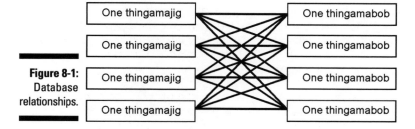

Figure 8-1:
Database
relationships.

One-to-many relationships: In a one-to-many relationship, each record in one database can be related to several records in another database. The relationship of the VIDCUST database to the VIDEOS database is an example: each customer can have more than one video tape rented out. The following are other examples of one-to-many relationships:

- A customer database and an invoice database: each customer can have more than one invoice.
- An invoice database and a line item database: each invoice can have more than one line item.
- A class database and a student database: each class can have more than one student.
- An instructor database and a class database: each instructor can have more than one class.
- A team database and a player database: each team can have more than one player.
- A department database and an employee database: each department can have more than one employee.

Notice that in a one-to-many relationship, *many* can mean zero, one, or more than one. Thus, a customer may not have any invoices. Likewise, a student may not have any classes, especially if he happens to be a basketball player at UNLV.

Many-to-one relationships: A many-to-one relationship is the opposite of a one-to-many relationship. It occurs when more than one record in a database can be related to a particular record in another database. For example, more than one invoice record can be related to the same customer record, and more than one employee record can be related to the same department record.

Note that any two databases that are joined in a one-to-many relationship also can be joined in the opposite many-to-one relationship. For example, if you join customers to invoices in a one-to-many relationship, you also can join invoices to customers in a many-to-one relationship.

Many-to-many relationships: A many-to-many relationship exists when records in one database can be related to many records in another database, and vice versa. For example, consider a suppliers and parts database in which each supplier can supply many different parts, and each part can be obtained from several different suppliers. The relationship between the parts database and the suppliers database is many-to-many.

Unfortunately, Approach cannot directly support a many-to-many relationship such as this one. To implement this kind of relationship, you need to create a third database that contains one record for each part/supplier combination. The Parts/Suppliers database has a one-to-many relationship with the Parts database and the Suppliers database, as shown in Figure 8-2.

Figure 8-2:
Many-to-
many
relationships
require an
intermediate
database.

Parts	
Part	**Description**
1000	Framis valve
1001	Transtator
1002	Infindibulator

Parts/Suppliers	
Part	**Supplier**
1000	100
1000	101
1001	100
1001	101
1001	102
1002	102

Suppliers	
Supplier	**Name**
100	Western Supply
101	Metalworks
102	Infinity Supplies

In Figure 8-2, a Parts/Suppliers database links the Parts and Suppliers databases in a many-to-many relationship. You can use this database to determine which suppliers provide Framis Valves (Western Supply and Metalworks) and which parts are supplied by Infinity Supplies (Transtators and Infindibulators).

Join fields

Creating a join establishes a relationship between two databases. This relationship is based on a *join field,* which is simply a field that the two databases have in common. In the video store example, the join field is Customer Number, which appears in both the VIDEOS database and the VIDCUST database. Whenever you call up a video tape record in the VIDEOS database, Approach automatically looks up the correct VIDCUST customer record by using the join field as a search key (assuming that the tape has been checked out).

Here are several things to be aware of concerning join fields:

✔ The join field must have unique values in at least one of the databases. The easiest way to ensure that the values are unique is to set up the join field as a serial number in one of the databases. Or the field can be some other unique value that identifies records. For example, video stores routinely use phone numbers to uniquely identify each customer. (Of course, you need to make sure that the number you use is unique for each record. In the case of phone numbers, what if two members of the same household want to open separate accounts?)

✔ The join fields do not have to have the same name in both databases. For example, the field may be named Customer Number in the VIDEOS database and Cust Phone in the VIDCUST database. Regardless of whether the fields have the same name, however, they should be of the same data type, and they should represent the same thing.

✔ If you want to join databases but the databases don't have a field in common, just create a field with which to join them. Make the field a serial number in one of the databases to ensure uniqueness.

✔ In Official Relational Database Jargon, the join field is called a *key*. In the database in which the key is unique, the join field is called the *primary key*. In the other database (in which the key does not have to be unique), the join field is called a *foreign key* or a *durn foreign key*.

Joining Databases

The procedure for joining databases is kind of like a wedding ceremony. Here is a suggested liturgy:

1. **Create the two databases that you want to join, paying special attention to the join field in both databases.**

   This step is the courtship phase of the relationship, in which the two databases get to know one another's likes and dislikes in an effort to find out whether they are compatible. If you cannot find common ground for a join (that is, a join field that is unique in at least one of the databases), the best thing to do is call the whole thing off right now, before anyone gets hurt.

2. **Open the Approach file in which you want to record the join.**

   This step is kind of like picking a church or other location for the wedding. The join doesn't actually reside in either of the database files but in the Approach file, along with the forms, reports, and other views that you use to access database data. Open the Approach file for the database that you want to be the main database for the view. For example, if you want to view customers' records to see which videos are currently rented to a particular customer, open the Approach file for the VIDCUST database. On the other hand, if you want to look up a specific video tape to see who has checked it out, open the Approach file for the VIDEOS database.

3. **Choose C̲reate⇨J̲oin.**

   The Join dialog box appears, as shown in Figure 8-3. Initially, only one database is shown in the Join dialog box, similar to the way the groom nervously stands alone at the front of the church, waiting for the processional to begin.

4. **Click the O̲pen button, select the database that you want to join to the main database, and click OK.**

   When you click O̲pen, you see an Open dialog box that is identical to the one that is displayed when you choose F̲ile⇨O̲pen. Select the database that you want to include in the join and click OK to open it. When you perform this action, the second database is added to the Join dialog box. It is customary to stand as the bride-to-be enters the dialog box.

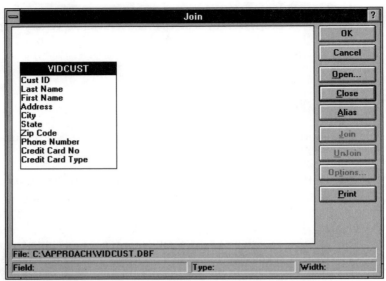

Figure 8-3:
The Join
dialog box.

5. Click the field that you want to use as the join field in both databases and then click the Join button.

Approach draws a line to indicate that the databases are joined on the field you selected, as shown in Figure 8-4. You may want to say something such as, "Do you, Cust ID in the VIDCUST database, take Cust ID in the VIDEOS database to be your lawfully wedded foreign key? If so, click OK."

6. Click OK.

The wedding is complete, so the Join dialog box vanishes, off on the honeymoon.

Here are a few additional thoughts to consider when you are joining databases:

✔ Instead of selecting the join field in both databases and clicking the Join button, you can use the more mousy technique of pointing at the join field in either one of the databases, pressing the left mouse button, and dragging the mouse to the join field in the other database. When you release the mouse button, Approach joins the databases on this field.

✔ You can create joins that involve three or more databases by opening the additional databases, selecting the join fields, and clicking the Join button or dragging the mouse as described in the preceding bullet. See the section "Database Polygamy" later in this chapter.

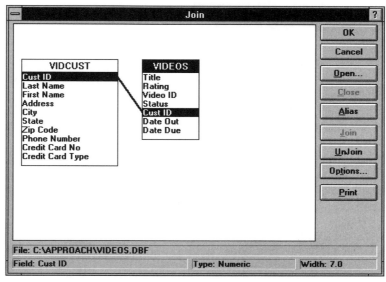

Figure 8-4:
Approach
draws lines
to show
joins.

✔ Unfortunately, the results of a successful join are not immediately visible. Database forms and reports are not automatically updated to reflect the joined database. Instead, you need to modify forms and reports to show fields from the joined databases. For more information about making those changes, turn to Chapters 9 and 10.

✔ To cancel a join, choose Create⇨Join, select the line that marks the join, and click the Unjoin command. (Having lawyers draw up papers first is best.)

✔ Don't forget that information about database joins is stored in the Approach files, not in the database files themselves. If you create a join between two databases and then close the Approach file and open a different Approach file (.APR) that includes one of the databases, the join will not be shown.

✔ Every database opened in the Join dialog box has to be joined to another database. If you open a database and then decide not to join it, select it by clicking one of its fields and then close it by clicking the Close button. This action is the database equivalent of calling off the engagement.

✔ You can print a graphic representation of a join by calling up the Join dialog box and clicking the Print button. The printed output will resemble the join diagram shown in Figure 8-4.

Database Polygamy

Unlike the real world (at least my home state), Approach permits joins between more than two databases. You can join three, four, or however many databases you want as long as all of the databases involved are consenting adults.

Note: Some database types are more adverse to polygamous relationships than others.

Figure 8-5 shows an example of a four-way join. In this example, the Customer database (CUST) is joined to the Invoice database (INVOICE) by using Cust No as the join field. As a result, each customer can have one or more invoices. The Invoice database is in turn joined to the Line Item database (LINEITEM) so that each invoice can have one or more line items. The line item database is in turn joined to the Item inventory database (ITEMS) in a many-to-one relationship; that is, each item can appear in more than one line item.

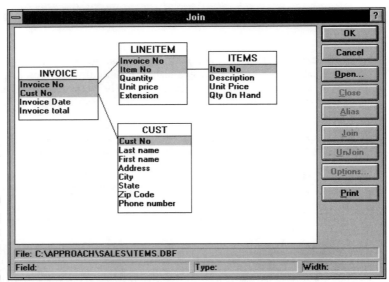

Figure 8-5:
Approach
permits
Polygamy.

The joins shown in Figure 8-5 enable you to print invoices that show the customer's name and address, which are obtained from the CUST database, line item details, which are obtained from the LINEITEM database, and an item description for each line item, which is obtained from the ITEMS database.

Note: Certain nonsensical types of polygamous joins are not allowed. In particular, you cannot create circular joins, in which database A is joined to database B, which is joined back to database A. Odds are you wouldn't want to attempt such a thing, but if you do, Approach will call a foul. (Well, Approach does allow a way to do this. It's called an *Alias,* but it's an advanced technique that only licensed database wonks should attempt.)

Join Options

Approach enables you to set several strange but useful options for database joins. These options are designed to help prevent weird situations from occurring within joined databases. For example, what happens if you delete the record for a customer who has invoices . . . should the customer's invoice records be deleted as well?

In the language of professional database gurus, such issues are referred to as *referential integrity.* Even if you don't understand what referential integrity is, you're bound to impress your friends by telling them that you've "taken every precaution to ensure referential integrity" in your database system.

To set join options, follow this procedure:

1. **In the Join dialog box, select the join whose options you want to set by clicking the line that marks the join.**

   You can set options independently for each join.

2. **Click the Options button.**

   The Relational Options dialog box appears, as shown in Figure 8-6. Notice how this dialog box names the databases that are involved. Aren't computers amazing?

3. **Check the options that you want Approach to enforce and then click OK.**

   You're done!

Figure 8-6:
The
Relational
Options
dialog box.

Relational Options	?

☒ Insert: If no records match the INVOICE record, typing into
    a blank CUST field inserts a new record.

☐ Delete: Deleting a record from INVOICE deletes matching records from CUST.

☒ Insert: If no records match the CUST record, typing into
    a blank INVOICE field inserts a new record.

☐ Delete: Deleting a record from CUST deletes matching records from INVOICE.

OK
Cancel

The relational options enable you to tell Approach what to do when it inserts and deletes records on both sides of the join. If you check either of the Insert options, records will automatically be created in the joined databases when you type a value in the join field. For example, if you type a customer number in the Cust No field of the Invoice database, a customer record will automatically be created.

The Delete options tell Approach whether to automatically delete related records when you delete joined records. For example, if you delete a customer record, should corresponding invoice records be deleted? Or, if you delete an invoice record, should corresponding customer records be deleted?

✔ The default settings for these options are to enable both Insert options and disable both Delete options, as shown in Figure 8-6. Usually, leaving the Insert options on is best. As for the Delete options, you should think carefully before enabling either of them. In the join shown in Figure 8-6, enabling the second Delete option probably makes sense. After all, if you delete a customer record, you should probably delete the customer's invoices as well. But deleting a customer record when you delete an invoice record makes no sense — what would happen if the customer had other invoices?

✔ If you disable the Insert options, you may want to set the validation options of the join fields so that the user cannot enter incorrect data. For example, if an Invoice database is joined to a Customer database by using the Cust No fields in both databases, it only makes sense that you should set the validation options of the Invoice file's Cust No field so that it will accept only values that exist in the Cust No field of the Customer database. (In Propellerhead Database Lingo, you're *ensuring the validity of a foreign key.*)

To set this option, choose Create⇨Field Definition. Select the database from the Database list and then select the join field from the field list. Click the Options button to reveal the field options and then click the Validation tab. Finally, check the In field check box and select the join field from the joined database in the field list that's next to the In field check box. Click OK and you're done. Whew!

Part II
Polishing
Your Database

The 5th Wave   By Rich Tennant

"FRANKLY, I'M NOT SURE THIS IS THE WAY TO ENHANCE OUR DATABASE."

In this part ...

You can use any database program to perform mundane
tasks, such as storing data, sorting and searching
records, and printing reports. Boring. What sets
Approach apart from other database programs is that it not
only lets you do those unimportant things, but it also lets
you do the really important stuff, such as changing colors
and using great-looking fonts and drop shadows and other
neat-looking effects. That stuff is what's *really* important,
because in today's world no one gives a whit about content.
Who *cares* if the report says that sales are dropping 20
percent each month as long as the report *looks* good!

The chapters in this part can help you gussy up your
database. You learn how to create fantastic forms and
reports that are suitable for royalty, how to draw cute
pictures on your views, and who knows what else. Read on.

Chapter 9

Creating World-Class Forms

● ●

In This Chapter

▶ Understanding forms and form objects

▶ Using Design mood

▶ Creating a new form

▶ Designing form fields

▶ Field formats

● ●

*W*ith brilliant swordsmanship, Peter Pan tosses Hook's wig from his head and then knocks Hook's sword from his hands and forces him to the ground. Peter slowly raises his sword to Hook's throat.

"Good Form, Peter," says Hook. "I am fallen." Glancing at his wig, Hook implores Peter, "At least give me my dignity. You took my hand; you owe me something."

Good Form is as important in Approach as it is in Neverland. When you first create a database, Approach automatically creates a default form that is functional but looks a bit like Hook without his wig. It works, but it's not exactly what Hook or any other pirate would call "Good Form."

This chapter is about Good Form. Or, if you prefer, it's about giving forms their dignity. You owe them that much.

Forms, Fields, and Objects

You already know this information (or you wouldn't have gotten this far), but a *form* is a view that enables you to access database records one at a time. Forms are the main portals through which you view and work with database data. You can use forms to enter data into a database, casually browse through the records of a database, or search for records whose fields match a search criteria that you specify.

Although Approach automatically creates a default form when you create a database, you won't be content to use that form for long. Soon you'll develop the urge to either modify the default form to make it easier to work with or to create additional forms that simplify certain tasks. You can create as many database forms as you want in a single Approach file. To switch from one form to another, just click the form tab that identifies the form that you want to call up.

A form (or any other view, for that matter) consists of a *background* and *objects*. The background is just that: the background of the form. You can change the color of the form background, and you can give it a border. Otherwise, you can't do much with it. The more interesting — and more troublesome — part of designing forms is working with the objects.

Most objects are simple field objects that display database data. If you're interested in other types of objects, read the sidebar about object types. Otherwise, just plow ahead.

I object to this meaningless dribble about Design objects

I don't really want to do this to you, but I feel compelled to point out that you can use several distinct types of objects on forms.

Field objects: A field object shows the data from the database. Besides your run-of-the-mill field boxes that provide an area for the contents of a database field and a label to identify the field, you also can create special types of fields, such as list boxes, radio buttons, and check boxes.

Text objects: A text object is an area that holds text that is displayed on the form. This text is a part of the form, not data obtained from the database. As a result, the same text is shown for every database record. The most familiar text field is the form label that usually appears at the top of the form.

Repeating panels: A repeating panel is a special area of a form that shows information from databases that are joined in one-to-many fashion. For example, the form for a Customer database can include a repeating panel to show all of the customer's invoices that were obtained from a separate Invoice database.

Shape objects: You can add shape objects, such as ellipses, rectangles, and lines. These objects are purely decorative. Chapter 11 covers the procedures for adding these ornaments.

Picture objects: You also can add pictures in several common graphics formats. These pictures are purely decorative, and Chapter 11 also covers them.

OLE objects: An OLE object is a picture, a chart, a portion of a spreadsheet, or some other bit of data that is created by another program. Chapter 12 covers OLE objects.

Macro buttons: A macro button enables the user to call up a macro by clicking the form button. Macro buttons are often used to invoke predefined Finds, switch from view to view, print reports, or do other useful tricks. Macro buttons are far too nerdy for this chapter, but you can find more information in Chapter 19 if you must.

Forget about everything except field objects for now. All the other object types are covered in later chapters.

Working in Design Mood

As you undoubtedly know by now, Approach is a rather moody program. To be specific, it has four distinct moods (which computer nerds are more likely to call *modes*): Browse mood, Design mood, Find mood, and Preview mood. To modify an existing form or to create a new form, you need to switch to Approach's Design mood.

You switch to Design mood in one of four ways:

- ✔ Click the Design icon in the icon bar.
- ✔ Choose <u>V</u>iew⇨<u>D</u>esign.
- ✔ Use the Design command from the pop-up mood menu in the status bar at the bottom of the screen.
- ✔ Press Ctrl+D.

When you switch to Design mood, the icon bar changes to provide icons that are useful when you design forms. Table 9-1 summarizes the most essential Design icons, along with their keyboard shortcuts.

Table 9-1	**Design Icons and Keyboard Equivalents**	
Icon	*Keyboard*	*What It Does*
📁	Ctrl+S	Saves design changes to the Approach file.
↩	Ctrl+Z	Undoes the most recent design change.
✂	Ctrl+X	Cuts the selection to the Clipboard (deletes the original).
🗐	Ctrl+C	Copies the selection to the Clipboard (leaves the original).
📋	Ctrl+V	Pastes the contents of the Clipboard on the view.
🖌	Ctrl+M	Copies the format of the selected object to other objects.
❶	Ctrl+E	Calls up the InfoBox for the selected object. (For details about the InfoBox, skip ahead to the section, "Playing with the InfoBox," later in this chapter.)

The wacky menu

When you work in Design mode, one of the menus on the menu bar — the one between <u>C</u>reate and <u>T</u>ools — changes, depending on what type of form object you're working with. Do not be alarmed! This change is entirely normal.

Here are the menus that appear:

Fo<u>r</u>m: Appears when no object is selected and a form view is displayed. (If another type of view is displayed, such as a report or mailing label, this menu changes again.)

<u>O</u>bject: Appears when an object is selected.

Te<u>x</u>t: Appears when text is selected.

<u>P</u>anel: Appears when a repeating panel is selected.

The commands that appear on the various menus are commands that are appropriate for the type of object that you have selected.

Using the Tools palette

The programmers who designed Approach wanted to provide so many useful Design icons that they couldn't fit them all in the icon bar, so they threw in a separate box of icons called the *Tools palette*. The Tools palette, shown in Figure 9-1, is a separate collection of Design icons that floats about on the screen. Table 9-2 summarizes the functions of the icons that are in the Tools palette.

Figure 9-1:
The Tools
palette.

Here are some juicy tidbits concerning the Tools palette:

- ✔ The icons on the Tools palette work just like the icons on the standard SmartIcon palette. To use most of them, you click an icon to select a drawing tool and then you drag the mouse to draw the selected shape on the form. The only tool that doesn't work this way is Add Field, which calls up a dialog box that enables you to drag database fields onto the form.

- ✔ If the Tools palette gets in the way, you can move it by dragging it gently by its title bar, just as you can move any other dialog box.

✔ To really get the Tools palette out of the way, move it down to the bottom of the screen so that only the title bar is still visible. Then it doesn't overlap anything except the status bar. You can quickly grab the title bar and drag the Tools palette back into view when you need it.

✔ To get rid of the Tools palette temporarily, double-click its control box (the rectangle in its upper-left corner). You can recall it into active service at any time by choosing View⇨Show Drawing Tools or by pressing Ctrl+L.

Table 9-2	Design Icons in the Tools Palette
Icon	*What It Does*
▲	Changes the mouse pointer back to the arrow pointer for selecting objects. Useful after you've used one of the other tools.
abc	Adds text to a form.
▢	Draws squares or rectangles.
▢	Draws squares or rectangles with rounded corners.
◯	Draws circles or ellipses.
╱	Draws lines.
▣	Draws a field.
⊠	Draws a check box field.
◉	Draws a radio button.
▢	Draws a macro button.
▤	Draws a PicturePlus field.
▣	Calls up the Add Field dialog box to add fields to the form.

Setting Design mood options

Design mood has a few options that make working with form objects easier. You set these options by using commands on the View menu or icons in the icon bar. The following paragraphs describe the options and tell you how to activate them:

Show Data: This option tells Approach what kind of information to display in fields when you work in Design mood. If Show Data is set, Approach displays actual data from the database. This setting gives you an idea of what the form will look like when you use it in Browse mood. If Show Data is not set, Approach displays the name of the field rather than sample data. Seeing the names of the fields can help you keep track of which field is which. To switch between data and field names, choose View⇨Show Data.

Show Grid: If the Show Grid option is set, a pattern of little dots is displayed on the form to help you line up form objects. Initially, 12 of these dots appear per inch. However, you can change the grid spacing by using the Tools⇨Preferences command.

 To show the grid, choose View⇨Show Grid or click the Show Grid icon in the icon bar. To hide the grid, choose View⇨Show Grid or click the Show Grid icon again.

Snap to Grid: If you want Approach to force objects to line up with the grid, activate the Snap to Grid option. Then anytime you draw a new object or move an existing object, Approach will line it up with the nearest grid mark. Using this method is the easiest way to create neat forms.

To snap objects to the grid, choose View⇨Snap to Grid or press Ctrl+Y. Use the command again to turn off the Snap to Grid option.

Show Ruler: The Show Ruler option displays rulers across the top and left edges of the Design window to help you line up objects. This option is useful when you are designing reports or merge letters, but you probably won't use it when you are working with forms.

 To display or hide the ruler, choose View⇨Show Ruler, press Ctrl+J, or click the Ruler icon.

Creating a New Form

Approach automatically creates a default form when you create a new database. In many cases, this form is all you need to use the database. However, Approach enables you to create more than one form so that you can access database data in different ways. For example, you may want to create a form for a Customer database that shows only the customer name and address fields so that you can easily enter name and address changes.

The easiest way to create a new form is to have the Form Assistant do it for you. Just follow this procedure:

1. **Open the database for which you want to create the new form.**

   Choose File⇨Open, click the Open icon, or select the file from the Welcome to Approach dialog box.

2. Conjure up the Create⇨Form command.

The first page of the Form Assistant appears, as shown in Figure 9-2.

Figure 9-2:
The Form
Assistant,
page 1.

3. Change the View name & title to something more memorable.

Approach suggests a brilliant name, such as *Form 2*. Change it to something more descriptive, such as *Cust Info*.

4. Select the SmartMaster style.

The styles govern the form color and other appearance factors. You can experiment with different SmartMaster styles if you want. The Sample Form box changes to give you an idea of what each style looks like.

5. Select the SmartMaster layout.

The four layout options are:

Blank: No fields are added to the form. If you choose this layout, skip ahead to Step 8.

Standard: Fields are added in a horizontal arrangement. This layout is the one that is most compact.

Columnar: Fields are added in a single column. This layout is nifty, but only a few fields fit on the screen without the use of scroll bars.

Standard with Repeating Panel: Use this layout if you want to include fields from a one-to-many join.

6. Click the Next button.

Page 2 of the Form Assistant appears, as shown in Figure 9-3.

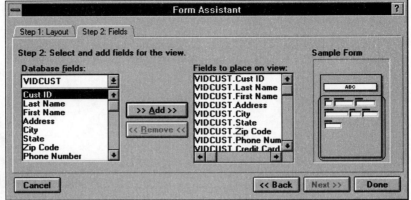

Figure 9-3:
The Form
Assistant,
page 2.

7. **Select the fields that you want to include on the form and click Add to add them to the list.**

   To add a field to the form, select it in the Database fields list and then click Add. (Each time you click Add, the next field in the list is selected. You can quickly add several successive fields by repeatedly clicking Add.)

   To add several fields at the same time, drag over them with the mouse. Or hold down the Ctrl key while you select the fields in the Database fields list and then click Add.

   To remove a field from the form, select the list in the Fields to place on view list and then click Remove.

8. **If you are creating a form that has a repeating panel, click Next; otherwise, skip ahead to Step 10.**

   Page 3 of the Form Assistant appears, as shown in Figure 9-4.

9. **Select the fields that you want to include in the repeating panel and click Add to add them to the list.**

   You can use the same techniques that you use to add fields to the form to add fields to the repeating panel.

10. **Click Done.**

   Lean back in your chair (not too far!) while the Form Assistant creates the form for you.

Figure 9-4:
The Form
Assistant,
page 3.

Deleting a Form

If you decide that you no longer need a form, or if you start to customize a form and mess it up so badly that you figure you may as well start over, you can delete a form by following this simple procedure:

1. Select the form that you want to delete by clicking its view tab.

The form is displayed.

2. Choose Edit➪Delete Form.

The confirmation dialog box shown in Figure 9-5 appears.

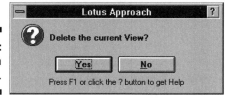

Figure 9-5:
Deleting a
form.

3. If you're really absolutely-positively-beyond-a-reasonable-doubt-no-turning-back-now sure you want to delete the form, click Yes.

The form is deleted.

Changing a Form's Name and Title

After you have created a form, you may want to change its name or title (the form *name* is what appears in the view tabs that you click to switch from form to form; the *title* is the text object that appears at the top of the form). You also may want to change the name and title of the default form to something more creative than *Form 1*.

To change the form name, follow this procedure:

1. **Double-click the form's view tab.**

   The tab widens, and a text insertion point appears in the form name.

2. **Type the new name for the form.**

3. **Press Enter.**

To change a form's title field, call up the form in Design mood and follow this procedure:

1. **Click the form's title text a couple of times until an insertion point appears.**

   This is a finesse move. The first click selects the text object, and the second click enables you to edit the text. Count to three between clicks to avoid double-clicking; if you double-click, the InfoBox dialog box appears. (For more information about the InfoBox, refer to the section, "Playing with the InfoBox," later in this chapter.)

2. **Edit the title text however you like.**

3. **When you're done, click the mouse anywhere outside the title object.**

Working with Fields

Field objects are the heart and soul of forms. The easiest way to make an Approach database more useful is to spend some time beefing up the fields on the database's forms. You can rearrange the fields into a more useful layout, add or remove form fields, change the tab order, and change the field formats. The following sections explain how to perform these tasks.

Moving and resizing fields

Often, one of the first things that you need to do to a new form is move and resize the form fields. This step is necessary when the fields that the Form Assistant automatically places on the form are not large enough to display the data contained in the field. When you enlarge a field, you often have to move other fields to avoid an overlapped, cluttered, Oscar Madison appearance.

To move a field, simply use the mouse to drag it to a new location. Move the mouse pointer over the field until the pointer changes to a grabbing hand and then press and hold the left mouse button. Move the hand to the new location (a rectangle representing the field moves with the hand) and then release the mouse button to move the field.

To resize a field, first select the field by clicking it. When you click it, handles (I call them *love handles*) magically appear around the field, as shown in Figure 9-6. You can then resize the field by dragging any of its love handles. Carefully position the mouse pointer over one of the handles until the pointer changes to a double-headed arrow. Then press and hold the left mouse button. Drag the love handle to change the size of the field and then release the button.

Figure 9-6:
Love
handles on
a form
object.

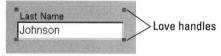

Love handles

Here are some crucial points about moving and resizing fields:

✔ You can move several fields at the same time by holding down the Shift key while you select the fields that you want to move. Then, when you move any of the selected fields, all of the fields move.

✔ Another way to select several fields is to point to a blank part of the form and then press and hold the mouse button while you drag a selection rectangle around all the fields that you want to select.

✔ Remember to select the field by clicking it before you attempt to move or resize it. When you see an outline box with love handles surrounding the field, you know that the field is selected.

✔ To maintain a neat, Felix Unger appearance to your form, turn on the Snap to Grid option by pressing Ctrl+Y or choosing View➪Snap to Grid. Then any fields that you move or resize will automatically fit neatly into the grid marks.

Adding fields to a form

If you omitted a field from a form when you used the form assistant, or if you later add a field to a database and want it included in a form, you can use the following procedure to add a form field:

1. **Select the form to which you want to add a field by clicking its view tab.**

   The form is displayed.

 2. **Switch to Design mood by clicking the Design icon.**

   You also can switch to Design mood by pressing Ctrl+D or choosing View⇨Design.

 3. **Click the Add Field icon in the Tools palette.**

   Alternatively, choose Form⇨Add Field (if an object is selected, choose Object⇨Add Field instead) or, using the right mouse button, click any form object to bring up the pop-up menu and then select the Add Field command.

   Either way, the all important Add Field dialog box appears, as shown in Figure 9-7.

4. **If the field that you want to add to the form is in a joined database, click the down-arrow next to the database name (VIDCUST in Figure 9-7) to reveal a list of joined databases and then select the database that you want to use.**

5. **Drag the field from the list in the Add Field dialog box to the location on the form where you want the field to appear.**

   The field is added to the form.

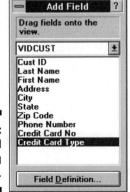

Figure 9-7:
The Add
Field dialog
box.

Here are some important variants to consider when you are adding fields:

 ✔ You can define a new database field from the Add Field dialog box by clicking the Field Definition button. The Field Definition dialog box appears, where you can define new database fields. For details, refer to Chapter 2.

 ✔ You also can add a field to a database by selecting the Field button from the Tools palette or by choosing Create⇨Drawing⇨Field. Position the mouse on the form where you want the field to be located and then hold down the mouse button and drag the mouse where you want the field to appear. Next, select the database field from the dialog box that appears. When you release the mouse button, the InfoBox for the field appears. Select the database field that you want to assign to the new form field. (Details about using the InfoBox are found later in this chapter, under the heading "Playing with the InfoBox.")

Deleting fields from a form

To remove a field from a form, follow this procedure:

1. **Select the form that contains the field that you want to remove by clicking its view tab.**

   The form is displayed.

2. **Select the field that you want to remove by clicking it.**

   Love handles appear to show that the field is properly selected.

3. **Press the Delete or Backspace key or choose Edit⇨Clear.**

   Poof! The field vanishes.

Consider the following:

 ✔ If you immediately realize that deleting the field was a foolish thing to do, press Ctrl+Z, click the Undo button, or choose Edit⇨Undo to make the field reappear.

 ✔ Deleting a field from a form does not delete the field from the database. The field — and data you have entered into it — is still safely kept in the database. You just can't see it in the form.

 ✔ To delete several fields at the same time, hold down Shift while you click the fields to select them or drag a selection rectangle around all the fields by using the mouse. You can choose from three methods to delete the fields: press Delete, press Backspace, or choose Edit⇨Clear to delete all of the selected fields.

Changing the data entry order

When you work with a form in Browse mood, you bounce from field to field by pressing the Tab key (or the Enter key if you have set the Preferences so that you can use the Enter key). Normally, the Tab key bounces from field to field in the order in which you added fields to the form. However, after an exhausting Design session in which you move fields here and there, you may discover that the Tab key seems to bounce about the form almost at random. When you have that problem, you need to change the data entry order. Here's how to change it:

1. **Call up the form whose data entry order is messed up.**

2. **Choose View➪Show Data Entry Order.**

   A big, boxy number appears next to each form field to indicate the data entry sequence, as shown in Figure 9-8. In this example, you can see that pressing Tab from the Cust ID field will bounce the cursor to the Last Name field, not to the Phone Number field. This data entry sequence should be changed.

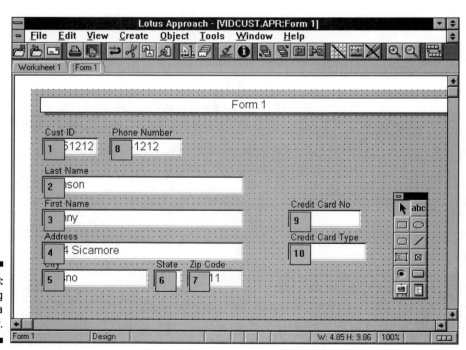

Figure 9-8:
Changing
the data
entry order.

3. **Click the number that you want to change and then type the new number.**

   For example, to change the Phone Number field to make it be second in line, click the *8,* delete the *8,* and then type **2**.

4. **Click any other number to see the new and improved data entry order.**

   When you click another number, all of the numbers are updated to show the new order. The old 2 becomes 3, the old 3 becomes 4, and so on.

To totally shake up the data entry order, use this procedure instead:

1. **Call up the form whose data entry order is messed up.**

2. **Choose <u>V</u>iew⬦Show Data <u>E</u>ntry Order.**

   The data entry sequence is shown.

3. **Double-click any of the numbers.**

   All of the numbers disappear, but the boxes remain.

4. **Click the empty boxes in the order that you want to establish as the data entry sequence.**

   The new data entry sequence number appears in each field as you click its box.

Changing a Field's Appearance

Approach gives you precise control over the way that fields appear on a form. For example, Figure 9-9 shows an Approach form that has various kinds of field formats. Of course, you wouldn't want to design a form like this one unless you already had another job lined up. Figure 9-9 is intended only to show that you can vary the font, size, and style of the text used to display the field's contents; the position and style of each field's label; and the border style and background color of the field itself.

Playing with the InfoBox

To change the appearance of the field, you have to contend with a special dialog box called the *InfoBox*. Here is the procedure:

1. **Click the field whose appearance you want to change.**

   Love handles appear, indicating that the field is selected.

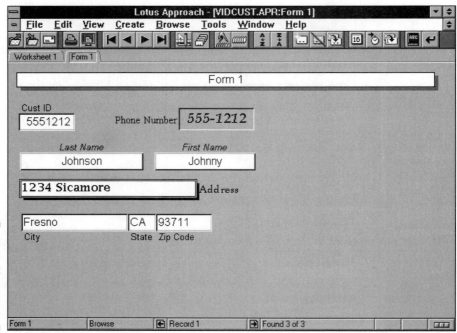

Figure 9-9:
A wacky
form that
has too
many field
styles.

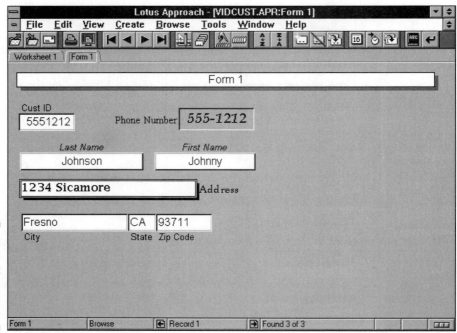

2. Click the Show Info icon to summon the InfoBox.

You also can choose Object⇨Style and Properties, Press Ctrl+E, or click the field with the right mouse button and then select Style & Properties from the shortcut menu. One way or the other, the InfoBox appears, as shown in Figure 9-10.

Figure 9-10:
The
infamous
InfoBox.

3. **Click the InfoBox tab that contains the field settings that you want to modify.**

   Because you can use the InfoBox to change so many different settings, the settings are organized into panels. Each panel is identified by a tab at the top of the InfoBox. You click a panel's tab to display the panel and its settings. (See Table 9-3, which follows these steps, for information on which field settings appear on each tab.)

   Also, you may notice that the tabs shown on the InfoBox vary depending on the type of object you select.

4. **Change whatever settings you want.**

5. **Repeat Steps 3 and 4 to change settings on other panels.**

6. **Double-click the InfoBox's control box (in the upper-left corner of the InfoBox) to dismiss it.**

   The results of the changed settings are immediately apparent.

Table 9-3 summarizes the field settings that are displayed for each of the InfoBox tabs.

Table 9-3	InfoBox Panels
Tab	**_Field Settings It Displays_**
✐	Font, size, style (bold, italic, and so on), color, alignment (left, center, right), and text relief style for field data
▤	Border width, color, fill color, shadow color, frame style, and border position
#	Number format
▭	Size and position of field
Basics	Database field and field type (text box, radio button, and so on)
Label	Font, size, style, color, alignment, position, and text displayed for the field label
Macros	Macros to be run when cursor enters or exits field or when data changes

Here are some important things to remember when you are working with the InfoBox:

- ✔ You can use two other methods to summon the InfoBox. Simply double-click the field or point to the field, hold down the right mouse button to summon the pop-up menu, and then choose Style and Properties.

- ✔ You don't have to dismiss the InfoBox to select another field. If you call up the InfoBox and then click another form field to select it, the InfoBox shows the settings for the second field. (If the InfoBox is in the way of a field that you want to select, just move the InfoBox by dragging it by its title bar.)

- ✔ If the InfoBox is really in the way, you can shrink it down to just a strip by double-clicking the InfoBox's title bar. The InfoBox rolls itself up into a nice little package that shows just the title bar and the tabs, as shown in Figure 9-11. To unravel the InfoBox, double-click its title bar again.

Figure 9-11:
The InfoBox
all rolled up.

- ✔ Approach has a particularly nerdy feature called *named styles* that enables you to assign a name to a frequently used combination of InfoBox settings. Then you can quickly apply those settings to a field by applying its style.

- ✔ A quick way to copy the InfoBox settings from one field to another is to use the Fast Format command, which is covered, uh, next.

Using Fast Format

The InfoBox has a large number of settings, and it can be tedious to use. Fortunately, Approach has a feature called *Fast Format* that enables you to quickly copy all of the InfoBox settings from one field to another. You can use this feature to quickly format all of the fields on a form so that they have a consistent appearance.

Follow this procedure to Fast Format fields:

1. **Play with the InfoBox settings for one of the form's fields until the field is perfect.**

2. **Click the perfect field to select it.**

3. Click the Fast Format icon.

You also can choose Object⇨Fast Format or press Ctrl+M. Either way, the mouse pointer changes to a paint brush.

4. Click the field to which you want to copy the format settings.

The format settings from the field that you selected in Step 2 are copied to the field that you click. The results should be instantly visible.

5. Click more fields.

The paint brush stays on the screen so you can Fast Format a whole gaggle of fields.

6. To make the paint brush go away, click the Fast Format icon again.

You also can choose Object⇨Fast Format or press Ctrl+M again.

Be sure to eradicate the paint brush before you resume your work. Otherwise, everything you click will be reformatted!

Chapter 10

Putting Your Database on Report

● ●

In This Chapter

▶ Understanding Approach reports

▶ Creating a report by using the Report Assistant

▶ Discarding an obsolete report

▶ Making sense of report panels

▶ Renaming a report

▶ Changing the heading

▶ Adding more summary fields

▶ Printing a report

● ●

*T*he previous chapters in this book focus on getting information *into* an Approach database. This chapter turns the tables and shows you how to get information *out* of a database by creating reports. Reports come in many shapes and sizes, ranging from simple listings of database records to complicated listings that group and summarize key data. It's all very interesting, if you're interested in that sort of thing.

Reports can be easy to create, or they can be nightmarish. This chapter focuses on the easy way to create reports, which is to have Approach create reports for you by utilizing a handy feature called the *Report Assistant*. Report Assistant asks you some questions about what you want your report to look like, and then it goes off and creates it for you. What could be easier?

Note: Throughout this chapter, I work with a sample database that records players' salaries for a fictional professional chess league. Each record in this database contains four fields: the chess team name (Team), the player's last name (Last Name), the player's first name (First Name), and the player's salary (Salary).

Understanding Approach Reports

In Approach, a *report* is just another view, like a form or a worksheet. Like a worksheet, a report shows data from more than one record on each page. Unlike a worksheet, though, reports have header lines at the top of the page and sometimes have footer lines at the bottom of the page. In addition, reports may have special summary lines that summarize related groups of records.

Although reports are born to be printed, you don't have to send a report to the printer in order for it to be useful. Approach enables you to view a report on-screen by switching to Preview mood, in which you see the report exactly as it will appear if you print it. (Well, the proper computer term is Preview *mode,* but humor me. I think Approach is moodier than most teenagers.)

Here are some more stunning facts about Approach reports:

- ✔ One of the weirdest, but sometimes most useful, features of Approach is that you can access most reports in Browse mood, which means that you can add, update, and delete database records from the report. All of the editing techniques that you learned in Chapter 4 apply to reports as well as to forms and worksheets.

- ✔ You can't set a sort sequence for a report. However, you can easily create a macro that sorts the database into whatever sequence you want whenever you call up the report. Instructions for creating such a macro are found in Chapter 19.

- ✔ The good folks at Lotus realize that when you need to design and create reports you can use a helping hand. So, out of the kindness of their hearts, they endowed Approach with a helpful feature called the *Report Assistant.* The Report Assistant asks you a few simple questions, such as what type of report layout you want, what fields you want to include in the report, and what you had for lunch. Then it magically creates a stunning report for you, right before your very eyes.

- ✔ After you create a report (or, more accurately, after Report Assistant creates a report for you), the report appears as a separate view. You can redisplay the report at any time by clicking its view tab or selecting it from the pop-up view menu at the left edge of the status bar.

- ✔ You don't have to use the Report Assistant to lay out your reports if you don't want to. You'd be crazy not to, though. Without Report Assistant, creating reports is tricky unless you really know what you're doing. Stick with the Report Assistant, at least for now.

- ✔ The Report Assistant can create six different types of report layouts, which are described, well, — oh here we are! — right now.

Approach Report Types

Although Approach enables you to create almost any type of report imaginable, at first you'll probably stick to the six predefined report types that the following sections describe. After you get the hang of working with the six predefined report layouts, you'll be ready to venture into more complex customized report layouts.

Columnar reports

A *Columnar report* is a simple listing of the records in a database, one row per record. The database fields are arranged into columns, which are labeled at the top of each report page. Figure 10-1 illustrates a Columnar report for the chess players database.

Players

Last Name	First Name	Team	Salary
Barnard	Bubba	Berkeley Braintrust	1500000
McPhearson	Bebe	Berkeley Braintrust	2000000
Bonnarolof	Meggski	Berkeley Braintrust	5125000
Anderson	Dutch	Berkeley Braintrust	1500000
Smith	Joanne	Boston Thinktank	2000000
Tranton	Dillard	Boston Thinktank	1750000
Adams	Melinda	Boston Thinktank	2250000
Daffomivich	Illych	Boston Thinktank	6500000
Johnson	Beverly	Los Angeles Lunatics	2500000
Lee	Sandy	Los Angeles Lunatics	2250000
McAllister	John	Los Angeles Lunatics	2250000
Bednarikoff	Vladimir	Los Angeles Lunatics	5500000
Anderson	Frenchy	Princeton Einsteins	1500000
Williams	Virginia	Princeton Einsteins	1750000
Curtevich	Karma	Princeton Einsteins	8000000
Phillips	Phil	Princeton Einsteins	2100000

Figure 10-1: A Columnar report.

- ✔ The column headings at the top of each page are initially set to the field names defined for the database. You can change these headings if you want.

- ✔ You also can change the width of each report column. Approach usually does a good job of picking the column width so that report data can be properly displayed.

Standard reports

A *Standard report* is a report in which each record is presented as a sort of miniform, with more than one row per record if necessary. Figure 10-2 shows an example of a Standard report.

Info

Last Name	First Name
Bernard	Bubba

Team	Salary
Berkeley Braintrust	1500000

Last Name	First Name
McPhearson	Bebe

Team	Salary
Berkeley Braintrust	2000000

Figure 10-2:
A Standard
report.

Last Name	First Name
Bonnarokof	Meggski

Team	Salary
Berkeley Braintrust	5125000

✔ Because data is not arranged neatly into columns, column headings are not used to identify database fields. Instead, field headings are printed separately for each database record in the body of the report. For this reason, Standard reports are not as concise as Columnar reports.

✔ Standard reports are often used when database records contain more fields than can be printed in a single row in a Columnar report.

✔ Another good use for Standard reports is to provide printed reports on which you can mark data entry changes. For example, you can print a Standard report for an Inventory database before you do a physical inventory count. Then you can mark any discrepancies between the computer inventory and the actual stock on hand on the report, and you can easily enter corrections into the database by using the Standard report view.

Leading Grouped Summary reports

A *Leading Grouped Summary report* is similar to a Columnar report, with the following differences:

✔ Records are sorted into order based on one of the fields.

✔ All records that have the same value for the sort field are grouped together. The sort field value is displayed once, on a separate line just before the group. This line is called the *Leading Summary*.

✔ A *Trailing Summary* line is displayed after each group of records that has the same sort field value. This summary line can include a total that represents the sum, average, or other calculation based on one database field.

✔ The report also includes a *Grand Summary* that totals a field for the entire report.

Figure 10-3 shows an example of a Leading Grouped Summary report. (The figure shows only the beginning of the report, so the Grand Summary isn't visible. Leading and Trailing Summaries are marked so you can tell which is which.)

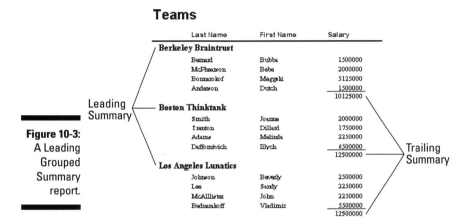

Figure 10-3:
A Leading
Grouped
Summary
report.

Trailing Grouped Summary reports

A *Trailing Grouped Summary report* is similar to a Leading Grouped Summary report, except that the leading summary is not shown. Instead, the value of the field that was used to sort and group database records is shown along with a total field on the trailing summary line. Figure 10-4 shows an example of a Trailing Grouped Summary report.

Team Salaries

Last Name	First Name	Salary
Berrard	Bubba	1500000
McPherson	Bebe	2000000
Bonnarolof	Maggski	5125000
Anderson	Dutch	1500000
Berkeley Braintrust		10125000
Smith	Joanne	2000000
Trenton	Dillard	1750000
Adams	Melinda	2250000
Daffomivich	Illych	6500000
Boston Thinktank		12500000
Johnson	Beverly	2500000
Lee	Sandy	2250000
McAllister	John	2250000
Bednarakoff	Vladimir	5500000
Los Angeles Lunatics		12500000

Figure 10-4:
A Trailing
Grouped
Summary
report.

Columnar with Grand Summary reports

A *Columnar with Grand Summary report* is a Columnar report that has a summary line, at the end of the report, that totals one of the database fields. Figure 10-5 shows a Columnar with Grand Summary report.

Player Salaries

Team	Last Name	First Name	Salary
Berkeley Braintrust	Bernard	Bubba	1500000
Berkeley Braintrust	McPhearson	Bebe	2000000
Berkeley Braintrust	Bonnarokof	Maggski	5125000
Berkeley Braintrust	Anderson	Dutch	1500000
Boston Thinktank	Smith	Joanne	2000000
Boston Thinktank	Irenton	Dillard	1750000
Boston Thinktank	Adams	Melinda	2250000
Boston Thinktank	Daffomivich	Illych	6500000
Los Angeles Lunatics	Johnson	Beverly	2500000
Los Angeles Lunatics	Lee	Sandy	2250000
Los Angeles Lunatics	McAllister	John	2250000
Los Angeles Lunatics	Bednarakoff	Vladimir	5500000
Princeton Einsteins	Anderson	Franchy	1500000
Princeton Einsteins	Williams	Virginia	1750000
Princeton Einsteins	Curtevich	Kazza	8000000
Princeton Einsteins	Phillips	Phil	2100000
			48475000

Figure 10-5: A Columnar with Grand Summary report.

Summary Only reports

A *Summary Only report* is similar to a Trailing Grouped Summary report, with one important difference: the database records themselves are not included in the report. In other words, the report shows only the summary lines that give totals for groups of database records that have the same value in the sort field. Figure 10-6 shows a Summary Only report.

Team Summary

Berkeley Braintrust	10125000
Boston Thinktank	12500000
Los Angeles Lunatics	12500000
Princeton Einsteins	13350000
	48475000

Figure 10-6: A Summary Only report.

Creating a Report by Using the Report Assistant

The Report Assistant is kind of like your own private computer nerd who already knows how to create Approach reports and is willing to do it for you. All you have to do to keep the Assistant happy is toss him an occasional Twinkie (or any suitable Hostess product) and make sure you let him outside twice a day.

Report Assistant asks you questions about the report you want to create, such as what type of layout to use for the report, what fields to include in the report, and what fields to use to create summary groups and totals. After you answer all the questions, Report Assistant unbegrudgingly creates the report for you.

Report Assistant can automatically create any of the six types of database reports described in the preceding section. In addition, you can use it to create a blank report to which you can add fields in any layout you desire.

To use Report Assistant to create a report, follow these steps:

Note: The following procedure describes how to create a Leading Grouped Summary report. The procedure for creating other types of reports is similar, except that you omit certain steps that don't apply. Don't worry, Report Assistant holds your hand through the whole process so you don't get lost.

1. **Open the database that you want to create a report for if it isn't already open.**

    Choose File➪Open, click the Open icon, or select Open an Existing File from the Welcome to Lotus Approach dialog box.

2. **Choose Create➪Report.**

   The Create➪Report command is always available, whether you're in Browse, Design, Preview, or Find mood. When you choose Create➪Report, the Report Assistant appears, as shown in Figure 10-7.

3. **Type a name for the report in the View name & title field.**

   This name will be used for the report view, so it has to be different from the name of any other view that already exists for the database. The name also will appear as the title at the top of each page of the report. It can be up to 30 characters long, and you can use more than one word.

4. **Select a report style from the SmartMaster style drop-down list.**

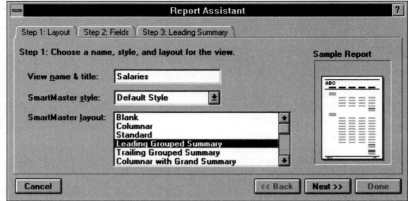

Figure 10-7:
The Report
Assistant
asks what
kind of
report you
want to
create.

The SmartMaster style governs the appearance of the report — colors, fonts, and so on. When you select a SmartMaster style, the sample report in the Sample Report box changes to give you a preview of what the report will look like.

5. Select Leading Grouped Summary from the SmartMaster layout list.

Pick Leading Grouped Summary to create a report that is sorted and grouped based on one database field and that has a summary line following each group that includes a total calculated from another database field.

Note: After you select a SmartMaster layout, the tabs at the top of the Report Assistant dialog box change according to the report layout you selected. For example, when you select Leading Grouped Summary, two additional tabs appear: *Step 2: Fields* and *Step 3: Leading Summary.* Not to worry. Remember, Report Assistant is holding your hand. You won't get lost.

6. Click the Next button to move to the next Report Assistant step.

The Report Assistant displays the options on the next tab in line, as shown in Figure 10-8.

7. Select each field you want to include in the report and click the Add button.

Each time you click the Add button, the selected field is copied to the Fields to place on view list, and the next field in the Database fields list is selected. To quickly include all database fields in the report, select the first field and then click the Add button repeatedly until all fields have been added.

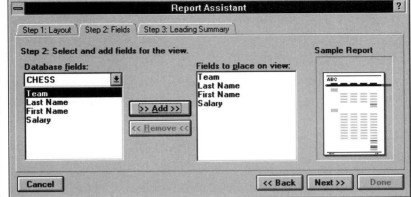

Figure 10-8:
The Report
Assistant
asks which
fields you
want in the
report.

8. **Click the Next button to move to the next Report Assistant step.**

   The Report Assistant displays the options on the third tab in line, as
   shown in Figure 10-9.

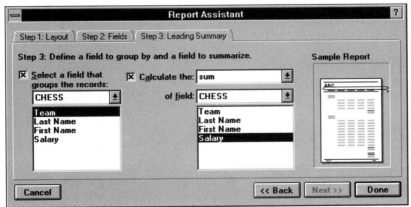

Figure 10-9:
The Report
Assistant
pesters you
for more
details
about the
report.

9. **Click a field in the Select a field that groups the records list.**

   This field will be used to sort and group database records and will be
   displayed in the leading summary line. For example, to group all players
   from the same team, select the Team field. Note that when you select a
   field in this list, the check box above the list box is automatically checked.
   So you don't have to check it manually.

10. **Indicate what type of calculation you want to include in the trailing summary line and select the field that you want to use for the calculation.**

    The Calculate drop-down list includes several types of calculations (sum, average, standard deviation, and so on). Pick the type of calculation you want and then pick the database field you want to use for the calculation. For example, to total the salaries for each player, pick the Salary field.

11. **Click Done and watch while Approach creates the report.**

When Report Assistant is finished, it dumps you into the new report in Browse, Design, Preview, or Find mood, depending on which mood you were in when you chose Create⇨Report.

Here are a few points to ponder during sleepless nights:

- ✔ The tabs that appear in the Report Assistant, and in some cases the options that appear on each tab, vary depending on the type of report you're creating. For example, Columnar Reports do not have leading or trailing summaries, so the summary tab doesn't appear. Similarly, a Columnar with Grand Summary report has a grand summary instead of a leading or trailing summary.

- ✔ If you make a mistake, you can return to any Report Assistant step by clicking the tab at the top of the Report Assistant dialog box or clicking the Back button. None of the options that you enter are set in stone until you click the Done button.

- ✔ Trust me, the Report Assistant saves you a ton of work. Don't take him for granted.

Deleting a Report

The following procedure is useful when you no longer need a report, or (more likely) when you create a beautiful report by using the Report Assistant and then mess it up beyond recognition so that the easiest way to proceed is to delete the report and start over:

1. **Select the report you want to delete by clicking its view tab.**

   The report is displayed.

2. **In Design mood, choose Edit⇨Delete Report.**

   The confirmation dialog box shown in Figure 10-10 is displayed.

3. **Click Yes if you think you know what you're doing.**

   The report is deleted.

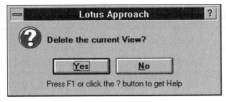

Figure 10-10:
Deleting a
report.

Fixing a Report

Report Assistant does a pretty darn good job of creating reports for you, good enough that you may be content to leave a report well enough alone after Report Assistant has finished its work. On the other hand, you may want to modify some aspect of the report's appearance to make it even better. The following sections explain how to improve on Report Assistant's work.

Note: Many of the procedures for working with form fields that are covered in Chapter 9 work equally well with report fields. Since they don't pay me by the page, I won't repeat all of those procedures here. Refer back to Chapter 9 for instructions on changing the size of fields, adding fields, and changing the text font and other field properties.

Working in Design mood

The procedures described in the following sections assume that you are working in Design mood. To switch to Design mood, click the Design icon in the icon bar, choose View➪Design, use the Design command from the pop-up mood menu in the status bar at the bottom of the screen, or press Ctrl+D.

When you switch to Design mood and display a report, the icon bar changes to provide icons that are useful when you design reports. Table 10-1 summarizes the most essential design icons, along with their keyboard shortcuts.

One of the items in the menu bar — the one between the Create menu and the Tools menu — has a tendency to change periodically when you're in Design mood. This Chameleon menu is nothing to be alarmed about; it simply provides commands that are specific to the type of object that's selected.

As when you work with forms in Design mood, you can call up the InfoBox to change the properties of any object in a report. See Chapter 9 for details about using the InfoBox.

Also, you can call up a pop-up menu that contains commands specific to any report object by pointing the mouse at the object and clicking the right mouse button.

Table 10-1		Report Design Icons and Keyboard Equivalents
Icon	*Keyboard*	*What It Does*
	Ctrl+S	Saves design changes to the Approach file.
	Ctrl+Z	Undoes the most recent design change.
	Ctrl+X	Cuts the selection to the Clipboard (deletes the original).
	Ctrl+C	Copies the selection to the Clipboard (leaves the original).
	Ctrl+V	Pastes the contents of the Clipboard on the view.
	Ctrl+M	Copies the format of selected object to other objects.
	Ctrl+E	Calls up the InfoBox for the selected object.
		Inserts a trailing summary panel to group records based on the selected field.
		Inserts a leading summary panel to group records based on the selected field.
		Creates an automatic sum field to sum the values in the selected field.
		Creates an automatic average field to calculate the average of the values in the selected field.
		Creates an automatic count field to count the values in the selected field.
		Displays or hides panel names.
		Switches between a display of actual database data and field names.

Understanding panels

The key to working with reports in Design mood is understanding the notion of *panels.* Approach carves a report up into various panels that contain the different pieces that make up the report. These panels serve as templates that govern how Approach prints the various report pieces. Figure 10-11 shows how these panels are displayed in Design mood.

 Note: If you switch to Design mode for a report view and you still see actual data in the report rather than the field names as in Figure 10-11, click the Show Field Names button.

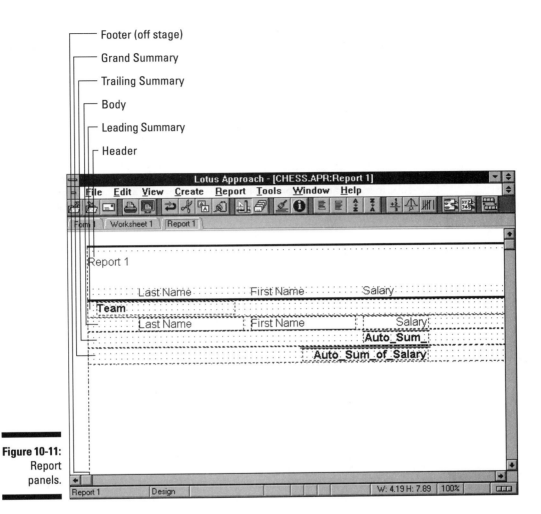

Figure 10-11:
Report
panels.

The following kinds of panels are shown in Figure 10-11:

- ✔ The *Header Panel,* which appears at the top of each report page and includes the report heading and the field headings.
- ✔ The *Leading Summary Panel,* which appears before each group of records.
- ✔ The *Body Panel,* which displays the fields for each record.
- ✔ The *Trailing Summary Panel,* which follows each group of records and usually includes a summary field.

✔ The *Grand Summary Panel,* which appears at the end of the report and usually includes a summary field.

✔ The *Footer Panel,* which appears at the bottom of each report page and usually contains the page number, date, and other information that you want on each page.

To select a panel, click in the panel outside of a field or other object. When the panel is selected, it will be surrounded by a heavy border. You'll know.

After you select a panel, you can resize it by positioning the mouse pointer directly over the top or bottom border. When the cursor changes from a hand to a double-sided arrow, you can drag the border up or down to increase or decrease the panel size. Increasing the height of a panel adds extra space between report lines.

 If you want to see the names of the panels that make up a report, choose <u>V</u>iew⇨Show Panel <u>L</u>abels or click the Show Report Panel Labels icon. Bright yellow labels are added to each panel. Unfortunately, the labels have a nasty habit of obscuring important report fields, so I usually leave them off.

 Another way to vary the appearance of the report in Design mood is to display the actual database field data rather than field names. You can switch between field names and data by choosing <u>V</u>iew⇨<u>S</u>how Data or by clicking the Show Data icon. When you display data, the various report panels are repeated as they will be in the printed report. When you show field names, only one occurrence of each panel is displayed on the report.

Changing a report's name and title

A report's *name* is the identifying text that appears in the view tabs that you click to switch from form to form; the *title* is the text object that appears in the heading at the top of each report page. You can assign a name and title that are more meaningful than "Report 1" when you use Report Assistant to create a report. However, if you want to change the name or title later, you can follow the procedures outlined in this section.

To change the report name, follow this procedure:

1. **Double-click the report's view tab.**

   The tab widens, and a text insertion point is placed in the report name.

2. **Type the new name for the report.**

3. Press Enter.

Or call up the InfoBox for the report and change the report name there.

To change a report's title, switch to Design mood, call up the report, and then follow this procedure:

1. Click the report's title text a couple of times until an insertion point appears.

Count to three between clicks to avoid double-clicking, which would bring up the unwanted InfoBox.

2. Edit the title text however you want.

3. When you're done, click the mouse anywhere outside the title.

Changing report headings

The Report Assistant always uses the database field names for column headings. If a field name is cryptic, like "Custno," you may want to change it to something a little more English-like, such as "Customer Number." Call up the report in Design mood and then follow this procedure:

1. Click twice on the report heading that you want to change.

Don't double-click, or you'll call up the InfoBox. Click the heading once to select the text object and then click again to edit it. Count to three between clicks.

2. Edit the heading text however you want to.

3. When you're done, click the mouse anywhere outside the title.

Adding additional summary fields

Although the Report Assistant can create a report that has a summary panel, it adds only one calculated field to the summary panel. That's fine if the report has only one field that you want to total, but what if you have several fields for which you want to see totals? No problemo. Just call up the report in Design mood and then follow these simple steps to add additional total fields:

1. In the body panel, click the field for which you want to create an additional total field.

For example, if the report is missing a total of the Sales field, click the Sales field in the body panel.

2. **Click the appropriate icon for the kind of total field that you want to create.**

   You can use three icons for creating total fields:

         Adds up all of the field values.

         Calculates the average value.

        Counts the values.

   When you click the icon, a field is added to the summary panel. You may have to adjust the position of the field a bit to get things lined up correctly.

Printing a Report

Printing a report is fairly simple: you just call up the report and click the print icon. However, to print a report *properly,* you need to attend to a few preliminaries. Here's the complete list:

1. **Call up the report that you want to print.**

2. **Sort the records.**

         To sort records into ascending sequence, click the field by which you want to sort the records and then click the Ascending Sort icon.

         To sort records into descending sequence, click the field by which you want to sort the records and then click the Descending Sort icon.

   For more complicated sorts, see Chapter 6.

3. **If you want to, you can use Find to select records that you want to include in the report.**

        To include all records in the report, click the Find All icon.

         To include just certain records in the report, click the Find icon, type search criteria into the database fields, and then click OK.

   For more information about finding records, see Chapter 5.

4. **Switch to Preview mood to check the report.**

         Click the Preview button, choose File➪Preview, or press Ctrl+Shift+B. This step helps preserve the Rain Forest.

5. **Now you can print the report.**

        Choose File➪Print, press Ctrl+P, or click the Print icon.

Chapter 11
Drawing on Forms and Reports

- -

In This Chapter

▶ Drawing simple lines and shapes

▶ Drawing text objects

▶ Creating drop shadows, embossed effects, and other fancy looks

▶ Understanding layers and groups

▶ Lining things up

▶ Stealing pictures from other programs

- -

C him-chiminey, chim-chiminey, chim-chim cheroo,
I draws what I likes and I likes what I drew. . . .

Art time! Everybody get your crayons and glue and don an old paint shirt.
You're going to cut out some simple shapes and paste them onto your Approach views so that people will either think you are a wonderful artist or scoff
at you for not using clip art.

This chapter covers Approach's crude but useful drawing features. Approach
isn't equipped with the artist's tools that you need to draw fancy pictures, but
it does give you some rudimentary drawing tools to spice up your forms with a
bit o' something here and a bit o' something there.

Some General Drawing Tips

Approach's drawing tools aren't as powerful as the tools provided with a full-
blown drawing program such as CorelDraw! or Illustrator, but they are powerful enough to create serviceable pictures to add some pizzazz to your views.
Before I get into the specifics of how to use these drawing tools, here are a
handful of general tips for drawing pictures.

Zoom in

When you work with Approach's drawing tools, you need to increase the zoom factor so that you can draw more accurately. Approach usually displays views full size (100%), but you can change the zoom factor to 25%, 50%, 75%, 100%, or 200%. For precision drawing, you should switch the zoom factor to 200%.

You can use any of the following techniques to change the zoom setting:

- ✔ Click the zoom setting in the status bar at the bottom of the screen to pop up a menu of allowable zoom settings and then choose the zoom factor you want.

 ✔ Click the zoom in icon or choose View➪Zoom In to zoom in to the next higher zoom setting.

 ✔ Click the zoom out icon or choose View➪Zoom Out to zoom out to the next lower zoom setting.

- ✔ To switch back to full size, choose View➪Actual Size.

After you zoom in, you have to play with the scroll bars a bit to find the portion of the view that you want to draw on.

Display the ruler

 If you want to be precise about lining up objects, consider activating the ruler. If the ruler isn't displayed already, choose View➪Show Ruler, use the handy keyboard shortcut, Ctrl+J, or click the Ruler icon to show the ruler. To make the ruler go away, repeat the command.

When you edit a text object, the ruler indicates the text margins and tab positions.

Use the grid

The grid is a pattern of dots that are superimposed on a view to help you line things up. You can display the grid to use as a visual guide to help you place objects, or you can activate the Snap to Grid feature to cause Approach to automatically align any object you draw with the nearest grid point.

To display the grid, choose View➪Show Grid. To hide the grid, choose the command again. (The View➪Show Grid menu item is checked when the grid is visible.)

To force any objects you draw to line up with the grid, choose <u>V</u>iew⇨Snap to <u>G</u>rid or its keyboard shortcut, Ctrl+Y. To disable the Snap To option, use the command again.

One thing to be aware of when you use the grid is that objects that have been automatically placed on a form by the Form Assistant (or on a report by the Report Assistant) are *not* aligned to the grid. As a result, any objects that you draw when the Snap To option is on will be misaligned with objects that are already on the screen. To rectify this situation, simply click each object and nudge it towards the nearest grid point.

Save frequently

Drawing can be tedious work. You don't want to spend an hour working on a particularly important drawing only to lose it all just because a comet strikes your building or an errant Scud lands in your backyard. You can prevent catastrophic loss from incidents such as these by pressing Ctrl+S frequently as you work. And always wear protective eyewear.

Don't forget Ctrl+Z

Don't forget that you're never more than one keystroke away from erasing a boo-boo. If you do something silly — such as forgetting to group a complex picture before trying to move it — you can always press Ctrl+Z to undo your last action. Ctrl+Z is my favorite and most frequently used key combination. (For left-handed mouse users, Alt+Backspace does the same thing.)

Drawing Simple Lines and Shapes

Approach's drawing tools are limited to lines and basic geometric shapes — circles and rectangles. Yet with these simple shapes, you can create some very good effects. For example, have a look at Figure 11-1. Here, I used a rectangle to group the customer name and address information together. Then I used a circle, two lines, and a text object to draw attention to a field that I don't want the user to overlook. (The box that contains the title was added by Approach when it created the form.)

The icons used to draw these shapes are found on the floating drawing Tools palette and are summarized in Table 11-1.

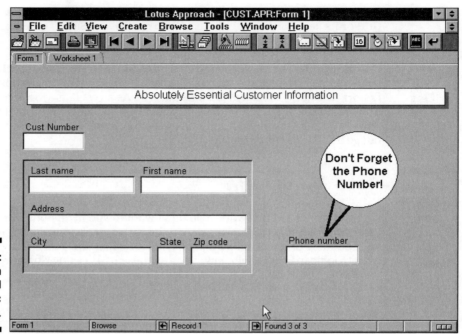

Figure 11-1:
A form
embellished
with graphic
shapes.

Table 11-1	Drawing Icons
Drawing Icon	*What It Does*
▶	Not really a drawing tool, but rather the generic mouse pointer used to choose objects.
abc	Adds a text object. Used to add explanatory text, instructions, or lawyer jokes to forms or reports.
▢	Used to draw rectangles. To make a perfect square, hold down Shift while you draw.
◯	Draws circles and ovals. To create a perfect circle, hold down Shift while you draw.
▢	Draws a rectangle with rounded corners. To draw a square with rounded corners, hold down Shift while you draw.
╱	Adds a line. You can later change the attributes of the line to make the line thicker or add a dashed pattern. To force the line to be horizontal, vertical, or 45-degree diagonal, hold down Shift while you draw.

To draw an object, follow this procedure:

1. **Click the icon for the shape you want to draw.**

2. **Point to where you want the object to start.**

3. **Click and drag the mouse button to where you want the object to end.**

   Approach stretches the object as you move the mouse.

4. **Release the mouse button when you reach your destination.**

Here are some pointers to keep in mind when you are drawing lines and shapes:

- ✔ Hold down Shift while you draw to force the object to be a perfect square or circle or to restrict lines to 45-degree angles.

- ✔ After you draw a shape, you can adjust it by clicking it to select it and then dragging one of the love handles that appear at the object's corners. (The official term for these love handles is just "handles," but my term is more colorful, don't you think?)

- ✔ If the floating drawing palette has mysteriously disappeared, you can call it back into view by choosing View➪Show Drawing Tools or pressing Ctrl+L.

- ✔ If you know in advance that you want to draw more than one object of the same type, double-click the drawing tool button. Then you can keep drawing objects of the selected type 'til who laid the rails. To stop drawing, click the arrow icon or any of the other drawing icons. (The icon you double-click turns blue in the face to remind you that you've selected it. It returns to normal color when you select another icon.)

- ✔ *Note:* I have no idea what the expression "'til who laid the rails" means. I heard one of the residents of River City (the mayor, I believe) use it in *The Music Man,* and I've liked it ever since.

Drawing Text Objects

A text object is a bit of text that's displayed in a view. Text objects are useful for displaying instructions, explanatory notes, or lawyer jokes.

Be sure not to confuse text objects with database fields, which display text contained in database records. Text objects are a part of the view, not the database. As such, the text does not change as different database records are retrieved.

To add a text object to a view, follow these steps:

1. **Click the Text Object icon in the floating drawing Tools palette.**

   As soon as you move the mouse away from the floating Tools palette, the pointer changes to a steel I-beam that's suitable for building bridges or editing text.

2. **Click the view where you want the text object to appear.**

   A default-style text object appears on the screen.

3. **Type whatever text you want.**

   As you type, the borders of the text object expand to accommodate the text.

4. **Click outside the text field when you're finished.**

Here are a few important pointers to keep in mind when you are working with text fields:

- As you type text into a text field, Approach expands the field to accommodate the text. After you're finished, you may want to resize the object if you don't like the way the text fits. Click the text object to select it and then drag any of the love handles that appear at the corners of the object.

- To edit the text in an existing text object, click the text object to select it and then click again to edit the text. Take your time between clicks; if you click too quickly, Approach thinks you're double-clicking the object and brings up the InfoBox instead of enabling you to edit the text.

- The default text style places text on a white background and uses a border style that creates a recessed appearance. To change the appearance, call up the InfoBox by selecting the object and pressing Ctrl+E or clicking the InfoBox icon. Then play with the InfoBox settings until you're satisfied.

- Figure 11-2 shows several text fields that have different formats to give you an idea of the effects that are possible. The formats shown in Figure 11-2 represent different combinations of text font and style, border style, background and shadow color, and text color (to create the white-on-black text). For the specifics on setting these options, see the following sections of this chapter.

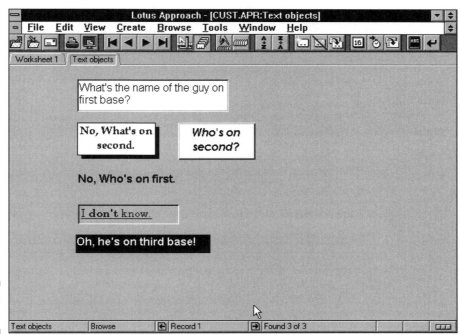

Figure 11-2:
Text objects.

Improving an Object's Appearance

No matter what they say, appearances do count. To create geometric objects that look as good as the ones in Figure 11-1, you have to spend some time tweaking the object settings.

The procedure for modifying an object's appearance is the same as the procedure for setting a field's appearance which was described in Chapter 9. The following is a summary of the procedure; if you want more detailed information, refer to Chapter 9.

1. Click the object whose appearance you want to change.

Love handles appear, as an indication that the object is selected.

 2. Call up the InfoBox by clicking the Info icon.

Or choose Object⇨Style and Properties, press Ctrl+E, or double-click the object. Either way, the InfoBox appears, as shown in Figure 11-3.

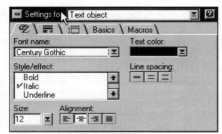

Figure 11-3:
The InfoBox.

3. **Click the InfoBox tab that contains the settings you want to modify.**

4. **Change whatever settings you want.**

5. **Repeat Steps 3 and 4 to change settings on other InfoBox tabs.**

6. **Double-click the InfoBox's control box (in the upper-left corner of the InfoBox) to dismiss it.**

   The results of the settings changes are immediately apparent.

Table 11-2 summarizes the settings that are displayed for each of the InfoBox tabs.

Table 11-2	InfoBox Panels
Tab	*Field Settings It Displays*
⬛	Used for text objects to change the font, size, style (bold, italic, and so on), color, alignment (left, center, right), and text relief style.
⬛	Border width, color, fill color, shadow color, frame style, and border position.
⬛	Size and position of object.
Basics	Stuff that's not very important for drawn objects.
Macros	Names a macro to be run when the user clicks the object.

Here are some important points to ponder when working with the InfoBox:

✔ You don't have to dismiss the InfoBox to select another object. If you call up the InfoBox and then click another object to select it, the InfoBox changes to show the settings for the second object. (If the InfoBox is in the way of an object that you want to select, just move the InfoBox by dragging it by its title bar.)

✔ If the InfoBox is *really* in the way, you can shrink it down to just a strip by double-clicking its title bar. The InfoBox will roll itself up into a nice little package that shows just the title bar and the tabs, as shown in Figure 11-4. To unravel the InfoBox, double-click the title bar again or click one of its tabs.

Figure 11-4:
The InfoBox
all rolled up.

✔ Approach has a feature called *named styles* that enables you to assign a
   name to a frequently used combination of InfoBox settings. Then you can
   quickly apply those settings to an object by applying the style. This feature
   is particularly nerdy, so just pretend I never mentioned it.

✔ A quick way to copy the InfoBox settings from one object to another is to
   use the Fast Format command. Click an object that's formatted the way
   you want and then click the Fast Format icon or press Ctrl+M. Next, click
   any objects to which you want to copy the formatting from the first object.
   When you're done, click the Fast Format icon or press Ctrl+M again.

The following sections outline the procedures for creating particular effects.

Creating a drop shadow

To create a shadow behind an object, as in the "No, What's on second" object in
Figure 11-2, select the object, call up the InfoBox, and click the Border tab. Then
set the shadow color to black. (You can use any color you want for the shadow,
but black usually works best.) To get rid of a shadow, set the shadow color to
Transparent (represented by a *T* in the color box).

Creating embossed effects

To create an embossed effect for an object, as in the "I don't know" object in
Figure 11-2, select the object, call up the InfoBox, and click the Border tab. Then
set one of the embossed frame styles — one of them creates a raised effect, the
other a recessed effect. Next, set the fill color to the same color as the view
background. (You can use an embossed frame style with any fill color, but the
effect is most pronounced when you use the view background color.)

Creating simple text with no border

To create simple text displayed without a border, as in the "No, Who's on first"
object in Figure 11-2, select a text object, call up the InfoBox, and apply these
formats:

✔ Set the border color to the same color as the view background or make it transparent (represented by a *T* in the color box). This setting renders the border invisible, so the border width and style settings don't matter.

✔ Set the fill color to the same color as the view background or make it transparent.

✔ Set the shadow color to transparent.

Creating white-on-black text

To create white-on-black text, as in the "Oh, he's on third base!" object in Figure 11-2, click a text object, call up the InfoBox, and then apply these formats:

✔ On the Border panel, set the border style to the simple rectangle outline.

✔ Set the border color to black.

✔ Set the fill color to black. The text disappears temporarily, but it reappears when you set the next setting.

✔ On the Text panel, set the text color to white.

Drawing Complicated Pictures

When you add more than one object to a view, several problems are bound to come up. What happens when the objects overlap? How do you line objects up so that they don't look as if they were thrown from a passing car? And how do you keep objects together that belong together?

This section explains how to use Approach's features to handle overlapped objects, align objects, and group objects.

Changing layers

Whenever you have more than one object on a view, the potential exists for objects to overlap one another. Like more sophisticated drawing programs, Approach handles this problem by layering objects like a stack of plates. The first object you add to a view is at the bottom of the stack; the second object is on top of the first one; the third object is on top of the second one; and so on. If two objects overlap, the one that's at the higher layer is the one that wins; objects below it are partially covered.

So far, so good — but what if you don't remember to draw the objects in the correct order? What if you draw an object that you want to tuck behind an object that you've already drawn, or what if you want to bring an existing object to the top of the pecking order? No problem. Approach enables you to change the stack order by moving objects toward the front or back so that they overlap just the way you want them.

Approach provides four commands for changing the stacking order:

Object⇨Arrange⇨Bring to Front: This command brings the chosen object to the top of the stack.

Object⇨Arrange⇨Send to Back: This command sends the chosen object to the bottom of the stack.

 Object⇨Arrange⇨Bring Forward: This command brings the chosen object one step closer to the front of the stack. The Bring Forward icon has the same effect.

 Object⇨Arrange⇨Send Backward: This command sends the chosen object one step closer to the top of the stack. The Send Backward icon has the same effect.

To use any of the preceding commands, first choose Object⇨Arrange. A submenu then appears, listing the Bring to Front, Send to Back, Bring Forward, and Send Backward commands.

Layering problems are most obvious when objects have a fill color. If an object is transparent, any objects behind it show through, and only the border overlaps objects that are beneath it.

To bring an object to the top of another object, you may have to choose Object⇨Arrange⇨Bring Forward several times. The reason is that even though the two objects may appear to be adjacent, other objects may occupy the layers between them.

Line 'em up and spread 'em out

Nothing looks more amateurish than objects that have been dropped randomly on a view with no apparent concern for how they line up with one another. Approach provides several features, some of which you already know about, that enable you to line up objects as you draw them:

 Show Grid: When Show Grid is on, a grid of dots, spaced 12 per inch, appears on the screen. You can use this grid to visually align objects. To turn the grid display on or off, choose View⇨Show Grid or click the Grid icon.

Snap to Grid: When Snap to Grid is on, any object you create or move automatically sticks to the nearest grid point. To turn Snap to Grid mode on or off, choose View⇨Snap to Grid or press Ctrl+Y.

Show Ruler: Choose View⇨Show Ruler or the handy keyboard shortcut, Ctrl+J, to show or hide a ruler to help line things up.

Align command: The Object⇨Align command enables you to choose several objects at a time and then line them up or space them out evenly. You can align objects horizontally to the left, center, or right of the objects, or vertically to the top, center, or bottom. You also can spread objects out evenly.

To align or distribute objects, follow this procedure:

1. **Select the objects that you want to align by clicking them while holding down Shift.**

   Alternatively, hold down the mouse button while you draw a selection rectangle that encloses all of the objects that you want to align. When you release the mouse button, all the objects will be selected.

2. **Choose Object⇨Align.**

   Or use its keyboard shortcut, Ctrl+I. Either way, the Align dialog box appears, as shown in Figure 11-5.

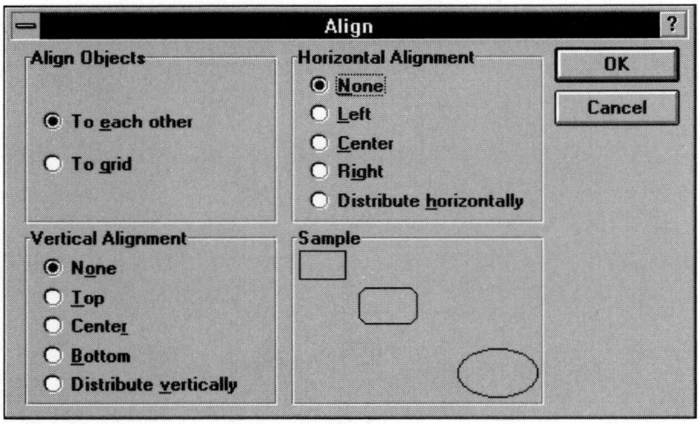

Figure 11-5:
The Align
dialog box.

3. **Select the horizontal and vertical alignment options you want.**

   As you select alignment options, the sample at the bottom right of the screen changes to indicate how the objects will be aligned. If you want to align only horizontally or vertically, make sure that you select None for alignment that you don't want. To space objects out, select one of the Distribute options.

4. Click OK.

Approach aligns or distributes the objects.

Figures 11-6 and 11-7 show how these Align commands work. Figure 11-6 shows three objects as they were originally drawn. Figure 11-7 shows the result of selecting all three objects and choosing the various Align commands.

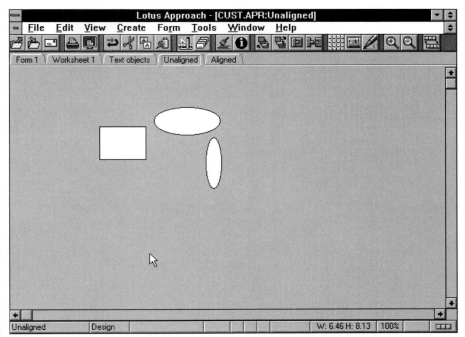

Figure 11-6:
Three
unaligned
objects.

To center two or more objects, choose the objects and then choose Object⊅Align. Choose Center for the Horizontal Alignment and Center for the Vertical Alignment and then click OK.

Unfortunately, Approach has no keyboard shortcuts or icon shortcuts for the Align command.

Group therapy

A *group* is a collection of objects that Approach treats as if they were one object. Using groups properly is one key to putting simple shapes together to

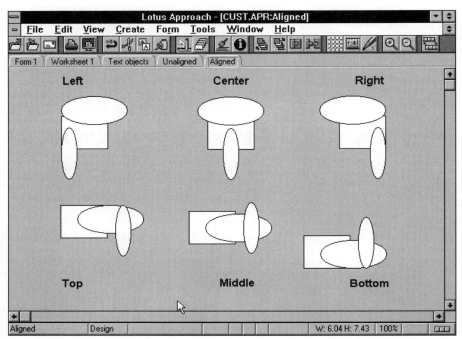

Figure 11-7:
Putting the
Align
commands
to work.

make complex pictures without becoming so frustrated that you have to join a therapy group. ("Hello, my name is Doug, and Approach drives me crazy.")

To create a group, follow these steps:

1. Choose all objects that you want to include in the group.

2. Choose Object⇨Group.

 Or use the keyboard shortcut, Ctrl+G, or click the Group icon.

To take a group apart so the objects are treated as individuals again, follow this procedure:

1. Choose the object that you want busted apart.

2. Choose Object⇨Ungroup.

 Or use the keyboard shortcut, Ctrl+U, or click the Ungroup icon.

Approach enables you to create groups of groups. This capability is useful because you can work on one part of the view, group it, and then work on the next part of the view without worrying about accidentally disturbing the part you've already grouped. After you have several such groups, choose them all and group them. You can create groups of groups of groups of groups, and so on, and so on, and so on, and so on.

Stealing Pictures from Other Programs

This chapter wouldn't be complete if I didn't point out that, frankly, Approach's drawing tools leave something to be desired. Sometimes using another program to create a picture is easier — even the simple Paintbrush program that comes free with Windows has advantages over Approach's drawing tools. Then you can copy the picture from the drawing program to the Clipboard, switch to Approach, and paste the picture into Approach. Here's the procedure:

1. **Draw a picture using your favorite drawing program.**

   Make sure that the background color of the picture matches the background color of the Approach view that you're going to paste the picture onto.

2. **Select the portion of the picture that you want to copy into Approach.**

3. **Press Ctrl+C to copy the picture to the Clipboard.**

4. **Switch to Approach.**

   If Approach is already running, press Alt+Tab until Approach appears. Otherwise, press Alt+Tab to switch to Program Manager, start Approach, and open the database that you want to paste the picture into.

5. **Press Ctrl+V.**

   The picture is pasted into the view.

6. **Grab the picture with the mouse and move it to the location where you want it.**

   The picture starts out in the upper-left corner of the view, which probably isn't where you want it to stay. Click the picture to select it and then move the mouse pointer over the picture. When the pointer changes to a hand, drag the picture to its new location.

7. **Resize the picture.**

   It's probably too big. Click the picture and then position the mouse pointer over one of its love handles. When the arrow pointer changes to a double-arrow pointer, drag the love handle to resize the picture.

Chapter 12

Adding Pictures and Grunts to a Database

*W*hat's all the rage about multimedia these days? You'd think that some computer geek in Sunnyvale had just invented talking movies. Multimedia technology has progressed almost to the point where a $3,000 computer can belch realistically and play six seconds of *The African Queen* almost as well as a $159 VCR can.

Oh, well. It's a trendy business. Multimedia features have infected just about every type of computer program you can buy, and database programs are no exception. I wouldn't be caught dead not including a chapter about multimedia in an Approach book, especially not when Approach devotes an entire database field type to multimedia gags: PicturePlus fields. You can use PicturePlus fields, as the name suggests, to store pictures or other "plus" stuff, such as sounds and videos.

What Is a PicturePlus Field?

A *PicturePlus* field is a special type of database field that is designed to store objects created by other programs. The most common type of object stored in a PicturePlus field is a picture created by a drawing program or, more likely, scanned in with a scanner. For example, you can use a scanner to scan photographs of your employees to store in an employee database or photos of your products to store in an inventory database.

Here are some important points to remember:

- ✔ *Note:* You use a PicturePlus field to store pictures in database records, and each record has its own picture. Pictures in PicturePlus fields are different from pictures drawn on views, as described in Chapter 11. Pictures drawn on views are not stored in the database file, but rather in the Approach file.

- ✔ A PicturePlus field can contain a picture drawn in a graphics program or an object that was created by a program that supports OLE. See the sidebar, "Stop me before I tell you about OLE," if you're interested in OLE.

- ✔ You can use a PicturePlus field to insert many different kinds of objects into a database record. You can insert a spreadsheet created by a spreadsheet program, a bit of text or a whole document created by a word processing program, a sound or a video clip, and who knows what else.

Stop me before I tell you about OLE

If you read anything about Windows these days, you can't avoid reading about OLE. Microsoft introduced OLE, which can be pronounced *oh-el-ee* or *ohlay!* (rhymes with the *o-Lay* part of Frito-Lay), with Windows 3.1.

OLE stands for *Object Linking and Embedding.* The idea behind it is that it enables you to create documents that contain different kinds of data. Perhaps you want to include some spreadsheet data in a word processing document. OLE enables you to simply insert a *spreadsheet object* in the word processing document. OLE remembers that the data was originally created by a spreadsheet program. If you want to edit the spreadsheet data, you just double-click it. OLE magically conjures up the spreadsheet program so that you can edit the data.

With regular OLE, a new window appears when you double-click an embedded object to edit it. Microsoft has recently introduced a new flavor of OLE, called OLE 2.0, in which embedded objects are not edited in separate windows. Instead, when you double-click an embedded object, the menus and toolbars from the embedded object's program appear, replacing the main program's menus and toolbars. You can then edit the object directly. Very strange, but not yet supported by Approach.

In OLE terminology, the document that contains an embedded object is called a *container,* and a program that creates a container document is called a *client.* An embedded object is called a *component,* and the program that creates it is called a *server.* These terms are important to the people who write OLE programs, but they're completely unimportant to normal people like you and me.

Spicing up records with pretty pictures

To use a PicturePlus field, you need to define a PicturePlus field in the database. If you didn't include a PicturePlus field when you created the database, you can add one later by following this procedure:

1. **Open the database to which you want to add the PicturePlus field.**

    Choose File➪Open, click the Open icon, or pick Open an Existing File from the Welcome to Lotus Approach dialog box.

2. **Switch to Design mood.**

    Press Ctrl+D, choose View➪Design, select Design from the pop-up menu in the status bar at the bottom of the screen, or click the Design icon.

3. **Choose Create➪Field Definition.**

   The Field Definition dialog box, which is shown in Figure 12-1, appears.

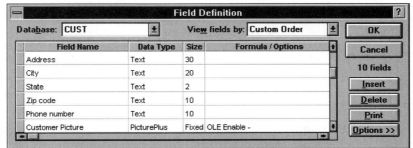

Figure 12-1: The Field Definition dialog box.

4. **Scroll to the bottom of the field list, type a field name in the first blank Field Name space, and press the Tab key.**

   Choose a good name for the PicturePlus field, such as Customer Picture.

5. **Select PicturePlus for the Data Type.**

   You can click the arrow that appears when you click in the Data Type column to drop down the list of data types and then click PicturePlus or press P to quickly select PicturePlus.

6. **Click Options.**

   The Field Definition dialog box expands to reveal the PicturePlus field options, as shown in Figure 12-2.

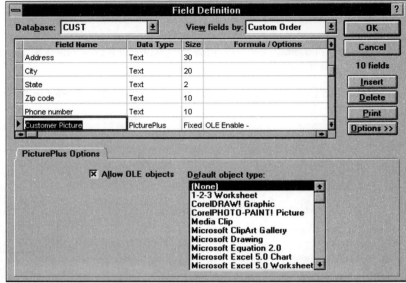

Figure 12-2:
The
PicturePlus
field options.

7. **Uncheck the A̱llow OLE objects check box if you want to restrict the field to pictures only (no OLE objects).**

8. **Select the default OLE object type if the field will usually contain a particular type of OLE object.**

   For example, if the field will usually hold a sound object, select Sound as the De̱fault object type. (If you unchecked the A̱llow OLE objects check box, you can skip this step.)

9. **Click OK.**

   You're done!

Adding a PicturePlus field to a view

Having added the PicturePlus field to the database, you'll probably want to add it to one or more of your views. Follow these steps:

1. **Switch to the view to which you want to add the PicturePlus field.**

   Click the view's tab or select the view from the pop-up menu on the status bar at the bottom of the screen.

2. **If the Add Field dialog box is not visible, click the Add Field icon in the floating icon palette.**

   Figure 12-3 shows the Add Field dialog box.

Figure 12-3:
The Add
Field dialog
box.

3. **Drag the PicturePlus field from the Add Field dialog box onto the view.**

   When you release the mouse button, the PicturePlus field is added to the view at the mouse location.

4. **Resize the PicturePlus field if necessary.**

   The default size is appropriate for most pictures, but you may want a different size or shape.

5. **That's it!**

   You're done.

Adding a Picture to a Database Record

Having created a PicturePlus field and added it to a database view, you use any of the following procedures to add a picture to the field. (To add an OLE object, see the remaining sections in this chapter.) You can paste the picture from an existing file or from the Clipboard.

Inserting a picture from a file

If the picture you want is already stored in a file, follow this procedure:

1. **In Browse mood, call up the record to which you want to add the picture.**

2. **Click the PicturePlus field.**

3. **Choose Edit⇨Paste from File.**

   The Paste from File dialog box appears, as shown in Figure 12-4.

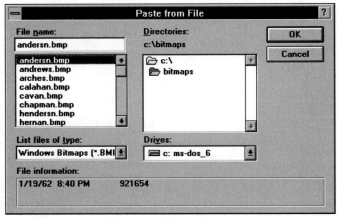

Figure 12-4:
The Paste
from File
dialog box.

4. **Rummage around your hard disk until you find the file you're looking for and then click OK.**

   If necessary, change the List files of type field to show the file type you're looking for (BMP, PCX, and so on).

   The rest of the dialog box contains the standard drive, directory, and file settings. Find the file that contains the picture you want to paste into the PicturePlus field. Then click OK.

   The picture is pasted into the PicturePlus field.

5. **Admire the picture.**

Table 12-1 summarizes the graphic file types supported by Approach.

Table 12-1	Graphic File Types
File Extension	*File Type*
BMP	Windows Bitmap file created by PaintBrush.
WMF	Windows Metafile, often used to exchange graphic data between Windows applications.
TIF	TIFF file, used by high-end paint programs.
PCX	Another graphics format, also used by PaintBrush.
GIF	Yet another graphics file format, this one frequently used by on-line bulletin board systems such as CompuServe.
TGA	Targa, still another graphics file format.
EPS	Encapsulated Postscript File, used by high-end drawing programs.

Pasting a picture from the Clipboard

Another way to insert a picture into a PicturePlus field is via the Clipboard. This technique is useful when the picture is in a file format that you can't directly paste into Approach. Here's the procedure:

1. **Use your favorite drawing program to draw a picture.**

2. **Select the portion of the picture that you want to copy into Approach.**

3. **Choose Edit⇨Copy to copy the picture to the Clipboard.**

   Or use the keyboard shortcut, Ctrl+C.

4. **Switch to Approach.**

   If Approach is already running, press Alt+Tab until Approach appears. Otherwise, press Alt+Tab to switch to Program Manager, start Approach, and open the database into which you want to paste the picture.

5. **In Browse mood, switch to the record to which you want to add the picture and then click the PicturePlus field to select it.**

6. **Choose Edit⇨Paste.**

   Or press Ctrl+V. Either way, the picture is pasted into the PicturePlus field.

Talking Fields

It used to be that the only sound you could get from your computer was a sterile *beep*. Nowadays, you can make your computer talk almost as well as the computers in the *Star Trek* movies. Or you can give it a sophomoric sense of audible distaste. At last, the computer can be as obnoxious as the user!

Note: There's a catch. Your computer has to be equipped with a sound card to play these kinds of sounds. Apple Macintosh users love to brag that every Macintosh ever made has had sound capabilities built right in while poor PC users still have to purchase a separate sound card to make their computers burp as well as a Mac. Fortunately, sound cards are getting less and less expensive. Cheap ones can be had for about $50 to $100 nowadays, and fairly good ones go for about $150 or more.

All about sound files

Computer sounds are stored in sound files, which come in two varieties:

Wave files: Contain digitized recordings of real sounds, such as Darth Vader saying, "I find your lack of faith disturbing," or Dr. McCoy saying, "He's dead, Jim." Windows comes with four WAV files: CHIMES.WAV, CHORD.WAV, DING.WAV, and TADA.WAV. Notice that these files all have names that end in WAV.

MIDI files: Contain music stored in a form that the sound card's synthesizer can play. Windows comes with one MIDI file: CANYON.MID. All MIDI files have names that end in MID.

To insert a sound into a database record, all you have to do is paste one of these sound files into a PicturePlus field. Then you can play the sound by double-clicking the field.

You're more likely to use wave files than MIDI files in an Approach database. MIDI files are great for playing music, but the wave files enable you to incorporate a voice or other actual recording into the database.

Sound files consume large amounts of disk space. A typical two-second sound clip can take up 25K of precious disk real estate. It doesn't seem like much, but it adds up. (The main reason that I use DoubleSpace — the disk compression program that comes with MS-DOS 6 — is to make room for my collection of Pink Panther sound files.)

Inserting a sound in Approach

To add a sound to an Approach database record, follow these steps:

1. **Call up the record that you want to add the sound to.**

2. **Click the PicturePlus field.**

3. **From Program Manager, start the Sound Recorder application.**

   Hold down Alt and press Tab repeatedly until Program Manager returns to the screen. Sound Recorder hides in the Program Manager's Accessories group. Figure 12-5 shows the Sound Recorder icon; double-click it to wake it up.

4. **Stare at the Sound Recorder window a minute to get your bearings.**

   Figure 12-6 shows what the Sound Recorder looks like. The wavy line in the middle is a waveform image of the current sound file.

5. **Choose File⇨Open to open the sound file you want to insert.**

Where to get great sounds

The four WAV sounds that come with Windows are pretty boring, but fortunately there is no national shortage of sound files. You can download them from just about any on-line system (such as CompuServe); purchase them in collections from computer software stores; or beg, borrow, or steal them from your computer geek friends. Most computer geeks will gladly offer you a disk full of *Star Trek* sounds in exchange for a large bag of Chee-tos and a six-pack of Jolt Cola.

If you have a microphone, you can plug it into your sound card and record your own sounds. Move your computer into the living room some weekend and rent the following movies:

- *Star Wars*
- Any Pink Panther movie
- *The Great Muppet Caper*
- *Star Trek IV* and *Star Trek VI*
- *The African Queen*
- *2001: A Space Odyssey*
- *Annie Hall, Bananas,* or *Sleeper*

These films should give you a good assortment of sounds to incorporate into your databases. For more information about recording sounds, check out *MORE Windows For Dummies* or *Multimedia and CD-ROM For Dummies,* both by Andy Rathbone.

Sound Recorder icon

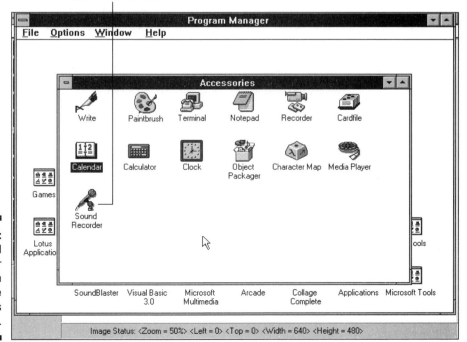

Figure 12-5: The Sound Recorder icon, which hides in the Accessories group.

Figure 12-6:
The Sound
Recorder
dialog box.

Reverse   Forward   Play   Stop

You may have to rummage through your hard disk until you find the file.
Keep looking; it's there somewhere.

6. Click the Play button to make sure that you found the right sound.

7. Choose Edit⇨Copy to copy the sound to the Clipboard.

Or use the familiar keyboard shortcut, Ctrl+C.

8. Pop over to Approach.

Press Alt+Tab until Approach comes back to life.

**9. Choose Edit⇨Paste Special and then check the Paste Link option button
and click OK.**

The sound is pasted into the PicturePlus field, and a microphone icon that
is identical to the Sound Recorder icon shown in Figure 12-5 appears in the
field.

Note: By using the Edit⇨Paste Special command, you are actually pasting
a *link* to the sound file into the database. If you used the regular
Edit⇨Paste command, the sound file itself would be copied into the
database. This can result in a lot of wasted disk space.

Playing a sound

Having pasted a sound into a PicturePlus field, you can play it easily. Just follow
this procedure, if you can:

1. Double-click the sound icon in the PicturePlus field.

2. Listen.

If you don't hear the sound, several things could be wrong:

✔ Your computer doesn't have a sound card.

✔ The sound card's driver file isn't properly installed.

✔ The sound card is working, but the speakers are unplugged or turned off, or the volume control is turned down too low.

✔ The kids are yelling too loudly in the other room for you to hear anything.

Removing a sound

If you finally come to your senses and realize that sounds are a bit frivolous, you can easily remove them. To remove a sound from a PicturePlus field, click the field to select it and press Ctrl+X.

Let's Go to the Movies

Welcome to the MTV era of computing. If your computer has the chutzpah, you can add small video clips to your database records and play them at will. This stuff is pretty exotic, but what the heck. It's a lot of fun.

Adding a video clip to a PicturePlus field is similar to adding a sound clip. The crucial difference, however, between video clips and sound bites is that video is meant to be seen as well as heard.

Oh, and you think sound files are big? Wait till you see how big video files are. Ha! The whole multimedia revolution is probably a conspiracy started by hard disk manufacturers.

✔ To work with video clips, you need to have the new version of the Windows Media Player. You can purchase Microsoft Video for Windows from a computer software store, or you can obtain a scaled-back version, called Run-Time Video for Windows, from CompuServe.

✔ As I said, video clips are big, big, big. Sure, you can find them on CompuServe, but downloading them costs a small fortune in connect charges. Your best bet is to buy them in a collection from a computer store. You need a CD-ROM drive because most movie clips are distributed on CDs.

✔ To learn more about video and multimedia in general, check out *MultiMedia and CD-ROM For Dummies* by Andy Rathbone. I don't get a nickel for this endorsement, but I figure you can probably use some more help here.

Adding a video clip

This procedure describes how to add a video clip to a database record:

1. **Call up the record to which you want to add the video clip.**

2. **Click the PicturePlus field.**

3. **From Program Manager, start the Media Player application.**

Media Player

Hold down Alt and press Tab repeatedly until Program Manager returns to the screen. Media Player is hiding in the Program Manager's Accessories group; double-click its icon to summon it.

4. **Behold the Media Player.**

Figure 12-7 shows what the Media Player looks like. The buttons that look like the buttons on your VCR work like the buttons on your VCR. Too bad Microsoft didn't throw in a blinking 12:00 to complete the VCR look.

Figure 12-7:
The Media
Player
dialog box.

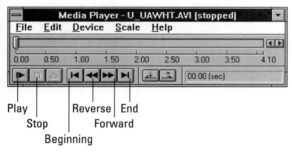

Play
Stop
Beginning
Reverse
Forward
End

5. **Choose File⇨Open to open the video file that you want to insert.**

Video files have names that end in AVI. If you can't find the movie you want, hunt around until you locate it.

6. **Click the Play button to make sure that you found the right video clip.**

7. **Choose Edit⇨Copy to copy the video to the Clipboard.**

Or use the familiar keyboard shortcut, Ctrl+C.

8. **Pop over to Approach.**

Press Alt+Tab until Approach comes back to life.

9. **Chose Edit⇨Paste Special and then check the Paste Link option and click OK.**

The video is pasted into the PicturePlus field, and a film reel icon that is identical to the Media Player icon appears in the field.

Note: The reason for using the more complicated Edit➪Paste Special command rather than the simpler Edit➪Paste command is to save disk space. If you use Edit➪Paste, a copy of the video clip is stored in the database file. When you use Edit➪Paste Special, only the name of the video file that contains the video clip is copied, not the entire video clip.

Playing a video

After you have pasted a video clip into a PicturePlus field, you can play it at any time by following this procedure:

1. **Make some popcorn.**

2. **Turn down the lights.**

3. **Double-click the film reel icon in the PicturePlus field.**

4. **Watch.**

Chapter 13

Using Calculated Fields

A *calculated field* is a database field in which a formula automatically calculates the field's value. For example, if a database has an invoice subtotal field, you can use a calculated field to calculate sales tax as a percentage of the subtotal. Then you can use another calculated field to calculate the invoice total by adding the sales tax to the subtotal.

Chapter 2 briefly introduces calculated fields. This chapter dives head first into the depths of creating formulas for calculated fields. If the water gets too deep here, you can use your mouse pad as a flotation device.

Using Simple Arithmetic

Approach uses a formula to figure out the value of a calculated field. Formulas can be simple or complex, depending on what value you want Approach to calculate for the field. The simplest Approach formulas use ordinary arithmetic — addition, subtraction, multiplication, and division. Here are some sample formulas that use nothing more than sixth grade math:

`TotalParts + TotalLabor`	Calculates an invoice total for an auto repair shop.
`Subtotal * .0725`	Calculates the sales tax assuming a tax rate of 7.25%.

```
AtBats / Hits          Calculates a batting average for a Little League
                       baseball database.
```

Notice that all of the database field names in the preceding formulas consist of one word. To use a field name that consists of two or more words with intervening spaces, you have to type a quotation mark on either side of the field name. For example, if the TotalParts and TotalLabor fields in the first example were named Total Parts and Total Labor, the formula would require quotation marks, like this: `"Total Parts" + "Total Labor"`.

Table 13-1 summarizes the *operators* (that is, math symbols) that you can use to create simple arithmetic functions.

Table 13-1	Simple Arithmetic Operators
Operator	*What It Does*
+	Addition
–	Subtraction
*	Multiplication
/	Division

Crazy but unavoidable formula jargon

After you start working with formulas, you inevitably bump up against some pretty crazy terminology. These terms were originally the result of a conspiracy between computer science majors and math majors to prevent outsiders from understanding their secret language. Here are the terms you need to know:

Expression: Nothing more than a computer and/or math geek's way of saying *formula*. Technically, an expression is a combination of operators and operands that yields a single result. Approach enables you to use three kinds of expressions: arithmetic expressions, comparison expressions, and logical expressions.

Operand: A value that is used in an expression. An operand can be a number, such as *23* or *689.58*, or a database field, as in `InvoiceAmount * TaxRate`.

Operator: A symbol that tells Approach what to do with a pair of operands. For example, the Plus operator (+) tells Approach to add two operands.

Arithmetic expression: An expression that produces a numeric result by adding, subtracting, multiplying, or dividing or by using special *functions* such as `Sqrt(64)` or `PMT(Principal,Rate,Months)`.

Comparison expression: An expression that produces a Yes or No result by comparing two values, such as `State = 'CA'`.

Logical expressions: An expression that produces a Yes or No result, usually by combining the results of several comparison expressions, such as

```
State = 'CA' OR State = 'NV'.
```

Creating simple formulas

To create a calculated field that uses a simple arithmetic formula, follow these steps:

1. **Choose Create⇨Field Definition to call up the Field Definition dialog box.**

   If the Field Definition dialog box is already visible, skip this step.

2. **Type a name for the calculated field in the Field Name column.**

   You may have to scroll down the field list to find a blank row in which to create the new field.

3. **Select Calculated as the Data Type for the new field.**

   When you select the Data Type, the Field Definition dialog box expands to show the field options for the calculated field, as shown in Figure 13-1.

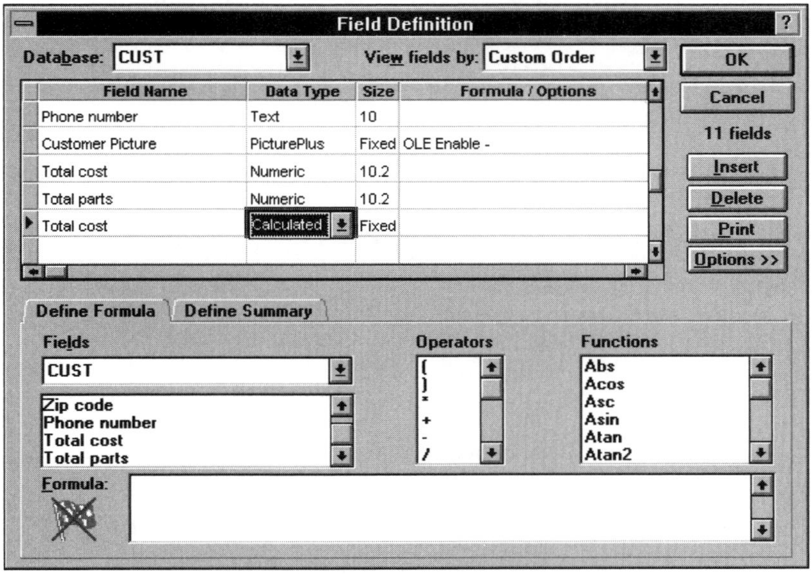

Figure 13-1:
Creating a
calculated
field.

4. **Create the formula for the field by clicking the field names and arithmetic operators that you want to include in the formula.**

   For example, to create the formula TotalParts + TotalLabor, click TotalParts, click the plus sign (+), and then click TotalLabor.

You can type numeric constants when you need them. For example, to create the formula `Subtotal * 0.0725`, click Subtotal, click the multiplication operator (*), and then type **0.0725**.

5. **When the formula is complete, click OK.**

Or type another field name in the next blank row to create another field.

Here are some things to watch for when you create simple formulas:

✔ Notice the checkered flag at the lower left of the Field Definition dialog box. It has a red stroke through it if the formula is incomplete. As soon as you complete the formula, the red stroke disappears, and the checkered flag lights up. (When you create more complex formulas, the stroke may flash on and off several times. Don't panic; this behavior is entirely normal.)

✔ When you click a field name to add it to the formula, Approach automatically adds quotation marks if they are needed.

✔ If the Approach file includes joined databases, the joined databases are listed in the drop-down list box above the field names.

✔ If you prefer to type the formula yourself instead of hunting and pecking for fields and operators, feel free to do so. Just make sure that you type the field names correctly and don't forget to use quotation marks when necessary.

Conehead formulas that look like algebra

Formulas can get more complicated than simple addition and subtraction. You also can use parentheses to make formulas that look like the kind of math you've been trying to forget since high school algebra. For example, consider how the parentheses affect the results of these two formulas:

✔ `5 + 3 * 2` equals 16, because Approach first adds 5 to 3 to get 8, and then it multiplies 8 by 2 to get 16.

✔ `5 + (3 * 2)` equals 11, because Approach first multiplies 3 by 2 to get 6, and then it adds 6 to 5 to get 11.

Approach normally calculates formulas from left to right, but parentheses change that order. Approach always calculates values within parentheses first.

If you really want to impress your friends who think you know more about math than you really do, try using parentheses within parentheses, as in `5 * (3 + (2 * 3))`, which equals 45 (2 x 3 = 6; 6 + 3 = 9; 9 x 5 = 45).

Here are some vital facts concerning parentheses:

- ✔ Sometimes parentheses do *not* affect the results of a calculation. For example, the formulas 5 + 3 * 2 and (5 + 3) * 2 both give the same result: 16.

- ✔ To add parentheses to a formula, click the left and right parentheses in the list of operators in the Field Definition dialog box or type the parentheses yourself.

- ✔ Make sure that you always use parentheses in matched pairs — one left parenthesis for every right parenthesis. If parentheses aren't properly matched, the red stroke appears over the checkered flag to indicate that the formula isn't finished. (Too bad they didn't also include a yellow caution flag, because crashing into the wall is pretty easy when you are creating formulas.)

Working with Functions

You can do a great deal with formulas that use only the basic math operators, but formulas get even more interesting when you start using Approach's functions in them. Functions perform a whole sequence of calculations to come up with a result, such as finding the square root of a number or determining the monthly payment for a loan, given the loan amount, interest rate, and number of payments.

To use a function in a formula, you type the function name (each function has its own name), followed by a left parenthesis, usually one or more arguments, and a right parenthesis. Each function requires either no arguments at all or a specific number of arguments. Usually, the arguments are field names or constant values such as numbers or text strings:

```
Sqrt(64)
PMT(Principal,Rate,Months)
```

Some functions do not use arguments. Even so, the parentheses are still required, as in the following example:

```
Pi( )
```

If you really want to get ambitious, you can use another function as a function argument, as in the following example:

```
DayOfWeek(Today( ))
```

In this example, the argument for the DayOfWeek function is the value of the Today function.

You also can combine functions with other calculations. The following are examples:

```
PMT(Principal,Rate,Months) / 2
Today( ) + 30
```

The following section outlines the more useful Approach functions.

Note: Many of Approach's functions are designed for playing with date and time values. These functions are covered in Chapter 14 rather than here.

Mathematical functions for eggheads

If you are the type of person who loved using a slide rule in high school, you'll love Approach's math functions. They let you calculate stuff that most of us have been trying to forget for years. Table 13-2 summarizes Approach's basic math functions, and Table 13-3 summarizes Approach's trigonometric functions.

Table 13-2	Approach's Math Functions
Function	*What It Does*
Abs(*number*)	Calculates the absolute value of *number*.
Avg(*list of numbers*)	Calculates the average of however many numbers you give it.
Exp(*number*)	Calculates *e* to the power of *number*.
Factorial(*number*)	Calculates the factorial of *number* (1*2*3 and so on, all the way up to *number*).
Ln(*number*)	Calculates the natural logarithm of *number*.
Log(*number*)	Calculates the logarithm (base 10) of *number*.
Mod(*number1, number2*)	Calculates the remainder when *number2* is divided into *number1*.
Pi( )	Returns the value of Pi: 3.14159.
Pow(*number1, number2*)	Calculates *number1* raised to the power *number2*.
Random( )	Returns a random number between 0 and 1.
Round(*number, precision*)	Rounds off *number* to the number of decimal places indicated by *precision*.

Function	What It Does
Sign(*number*)	Returns −1 if *number* is negative, 1 if *number* is positive, or 0 if *number* is zero.
Sqrt(*number*)	Calculates the square root of *number*.
STD(*list of numbers*)	Calculates the standard deviation of however many numbers you give it.
Trunc(*number, precision*)	Truncates *number* to the number of decimal places indicated by *precision*.
Var(*list of numbers*)	Returns the variance of however many numbers you give it.

Table 13-3	Approach's Trig Functions
Function	**What It Does**
Acos(*number*)	Calculates the arc cosine of *number*.
Asin(*number*)	Calculates the arc sine of *number*.
Atan(*number*)	Calculates the arc tangent of *number*.
Atan2(*number1,number2*)	Calculates the arc tangent of *number1/number2*.
Cos(*angle*)	Calculates the cosine of *angle*.
Degree(*radians*)	Converts *radians* to degrees.
Radian(*degrees*)	Converts *degrees* to radians.
Sin(*angle*)	Calculates the sine of *angle*.
Tan(*angle*)	Calculates the tangent of *angle*.

Of the functions listed in Tables 13-2 and 13-3, the only one that doesn't require a pocket protector and a love of higher mathematics is Round( ). You can use Round( ) whenever a monetary calculation involves division to avoid charging a customer $10.9863. The first parameter that you use with Round( ) is the number that you want rounded; the second parameter is the number of decimal places that you want to preserve. For example, if the field Credit has a value of 10.9863, the formula `Round(Credit,2)` returns the value 10.99.

Trunc( ) is similar to Round( ), but there's a crucial difference. Round rounds a number up if the first unused digit is 5 or greater, but Trunc simply lops off unwanted digits. Thus, if the value of Credit is 10.9863, the function `Trunc(Credit,2)` returns the value 10.98, not 10.99. For most business purposes, Round( ) is the one you want. (Use Trunc( ) if you're trying to embezzle millions of dollars, half a penny at a time.)

Interesting financial functions

If your idea of good reading is an amortization table, you'll love Approach's financial functions, which Table 13-4 summarizes.

Table 13-4	Approach's Financial Functions
Function	*What It Does*
FV(*payment, rate, periods*)	Tells you the future value of *payment* invested at a given interest *rate* for a certain number of *periods*.
NPeriods(*rate,principal,payment*)	Tells you how many periods will be necessary to pay off *principal* at a given interest *rate* and *payment*.
PMT(*principal,rate,periods*)	Tells you what the payment will be if you borrow *principal* at a given interest *rate* for a certain number of *periods*.
PV(*payment,rate,periods*)	Tells you the present value of an annuity with a given *payment*, interest *rate*, and number of *periods*.
SLN(*cost,salvage,life*)	Calculates straight-line depreciation for an asset with a given *cost*, *salvage* value, and *life*.

Notice that several of these functions use the same arguments — *principal, rate,* and *periods* — but in different orders. For example, the NPeriods function is NPeriods(*rate,principal,payment*), but the PMT function is PMT(*principal,rate,periods*). Very confusing. You have to check for the correct sequence of arguments when you use one of these functions because Approach doesn't tell you if you've listed the arguments in the wrong order.

When you use these financial functions, you need to keep in mind that the interest rate is the rate *per period.* Thus, if you make payments once per month, the interest rate argument must provide the monthly interest rate. For example, perhaps you want to know the monthly payment for a three-year (36-month) loan of $15,000 at an annual interest rate of 12 percent. In this case, the monthly interest rate is 1 percent, so you use the PMT function like this:

```
PMT(15000,.01,36).
```

If you don't deal much with financial calculations, you won't need these functions. If you do, you may be better off using a spreadsheet program such as Lotus 1-2-3, which has more powerful financial functions and provides more ways to manipulate and analyze financial data.

Using logical functions

Logical functions are the weirdest functions in Approach's function goody box. They return one of two different values, depending on the results of a conditional test. Table 13-5 summarizes the logical functions.

Table 13-5	Approach's Logical Functions
Function	*What It Does*
If(*condition, true value, false value*)	Evaluates the *condition* expression, then returns *true value* if the condition is true or *false value* if the condition is false.
Blank(*field,value*)	Returns the value of *field,* unless *field* happens to be blank, in which case *value* is returned instead.
IsBlank(*field*)	Returns Yes if *field* is blank; otherwise, returns No.

The If function is Approach's main logical function. You use it to set a field to one of two different values depending on the result of a conditional test. For example, suppose that you need to charge 7.5 percent sales tax for sales to customers who live in California (as indicated by a field named State) but no sales tax for customers who live outside of California. You can use an If function:

```
If(State = 'CA',.075,0)
```

In this example, the *condition* argument is `State = 'CA'`. Approach analyzes this comparison expression to see whether the State field is indeed equal to CA. If it is, the If function uses the true value, .075. If it is not, the false value, 0, is used. (Also, notice how I used apostrophes to mark the value CA. Double-quotation marks (") are used to enclose field names that include spaces; apostrophes are used to enclose all text field values.)

You can use the preceding If function to set the value of a Tax Rate field, or you can use it as a part of a more complicated formula to calculate a sales tax amount:

```
Subtotal * If(State = 'CA',.075,0)
```

In this example, the value of the Subtotal field is multiplied by .075 or 0, depending on whether the State field equals CA.

You can use the Blank function to set a value for fields that are blank. For example, perhaps you want to charge $2.00 shipping and handling if no other value is typed in the Shipping field. In that case, you can use a formula such as `Blank(Shipping,2.00)`. This formula returns the value of the Shipping field as long as the Shipping field is not blank. If the Shipping field *is* blank, 2.00 is used.

The IsBlank function provides a convenient way to test whether a field has a blank value. The formula `IsBlank(State)` returns a value of Yes if the State field is blank, or No if the State field is not blank.

You can use IsBlank within an If function, as in the following:

```
If(IsBlank(State),.075,0)
```

In this example, 0.075 is used if the State field is blank, otherwise 0 is used.

You can see from the preceding examples that you can really get yourself tied up in knots if you overuse these logical functions. Use them only if you must, and be extra careful when you do. Make sure that you thoroughly test them with every possible combination of field values to make sure that they work the way you expect them to work.

Functions for doing funny things with text fields

Some of Approach's functions enable you to do strange things with text fields, such as extracting characters from the left, right, or middle of a text field; combining text fields; or capitalizing each word in a text field. These functions are too numerous for me to describe all of them, but most of them are reserved for computer nerds. Table 13-6 lists the functions that ordinary mortals commonly use.

The text function that you're most likely to use is Combine( ). It gangs up two or more strings to create a single string, and it is most often used to combine a first and last name to create a full name:

```
Combine("First Name", ' ', "Last Name")
```

This function produces results such as the following:

```
John Smith
Mary Hernandez
Silvia Hancock
```

Notice that *three* arguments are used in the preceding Combine( ) function: the first name, a space, and the last name. If you omit the space between the first and last names, the names will be jammed together.

If you want to list names last name first, use a Combine( ) function such as this one:

```
Combine("Last Name", ', ', "First Name")
```

This function produces results such as the following:

```
Smith, John
Hernandez, Mary
Hancock, Silvia
```

In this example, the second argument is a text constant that consists of a comma and a space.

Table 13-6	Approach's Text Functions
Function	**What It Does**
Combine(*list of strings*)	Combines all of the text strings that you give it to create a single text string.
Fill(*text,number*)	Repeats *text* as many times as indicated by *number*.
Like(*text1,text2*)	Compares the two text fields, ignoring case. You can use the wildcards * and ? to stand for multiple or single characters. Returns Yes if the strings match; otherwise, returns No.
Lower(*text*)	Changes all of the characters in *text* to lowercase.
Proper(*text*)	Converts the first letter of each word in *text* to uppercase; converts all other letters to lowercase.
Soundslike(*text1,text2*)	Compares two text fields to see whether they are phonetically similar. Returns Yes if they are or No if they are not.
Trim(*text*)	Removes extraneous spaces from the left and right of *text*.
Upper(*text*)	Converts *text* to all uppercase.

Summary functions

The last group of functions that I want to present in this chapter is summary functions. These functions are applied to field values from more than one record. Usually, you use these summary functions when you create a form that includes a repeating panel or a report that includes summary totals. However, you also can use them when you define fields by using the Field Definition dialog box.

The summary functions are listed in Table 13-7.

Table 13-7	Approach's Summary Functions
Function	*What It Does*
Saverage(*field*)	Calculates the average value for *field* in a range of records.
Scount(*field*)	Counts the number of records that have a value for *field* in a range of records.
Smax(*field*)	Tells you the largest value for *field* in a range of records.
Smin(*field*)	Tells you the smallest value for *field* in a range of records.
SSTD(*field*)	Calculates the standard deviation for *field* in a range of records.
SSUM(*field*)	Adds up the values for *field* in a range of records.
SVAR(*field*)	Calculates the variance for *field* in a range of records.

The 5th Wave

By Rich Tennant

"IT WAS BETWEEN THAT AND THE NEW DATABASE PROGRAM FOR THE CLASSROOM COMPUTERS."

Chapter 14
Working with Date and Time Fields

∙ ∙

In This Chapter

▶ Entering values into date and time fields

▶ Using fancy date and time formats

▶ Performing simple date and time calculations

▶ Using date and time functions

∙ ∙

*I*f you've ever been late for a very important date, you'll be relieved to know that Approach is quite sophisticated at working with date and time fields. This chapter covers the ins and outs of working with these kinds of fields. You learn how to enter values into date and time fields and how to perform various calculations on these fields.

Entering Values into Date and Time Fields

Aside from simply being able to type a date or time into a date or time field, you need to know about several techniques that enable you to enter date and time values more efficiently. The following sections cover these techniques.

Entering values into date fields

To enter a date into a date field, type the month, day, and year, using numbers separated by nonnumeric characters. For example, you type **5/16/94** or **12-31-95.** You can use any nonnumeric character you prefer to separate the month, day, and year, but slashes or hyphens are the most common. Approach uses slashes whenever it displays a date field.

If you leave out the month and year, Approach assumes that you mean the current month and year. For example, if you type **20** during November of 1994, Approach assumes that you mean November 20, 1994.

You can type two or four digits for the year. If you type two digits, Approach assumes that you mean the twentieth century. Thus, **94** is interpreted as 1994. If you type four digits, Approach accepts whatever year you type. (If you type just one digit, Approach also assumes the twentieth century. Thus, **5** is interpreted as 1905.)

For the months January through September, you can type a single digit (**0 – 9**) or two digits (**00 – 09**). It doesn't matter.

Note: If you defined a fancy date format for a date field, the format of the date changes the moment the insertion point leaves the date field. For example, if you type **5-16-94** into a date field, the date may change to something such as Monday, May 16, 1994, when you move the cursor out of the field. Do not be alarmed; this behavior is normal. (For more information about using fancy date formats, see the section "Using Fancy Date and Time Formats" later in this chapter.)

If the Show data entry format option is selected for the field (via the InfoBox), slashes and underlines appear on-screen to indicate how to type the date. To enter a date into this type of field, you type only the month, day, and year values; you do not need to type any separator characters.

Entering values into time fields

To enter a time into a time field, type the hours and minutes, using a normal person's 12-hour clock or a military-style 24-hour clock. Either way, you have to type the hour and minutes as numbers separated by colons. For example, you type **12:15** or **9:30**.

If the hour is 12 or less, Approach assumes that you mean morning. To type an afternoon or evening time when you are using a 12-hour clock, you have to type **PM**, as in **6:00 PM**.

If you're into Spockish precision, you can type seconds, and even hundredths of seconds. For example, you can type **11:30:45** or **11:30:45.99**.

On the other hand, if all you're interested in is the hour, just type the hour. Approach assumes that a single number typed by itself is an hour. Thus, **8** becomes 8:00, and **12** becomes 12:00.

Note that if you define a time format for a time field, the time that you enter into the field is reformatted according to the time format the moment the cursor leaves the time field. For more information about time formats, see the section "Using Fancy Date and Time Formats" later in this chapter.

If the Show data entry format option is selected for the field (via the InfoBox), colons and underlines appear on-screen to indicate how to type the time. To enter a time into this kind of field, you type only the hours, minutes, and seconds. Approach supplies the colons, so you don't have to type them.

Automatically entering the current date and time

You can quickly enter the current date in a date field by using one of the following techniques:

- ✔ Click the Insert Today's Date icon.
- ✔ Press Ctrl+Shift+D.
- ✔ Choose Browse⇨Insert⇨Today's Date.

To enter the current time in a time field, use one of the following techniques:

- ✔ Click the Insert Current Time icon.
- ✔ Press Ctrl+Shift+T.
- ✔ Choose Browse⇨Insert⇨Current Time.

If your computer's system clock has the wrong date or time setting, these techniques will put the wrong date or time values into the database. To check and correct the system clock, switch to Program Manager and open the Main group. Double-click the Control Panel icon and then double-click the Date/Time icon. Adjust the date and time settings if necessary and then click OK.

Using Fancy Date and Time Formats

Date and time fields would be pretty boring if the only ways to format them were 05/16/94 and 12:30 PM. Fortunately, Approach gives you a plethora of choices for formatting dates and times on forms, reports, and other views. If you prefer, you can display a date as May 16, 1994 or even Monday, May 16, 1994. You can even leave parts of the date off, such as May 16 or just May.

Times aren't quite as flexible as dates, but you can use a 12-hour or 24-hour clock; specify which suffixes to use (AM and PM, am and pm, or whatever), and decide whether to include all of the date, just the hours and minutes, or just the hours.

Keep in mind that these date and time formats apply only to how the date or time is displayed on a form, report, or other view. The format does not affect how the date or time is actually stored in the database.

Setting a fancy date format

To set a fancy date format, follow this procedure:

1. **Switch to Design mood and select the view that you want to modify.**

   Click the design icon, select Design from the pop-up mood menu in the status bar, choose View⇨Design, or press Ctrl+D. My, aren't there a lot of ways to switch to design mood? ("Design Mode" for those who insist upon proper technobabble terminology. I just think Approach is kind of a moody program.)

   To select the view, click the appropriate view tab or choose the view from the View menu or the pop-up view menu in the status bar.

2. **Click the date field whose format you want to modify.**

3. **Call up the InfoBox.**

   Click the Info icon or press Ctrl+E. The InfoBox for the date field appears.

4. **Click the Number Format tab in the InfoBox.**

   The date format options appear, as shown in Figure 14-1.

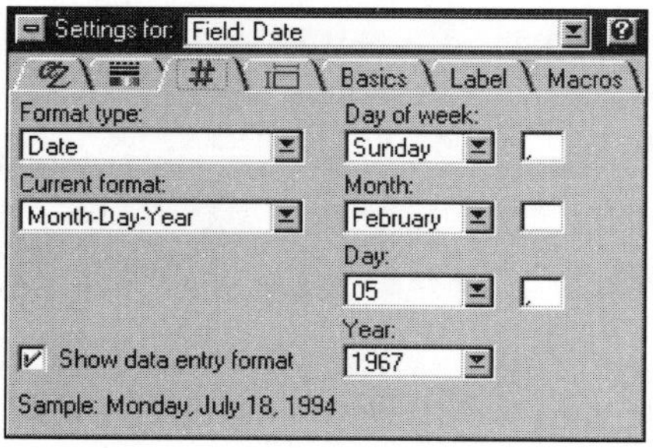

Figure 14-1: The date format options in the InfoBox.

5. **Change the Format type from Display as entered to Date.**

   When you click the Number Format tab, most of the formatting options shown in Figure 14-1 are hidden until you change the Format type to Date.

6. **Use the various date options to customize the format of the Day of week, Month, Day, and Year.**

For example, to change the format of the month, select the month format that you want from the list of options in the Month field. Here is the lowdown on each of these options:

Current format: Tells Approach what parts of the date you want to include and in what order. For example, Month-Day-Year means you want to include the month, day, and year in that order. If you want to create a sophisticated European-style date to confuse and impress your friends, switch to Day-Month-Year.

Day of week: The format for the day of the week, which appears at the beginning of the date. You can pick the full day of the week (for example, Sunday) or an abbreviated day of the week (Sun). Or you can omit the day of the week altogether by picking the blank space at the top of the list. Next to the Day of week box is a separator text box. The separator is usually a comma.

Month: The format for the month. You can pick the month number with or without a leading zero (02 or 2), the full month name (February), or the abbreviated month name (Feb). Or you can omit the month altogether by clicking the blank space at the top of the list. Another separator text box appears next to the month box. For the full or abbreviated month name, you usually leave the separator text box empty. For the month number, change the separator to a slash or hyphen.

Day: The format for the day of the month. You can tell Approach to always use two digits even if the first digit is a zero (05) or to omit the leading zero (5); or you can omit the day field by clicking the blank space at the top of the list. Once again, a box for a separator character follows the Day box. Use a comma, hyphen, or slash.

Year: The year, which can be two digits (67) or four digits (1967), or you can omit it by clicking the blank space at the top of the list.

Show data entry format: If you check this check box, the field is filled with underscores and slashes to make entering an acceptable date value easier.

7. **Double-click the control box (in the upper-left corner of the InfoBox) to dismiss the InfoBox.**

   You're done!

Here are some points to consider when you define date formats:

✔ As you adjust the various date format options, you can see the results of the changes in the sample date shown at the bottom of the InfoBox. Keep your eye on this sample date to make sure that the date is formatted as you expect.

> ✔ You use the unlabeled boxes to the right of the Day of week, Month, and Day boxes in Figure 14-1 to change the separator character that appears between the various pieces of the date. Depending on the type of date format that you want to use, you may need to change these separator characters.

> ✔ When you change the Current format, the rest of the InfoBox changes to reflect the new order. For example, if you change the Current format to Year-Month-Day, the order of the other date format options in the InfoBox changes accordingly.

> ✔ If you pick Other for the Current date format, you are presented with the additional formatting options that are shown in Figure 14-2. These options enable you to pick a date format that includes a period, such as a quarter, third, or half year. The predefined formats provide various options for quarters. To set up a trimester or half year, you have to type your own format code. For more information about special periods, see the sidebar "All about periods, period."

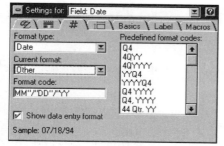

Figure 14-2:
Other date
format
options.

Setting a fancy time format

Mercifully, you don't have as many options for setting time formats as you do for setting date formats. Here's the procedure:

1. **Switch to Design mood and select the view that you want to modify.**

   Click the design icon, select Design from the pop-up mood menu in the status bar, choose View⇨Design, or press Ctrl+D. There are, indeed, many ways to switch to Design mood.

   To select the view, click the appropriate view tab or choose the view from the View menu or the pop-up view menu in the status bar.

2. **Click the time field whose format you want to modify.**

All about periods, period

Approach enables you to use date formats that show periods of the year, such as quarters, trimesters, and halves. For example, Approach can display the date 6/20/94 as 2Q94, First half of 1994, or 2nd trimester, 1994.

To use these special periods, you have to create your own date formats. You can include any text in the format, plus any of the following special codes:

Code	What It Stands for
4	The quarter, as a number (1, 2, 3, or 4).
44	The quarter, as an "ordinal" number (1st, 2nd, 3rd, or 4th).
444	The quarter, spelled out (First, Second, Third, or Fourth).
3	The trimester, as a number (1, 2, or 3).
33	The trimester, as an "ordinal" number (1st, 2nd, or 3rd).
333	The trimester, spelled out (First, Second, or Third).
2	The half, as a number (1 or 2).
22	The half, as an "ordinal" number (1st or 2nd).
222	The half, spelled out (First or Second).
YY	The year, two digits (as in *94*).
YYYY	The year, four digits (as in *1994*).

Here are some sample formats that use the above codes:

Format Code	Example with Date 6/20/94
4QYY	2Q94
222 half of YYYY	First half of 1994
33 trimester, YYYY	2nd trimester, 1994

3. Summon the InfoBox.

Click the Info icon or press Ctrl+E. The InfoBox for the time field appears.

4. Click the Number Format tab in the InfoBox.

The time format options appear, as shown in Figure 14-3.

5. Change the Format type from Display as entered to Time.

Most of the formatting options shown in Figure 14-3 are hidden until you change the Format type to Time.

6. Play with the settings to customize the time format.

Here's the lowdown on each option:

Current format: Tells Approach which parts of the time you want to include: hours only; hours and minutes; hours, minutes, and seconds; or hours, minutes, seconds, and hundredths of seconds.

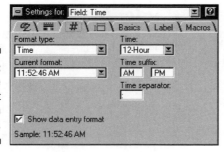

Figure 14-3:
The time
format
options in
the InfoBox.

Time: You can choose a 12-hour clock or a 24-hour clock.

Time suffix: You can change the suffix from AM and PM to whatever you prefer, perhaps am and pm or a.m. and p.m.

Time separator: You pick the character to use to separate the parts of the time. Best leave this as a colon, unless you want to impress your friends with a Euro-looking period.

Show data entry format: If you check this check box, the field is filled with underscores and colons to make entering an acceptable time value easier.

7. **Double-click the control box (in the upper-left corner of the InfoBox) to dismiss the InfoBox.**

That's all there is.

Here are some timely thoughts:

✔ As you adjust the time format, the sample at the bottom of the InfoBox shows a sample of the time format that you have chosen. Keep one eye on this sample at all times.

✔ You can usually coax your friendly computer guru into formatting time fields for you by offering a six pack of beer as a bribe. If you've got the beer, he's got the time.... .

Using Dates and Times in Calculations

Besides simply storing and displaying dates and times, Approach enables you to perform various calculations on date and time fields. For example, you can use a date field in an Invoice database to calculate the age of an invoice so that you can send annoying collection notices to customers who have overdue bills. Or you can calculate the number of days since the last time a customer ordered, or the date on which a bill will be due.

Simple date and time calculations

You can use date and time fields in simple formulas, but you need to be aware of a few key points when you use dates and times in calculations:

- ✔ If you subtract one date from another, the result is a number that represents the number of days between the dates. For example, the formula Today()-InvoiceDate tells you how many days old an invoice is.

- ✔ If you add or subtract a number to or from a date, the result is another date. Thus, to determine the date 30 days from today, you can use the formula Today()+30.

- ✔ Although Approach can do it, multiplying or dividing date or time values make no sense. Don't even think about it.

- ✔ To incorporate a constant date value into a formula, you have to use the TextToDate() function, which is described in the next section, "Functions for date and time calculations."

- ✔ If you subtract one time value from another, the result is the difference between the two times in hundredths of seconds. For example, suppose that the value of a field named Time1 is 4:30:00 PM, and the value of another field, named Time2, is 4:30:15 PM. The formula Time2 − Time1 gives the result 1,500.

  To determine the number of seconds between two times, divide the result by 100, as in the formula (Time2 − Time1) / 100.

- ✔ To add or subtract a value to or from a time, express the value in hundredths of seconds. Thus, to add 10 seconds to a field named Time, use a formula such as Time + 1000.

Functions for date and time calculations

Approach provides several functions that you can use with Date and Time values to make date and time calculations easier. The date functions are summarized in Table 14-1, and Table 14-2 summarizes the Time functions.

Table 14-1	Approach's Date Functions
Function	*What It Does*
Today()	Returns the current date.
Date(*month,day,year*)	Converts separate *month*, *day*, and *year* values to a date value.
Month(*date*)	Returns the month for *date*.

(continued)

Table 14-1 *(continued)*

Function	What It Does
Day(*date*)	Returns the day of the month for *date*.
Year(*date*)	Returns the year for *date*.
DayOfWeek(*date*)	Returns the day of the week (1 – 7) for *date*.
DayOfYear(*date*)	Returns the day of the year (1 – 365) for *date*.
WeekOfYear(*date*)	Returns the week of the year (1 – 52) for *date*.
DayName(*number* or *date*)	Returns the name of the day for *number* (1 – 7) or *date*.
MonthName(*number* or *date*)	Returns the name of the month for *number* (1 – 12) or *date*.
DateToText(*date*)	Converts *date* to a text string that can be displayed.
TextToDate(*text*)	Converts a text string to a date.

Table 14-2 Approach's Time Functions

Function	What It Does
CurrTime( )	Returns the current time.
Time(*hours,minutes, seconds,hundredths*)	Converts separate *hours*, *minutes*, *seconds*, and *hundredths* to a time value.
Hour(*time*)	Returns the hour for *time*.
Minute(*time*)	Returns the minute for *time*.
Second(*time*)	Returns the second for *time*.
Hundredth(*time*)	Returns the hundredths of a second for *time*.

The two functions that you are most likely to use are Today( ) and CurrTime( ), which tell you the current date and time. The other functions are useful for special types of date calculations, most of which are best performed while you are wearing a propeller cap and a pocket protector. Having summarized these functions in Tables 14-1 and 14-2, I therefore guiltlessly leave it to you to figure out how and when to use them.

Part III

Getting Real
Work Done

"I STARTED DESIGNING DATABASE SOFTWARE SYSTEMS AFTER SEEING HOW EASY IT WAS TO DESIGN OFFICE FURNITURE."

In this part ...

So far, this book has shown you how to work with two types of database views: forms and reports. Approach enables you to work with database data in five additional kinds of views, too: form letters, mailing labels, worksheets, crosstabs, and charts.

Although these alternative views are kind of fun to play with, they also are very useful for getting real work done. So, get to work!

Chapter 15

Printing Form Letters

- -

In This Chapter

▶ Understanding form letters

▶ Creating a form letter with the Form Letter Assistant

▶ Printing form letters

- -

*F*orm letters enable you to send junk mail to the unsuspecting people who are on file in your Approach database. Of course, so many other people are sending those same people form letters every day that probably no one will even open your letter. So you may as well not bother. But in case you're more optimistic than I am, this chapter shows you how to do it.

In the old days, creating form letters was about as much fun as having oral surgery. If you've ever done a mail merge with WordPerfect, you know what I'm talking about. You started by creating a primary document that was filled with a bunch of weird codes. Then you had to create a secondary document that contained all of the names and addresses plus more weird codes. Then you had to spread votive candles about the room and offer sacrifice to the Mail Merge gods. Then you had to . . . well, you get the idea.

Approach makes creating and printing form letters easy. In fact, a built-in Form Letter Assistant does most of the dirty work for you. All you have to do is answer a few questions, type the letter, and — voilà! — you're in the junk mail business.

After your friends find out that you know how to create form letters on your computer, they will assume that you are a computer expert and will come to you with their computer problems until you eventually decide to leave town and begin a new life. A word of advice: Don't let on that you know the first thing about printing form letters. Tell them that you paid Ed McMahon to do it for you.

The Big Picture

Suppose that you weren't at the Parents Club meeting last night, so they elected you secretary. Now you have the job of sending a letter to all the parents at the school begging them to join the Parents Club. The Parents Club has decided that sending a note home with the kids isn't good enough; a *personalized* letter must be sent to each parent's home.

Preparing a personalized form letter is a three-step affair:

1. **Collect the names and addresses in an Approach database.**

   Hope that someone has already typed the names and addresses of all the parents into a computer. In the best of all worlds, that person typed the names into an Approach database, so you're all set. In the OK-but-still-unlikely world, someone has indeed already entered the names, but they were entered in PC CheaperBase or something worse, such as Microsoft Access. You then have to figure out a way to convert the data into a format that you can use with Approach. Chapter 22, "Conversion Experiences," can help you convert the data.

   Most likely, though, you have to plead with the principal to get permission to have the kids take home a form on which parents can write their names and addresses, with a request that the kids bring back the forms the following day. If you're lucky, about half of the forms will come back within a week. You can safely figure that the other half probably got turned into paper airplanes or spit wads and never made it home, so you have to send reminder notes home a week later, hoping — as they say in the direct-mail business — to "improve your response rate." After two or three weeks, you'll have a stack of 400 forms that have barely legible names and addresses just waiting to be typed into your computer. Oh, the joy of database.

   Now you go through the process of defining an Approach database and spending two or three evenings entering the names and addresses when you could be watching reruns of "Rosanne." Oh boy.

2. **Create the form letter.**

   Next, you have to figure out what to say to all those unsuspecting parents. You can use the Form Letter Assistant to create a skeleton form letter that contains the special codes necessary to insert database fields in the letter for the inside address and the salutation (Dear John).

   Then you get to toil over the body of the letter for hours, trying to be firm yet inoffensive. To come up with the body of the letter, you use Approach as if it were a word processing program. On occasion, you may wish that Approach were a word processing program, which it isn't, so don't get all excited.

The most important thing to remember about this step is that a form letter is nothing more than a special type of database view, just like a form or report. The step-by-step procedure for creating a form letter is in the section "Creating a Form Letter" later in this chapter.

3. Print the form letters.

This part is easy. After you create the database records with the names and addresses, and after you create a form letter, all you have to do is click the Print button, and away she goes. (If you want to send the letter to only a certain privileged few, you can use the Find command before you print the form letters.)

Creating a Form Letter

So you've got your database all stuffed full of names and addresses, and you're dying to drop some junk mail on those poor unsuspecting folk. No problem. Just summon the Form Letter Assistant, which will promptly ask you about the details of the letter you want to create and then create the letter for you. No fuss, no muss.

Open the database that contains the names and addresses to which you want to send junk mail, and then follow these steps:

1. Choose Create⇨Form Letter.

The Form Letter Assistant appears, as shown in Figure 15-1.

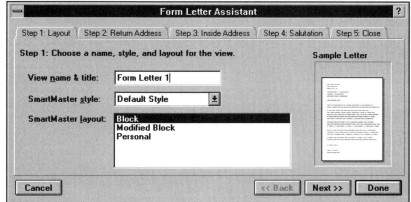

Figure 15-1:
The Form Letter Assistant's layout options.

As you can see, the Form Letter Assistant has five tabs, corresponding to five steps for creating form letters. If you realize that you've made a mistake in any of these steps, you can go back by clicking the Back button or by clicking directly on the tab to which you want to return.

2. **If you prefer, you can change the View name & title to something more meaningful than Form Letter 1.**

3. **Select the SmartMaster style.**

   You use the SmartMaster style setting to pick one of four styles for the letter: default (a generic, inoffensive layout), business, classic, and informal. (All this last setting does is change the font.)

4. **Pick the SmartMaster layout.**

   In the SmartMaster layout box, you can choose the Block, Modified Block, or Personal letter layout. Pick the layout that suits your fancy.

5. **Click Next.**

   The Form Letter Assistant's return address options appear, as shown in Figure 15-2.

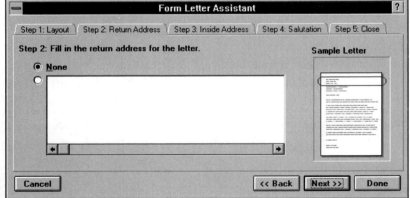

Figure 15-2:
The Form
Letter
Assistant's
return
address
options.

6. **If you want to include a return address in the letter, type the address in the box. Otherwise, click None.**

   Omit the return address if you plan to print the form letters on preprinted letterhead or if you don't want people to know where you live.

7. **Click Next.**

   The Form Letter Assistant's inside address options appear, as shown in Figure 15-3.

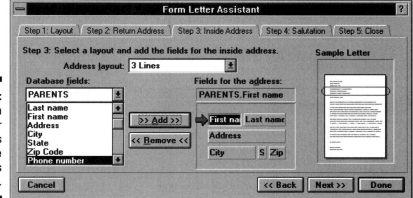

Figure 15-3:
The Form
Letter
Assistant's
inside
address
options.

8. **Pick the Address layout.**

   In the Address layout setting, you pick the number of lines to include in
   the inside address. When you are mailing to residences, three lines are
   usually adequate. For business mailings, you may need to use four or five
   lines.

9. **Select the fields that you want to appear in each portion of the inside
   address.**

   When you pick the address layout, the boxes in the Fields for the address
   section of the Form Letter Assistant dialog box change to indicate where
   you can insert fields in the inside address. For the three-line layout, the
   first line contains two fields (typically, first name and last name), the
   second line contains one field (the street address), and the third line
   contains three fields (city, state, and zip code). Other layouts have similar
   arrangements of fields.

   To add a field to the inside address, click the field in the Database fields
   list and then click the Add button. The field name appears in the inside
   address box, and the next box in the inside address is selected. Continue
   until all of the address fields have been added to the inside address.

10. **Click Next.**

    The Form Letter Assistant's salutation options appear, as shown in Figure
    15-4.

11. **Select one or two fields to include in the salutation.**

    Notice that the Form Letter Assistant provides text boxes that you can use
    to enter text before and after the database fields. You can use these boxes
    to customize the salutation however you choose.

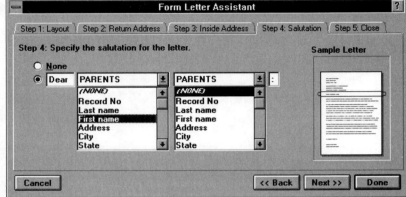

Figure 15-4:
The Form
Letter
Assistant's
salutation
options.

12. Click Next.

The Form Letter Assistant's close options appear, as shown in Figure 15-5.

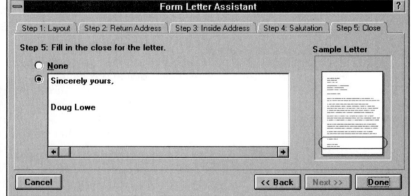

Figure 15-5:
The Form
Letter
Assistant's
close
options.

13. Edit the close however you choose.

It initially says "Sincerely yours," but you can edit it to say anything you choose. It also inserts your name in the closing, assuming that you told Approach your real name when you installed it.

14. Click Done.

Approach spins and whirs for a few moments, and then it spits out a skeleton form letter that is similar to the one shown in Figure 15-6.

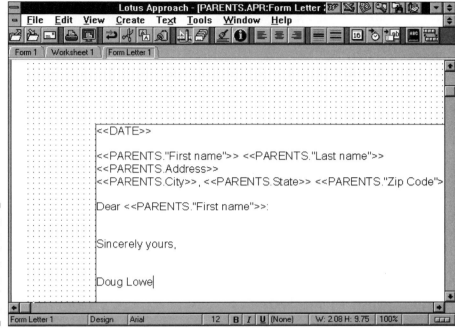

Lotus Approach - [PARENTS.APR:Form Letter
File Edit View Create Text Tools Window Help

Form 1 / Worksheet 1 / Form Letter 1

<<DATE>>

<<PARENTS."First name">> <<PARENTS."Last name">>
<<PARENTS.Address>>
<<PARENTS.City>>, <<PARENTS.State>> <<PARENTS."Zip Code">>

Dear <<PARENTS."First name">>:

Sincerely yours,

Doug Lowe

Form Letter 1   Design   Arial   12   B I U (None)   W: 2.08 H: 9.75   100%

Figure 15-6:
A skeleton
letter
created by
the Form
Letter
Assistant.

15. Type the body of the form letter.

Sending out form letters that don't say anything is pretty silly, so you'll
undoubtedly want to add some text to the letter. Just move the pointer to
the end of the salutation, click to position the insertion point there, press
the Enter key to create a new line, and start typing.

When you're done, the letter should look something like the one in Figure
15-7.

16. You're done!

Here are a few important points to ponder when you create form letters:

✔ Within the text of a form letter, database fields appear between two angle-
brackets (for example, <<FirstName>>). Do not be alarmed. Actual database data replaces the brackets and the field name when you print the
form letters.

✔ To apply formatting to portions of text, highlight the text with the mouse
and then use the Text commands listed in Table 15-1 to apply the formatting.

Figure 15-7:
A form letter
all ready to
go.

Table 15-1   Commands for Formatting Text in Form Letters

Command	*What It Does*
Text⇨Normal	Removes character formats.
Text⇨Bold	Makes the text bold.
Text⇨Italic	Makes the text italic.
Text⇨Underline	Underlines the text.
Text⇨Strikethrough	Draws a strikethrough line through the text.
Text⇨Align	Enables you to pick left, right, center, or justified alignment.
Text⇨Spacing	Enables you to pick single, 1.5 lines, or double for the spacing.

✔ To add a field to the body of the letter, click where you want the field to be added and then choose Text⇨Insert⇨Field. Select the field that you want to insert and then click OK.

✔ You also can use the Text⇨Insert command to insert the current date, time, or page number.

✔ Don't embarrass yourself by sending out 1,000 letters that contain a simple spelling error! Spell check your letters before printing them. See Chapter 7 for more information about the spell checker.

Printing Form Letters

You can print form letters pretty much the same way you print a report. Just follow these steps:

1. **If you want to print letters for only certain records, use the Find command to find the records for which you want to print letters.**

   Chapter 5 contains the lost secrets of finding records.

2. **If you want the letters printed in a certain order, sort the database.**

   See Chapter 6 for orderly instructions on sorting.

3. **Make sure that the printer is on, ready, and loaded with the right paper.**

   If you're printing on letterhead, insert the letterhead into the printer.

4. **Click the Print icon, choose File⇨Print, or press Ctrl+P.**

   When the Print dialog box appears, resist the urge to play with its settings. Usually, the Print dialog box is already set up just right.

5. **Click OK.**

   Away you go!

Chapter 16

Printing Mailing Labels

In This Chapter

▶ Creating mailing labels by using the Mailing Label Assistant

▶ Creating your own label formats

▶ Printing mailing labels

*I*f you've ever spent 20 minutes printing 100 form letters and then spent two hours hand-addressing the envelopes, you'll appreciate Approach's ability to prepare mailing labels for your database quickly. You'll never hand-address an envelope again.

As you read this chapter, keep in mind that although the mailing labels feature is usually used to create, well, *mailing* labels, you can use it for other kinds of labels as well. For example, you can use it to create a file folder label for each of your customers. Or you can create floppy disk or videotape labels, or even name tags.

Creating Mailing Labels

Creating mailing labels from your data is easy because Approach provides a Mailing Label Assistant that is simple to use. Like forms, reports, and form letters, mailing labels are another type of database view in Approach. The Mailing Label Assistant merely sets up this mailing label view for you.

The Mailing Label Assistant stayed up all night memorizing the Avery label catalog. Thus, it already knows the exact size of each type of label created by Avery. All you have to do is tell it the Avery label number and what fields you want to include on the labels. Producing labels couldn't be easier.

Note: Although Approach is designed to work best with Avery brand labels, you can use other brands. Some brands include Avery numbers on their packages. If you can find an Avery number on the package, use it. Otherwise, you can create a custom label format that fits your labels perfectly. See the section "Using a Custom Label Format" later in this chapter if you must.

To create mailing labels, open the database that contains the names and addresses you want to send junk mail to. Then follow these steps:

1. **Choose Create⇨Mailing Label.**

   The Mailing Label Assistant appears, as shown in Figure 16-1.

   Unlike many other Approach Assistants, the Mailing Label Assistant has only two tabs: Basics and Options. Better yet, you usually only have to mess around with the settings on the Basics tab. You use the Options tab only for oddball labels that don't match any of the predefined Avery label types.

Figure 16-1:
The Mailing
Label
Assistant's
Basics
settings.

2. **Change the Mailing label name field to something more meaningful than Mailing Labels 1 if you're compulsive about such things.**

3. **Pick the SmartMaster address layout.**

   In the address layout setting, you pick the number of lines to include on the label. When you are mailing to residences, three lines are usually adequate. For business mailings, you may need to use four or five lines. The other layouts are for oddball uses.

4. **Select the fields that you want to appear in each portion of the address.**

   When you pick the address layout, the boxes in the Fields to place on label option of the Mailing Label Assistant dialog box change to indicate where you can insert fields on the label. For the three-line layout, the first line contains two fields (typically, first name and last name), the second line contains one field (the street address), and the third line contains three fields (city, state, and zip code). Other layouts have similar arrangements of fields.

To add a field to the address, click the field in the Database fields list and then click the Add button. The field name appears in the Fields to place on label section, and the next Fields to place on label box is selected. Keep adding fields until you have added all the fields you want to place on the label.

5. Pick a Label type.

The drop-down list for the Label type field lists a whole bunch of Avery label formats. If you're using Avery labels, check the package of labels to find the label number and then pick that number from the list. If you're not using Avery labels, check the package anyway. Sometimes other companies list Avery numbers on their packages if the labels are the same size.

6. Click OK.

After a few moments, the labels appear on-screen, as shown in Figure 16-2.

7. You're done!

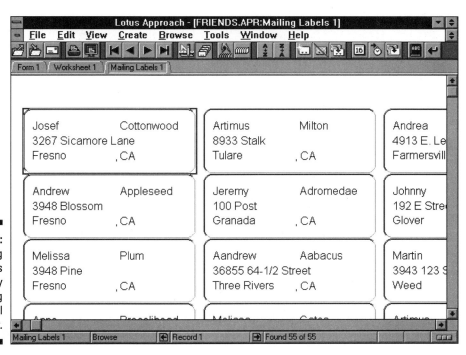

Figure 16-2:
Mailing
labels
created by
the Mailing
Label
Assistant.

That's all there is to it, although you should keep the following points in mind:

- ✔ When you view mailing labels in Browse mood, the fields on the label are spaced out. For an example, look at the labels in Figure 16-2. There's way too much space between the first and last names and the city and state fields. Don't worry; this extra space will be removed when you print the labels. For a sneak peek at what the labels will look like with the extraneous space removed, call up Preview mood (or mode, if you prefer). Choose File⇨Preview or press Ctrl+Shift+B to switch to Preview mood.

- ✔ When you are working in Browse mood, you can actually enter and edit data through a mailing label view. Just click the field you want to enter or edit and start typing.

- ✔ Unfortunately, the default arrangement of fields on mailing labels sometimes doesn't leave enough room to print longer city names. If you encounter this problem, switch to Design mood and drag the state and zip code fields a bit to the right. Then grab the edge of the city field and extend it to the right to fill up the space that you opened up between the city and state fields. You should have enough room to print the names of most American cities. You may have trouble with addresses in Germany, though, where city names such as Oberunteruntaroundentowne are common.

- ✔ If the labels shown in Figure16-2 are too plain for you, switch to Design mood and make whatever changes you want. If more than one label appears when you switch to Design mood, choose View⇨Show Data to display field names rather than actual database data. Then the display should look something like Figure 16-3. With this display, you can customize the label format easily by changing the size of fields, moving fields around, or adding additional text or drawing objects to the label.

Using a Custom Label Format

Skip this section if you possibly can. Stick to Avery labels or labels that have equivalent Avery numbers, and all shall go well for you, your children, and your children's children. If you're stuck with using nonstandard labels because your cheapskate boss got a great deal on a case of them at the local office warehouse store, you'll have to design a custom layout. Here's the procedure:

1. **Find a ruler and measure the labels.**

   Make a note of the following measurements:

   Top margin: The space between the top of the page and the top of the top row of labels

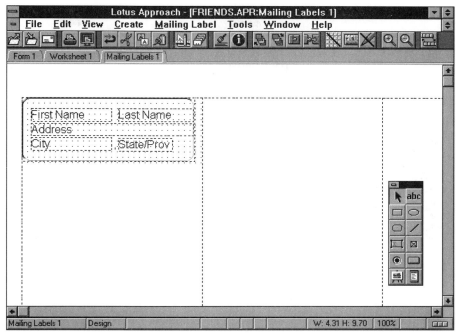

Figure 16-3:
Working
with mailing
labels in
Design
mood.

Left margin: The space between the left edge of the page and the left edge of the leftmost column of labels

Height: The height of each label

Width: The width of each label

Vert. gap: The amount of vertical space between the bottom of each label and the top of the label beneath it

Horiz. gap. The amount of space between the right edge of each label and the left edge of the label next to it

2. **Choose Create⇨Mailing Labels and click the Options tab.**

   The Mailing Label Assistant Options panel appears, as shown in Figure 16-4.

3. **Type a name for the custom label format in the Custom label box.**

4. **Type the measurements from Step 1 in the corresponding text boxes.**

5. **Type the number of labels across and down each page in the Across and Down text boxes.**

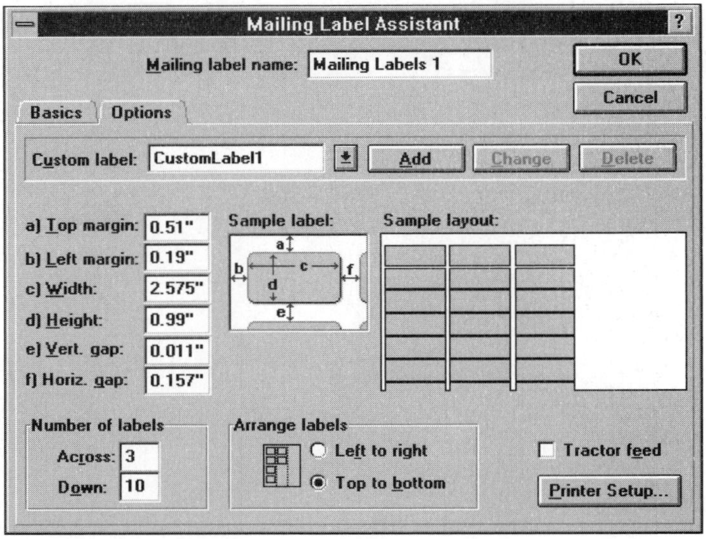

Figure 16-4:
Creating a
custom label
format.

6. **Select the printing order (Left to right or Top to bottom).**

   If you select Left to right, labels will be printed across the page, filling up one row before starting the next. If you select Top to bottom, labels will be printed down the page, filling up the first column before starting the second, and so on.

7. **If the labels are on continuous feed paper for use in an old-fashioned dot-matrix printer, click Tractor feed.**

   When you click Tractor feed, Approach ignores the top and bottom margins because continuous feed labels print right to the very top and bottom of each sheet of labels.

8. **If you think that you'll need to use this label format again, click Add.**

   From then on, the custom label will appear as one of the label format options on the Basics tab, so you won't have to return to the Options tab again.

9. **Click OK.**

   You're done!

Keep the following two points in mind when customizing label formats:

✔ After you create a mailing label view, you can change the layout options by displaying the labels in Design mood, calling up the InfoBox Basics tab for the labels by pressing Ctrl+E, or clicking the Info icon, and then clicking the Edit Label Options button that appears in the InfoBox. To save any changes that you make to a custom layout, click the Change button.

✔ You can remove a custom label setting by calling up the Mailing Label Assistant Options panel, selecting the custom layout that you want to delete, and clicking the Delete button.

Printing Mailing Labels

You print mailing labels the same way that you print reports or form letters. Here's the procedure:

1. **If you want to print labels for only certain records, use the Find command to find the records for which you want to print letters.**

   See Chapter 5 for more information about finding records.

2. **If you want the labels printed in a certain order, sort the database.**

   See Chapter 6 for information about sorting.

3. **Make sure that the printer is on, ready, and loaded with the correct labels.**

4. **Click the Print icon, choose File⇨Print, or click Ctrl+P.**

5. **Click OK.**

   The labels will be printed.

If you're unsure about the label format, try printing the labels on plain paper first. Then you can hold up the names and addresses printed on plain paper to a blank sheet of labels to see whether everything lines up correctly.

The 5th Wave — By Rich Tennant

"OUR NEW DATABASE HAS BEEN ON THE MARKET FOR OVER 6 MONTHS, AND NOT ONE INTELLECTUAL PROPERTY LAWSUIT BROUGHT AGAINST US, I'M WORRIED."

Chapter 17

Working with Worksheets and Cursing at Crosstabs

A *worksheet* is a special type of database view that you can use to display the fields and records in an Approach database in an arrangement that is similar to a spreadsheet program such as Lotus 1-2-3. In a worksheet view, each database record is represented as a row in the worksheet, and each field is represented as a column. The intersection of a row and column is called a *cell*.

Worksheets are simple enough. Crosstabs are harder to swallow. A *crosstab* is a special type of view in which each cell shows summary information — such as a total, an average, or a count — for a group of database records. For example, you can use a crosstab to summarize information from a Sales database by sales district, salesman, or product.

This chapter shows you how to work with worksheets and how to set up simple crosstabs.

Working with Worksheets

When you create an Approach database, a default worksheet view named Worksheet 1 is automatically created for you. To switch to this worksheet view, click the tab labeled Worksheet 1 at the top of the file window. Figure 17-1 shows a worksheet view of a database.

Unlike forms, which show one database record at a time, worksheets show as many database records as will fit on the screen, each record in a separate worksheet row. If the database contains more records than can fit on the screen at one time, use the scroll bars to display them all.

✔ If you are experienced with Lotus 1-2-3 (or any other spreadsheet program), you're already way ahead of the worksheet game. The basics of finding your way around Approach worksheets — such as using the arrow keys to move from cell to cell — are the same.

✔ You can edit database fields while you are working in worksheet view. Just click a cell and start typing.

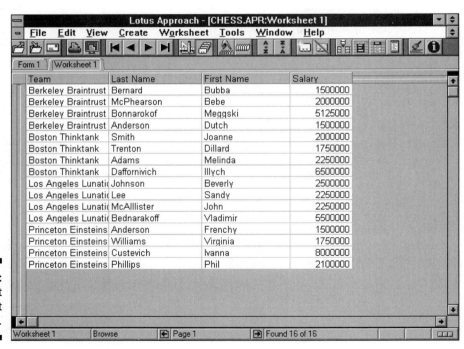

Figure 17-1:
A default
worksheet
view.

✔ Inserting a new record in worksheet view is the same as inserting a new record in a form. Click the New Record icon or type Ctrl+N. Approach inserts a new row for the new record.

✔ To change the text in a column heading, triple-click the header and then type the new text. Click, click, click!

✔ The default worksheet for a new database includes a column for each database field. The column headings are the field names, and each column is set up just wide enough for the field name to fit. If you're picky, you can change many aspects of this basic layout: rearrange columns, remove columns you don't need or want, change the column width, change the column headings, and who knows what else.

Creating a new worksheet

Approach automatically creates a worksheet for you when you create a new database. For most databases, one worksheet is more than enough. If you need to create an additional worksheet, though, follow this procedure:

1. **Open the database for which you want to create a new worksheet.**

   Choose File⇨Open, click the Open icon, use the keyboard shortcut Ctrl+O, or select Open an Existing File from the Welcome to Lotus Approach dialog box.

2. **Choose Create⇨Worksheet.**

   The Worksheet Assistant appears, as shown in Figure 17-2.

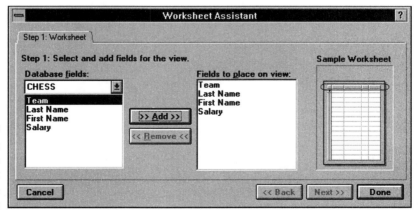

Figure 17-2: The Worksheet Assistant.

3. **Select the fields that you want to include on the worksheet and click Add to add them to the list.**

   To add a field to the worksheet, select it in the Database fields list and then click Add. (Each time you click Add, the next field in the list is selected. You can quickly add several successive fields by repeatedly clicking Add.)

   To add several fields at the same time, hold down the Ctrl key while you select them in the Database fields list and then click Add. Or you can hold down the Shift key to mark a range of fields or click the first field and then hold down the left mouse button and drag to mark a range of fields.

   To remove a field from the worksheet, select the list in the Fields to place on view list and then click Remove.

4. **Click Done.**

   The worksheet is created.

Moving around in a worksheet

The most common way to move around a worksheet is to use the arrow cursor-control keys. Pressing one of these keys moves the cell pointer up, down, left, or right one cell.

You can move directly to any cell by clicking it with the mouse. If the cell you want to move to isn't visible, use the scroll bars to bring the cell into view.

You also can use the following keyboard shortcuts for moving about the worksheet:

Tab	Moves to the next cell.
Shift+Tab	Moves to the previous cell.
PgDn	Scrolls the worksheet forward one screenful.
PgUp	Scrolls the worksheet backwards one screenful.
Ctrl+Home	Moves to the first record.
Ctrl+End	Moves to the last record.

Selecting worksheet cells

Here are the all-important techniques for selecting cells in a worksheet:

- To select a single cell, click it.
- To edit a cell, double-click it.

- ✔ To select a range of cells, point to the cell at one corner of the range, press and hold the left mouse button, and drag the mouse to highlight the cell range.
- ✔ To select an entire column of cells, click the column heading.
- ✔ To select several columns, point to the column heading of the first column that you want to select and then press and hold the left mouse button as you drag the mouse to select additional columns.
- ✔ To select an entire row of cells, click in the border immediately to the left of the row.

- ✔ Unfortunately, accidentally moving a field or creating a crosstab is all too easy when you are mousing around with the column headers. Be careful not to release the mouse button after first selecting the column and then clicking. If the mouse pointer changes to a hand, release the mouse button immediately!
- ✔ To select several rows, point to the border immediately to the left of the first row that you want to select, press and hold the left mouse button, and drag the mouse to select additional rows.
- ✔ To select the entire worksheet, click the box at the upper-left corner of the worksheet.

Resizing a column or row

When Approach creates worksheet columns, it sets the column width so the column is just wide enough to display the name of the field that is displayed in the column. You'll more than likely need to change the width of one or more columns so that the column is wide enough to display the data.

✛ To resize a column, position the mouse pointer at the border between the heading of the column that you want to change and the heading of the column immediately to its right. When you get the mouse in the right spot, the arrow pointer changes to a funny-looking double arrow. After the double arrow appears, you can press the left mouse button and drag the column to a new width.

✛ If the worksheet rows are not high enough to display your data — perhaps because you increased the size of the font in the field — you can increase the row height. Just position the mouse pointer at the border to the left of the rows until the arrow pointer changes to a double arrow. Then press the left mouse button and drag the row to new heights.

Note: Although each worksheet column can be a different width, all rows in the worksheet are the same height. So when you adjust the height of any worksheet row, the height of all rows is automatically adjusted.

Adding a column to a worksheet

You can add a new column to a worksheet to contain a field that you accidentally omitted when you created the worksheet. You also can add a column that contains a formula.

If you left out a field when you created a worksheet and want to add it later, follow this procedure:

1. **If the Add Field dialog box is not already visible, choose Worksheet⇨Add Field.**

   The Add Field dialog box appears, as shown in Figure 17-3.

Figure 17-3:
The Add
Field dialog
box.

2. **Point the mouse pointer at the field that you want to add to the table and then press the left mouse button and hold it down while you drag the field to the position among the column headings where you want to add the new column.**

   As you drag the field, the mouse pointer turns into a hand and the field name follows the handy little mouse pointer.

3. **Release the mouse button.**

   A new column is added to the worksheet.

To add a column that contains a formula, follow these steps:

1. **Position the mouse at the top of the column heading area, between the columns where you want to insert the new column.**

   When you get the mouse at the right spot, the arrow pointer changes to a wedgie.

2. **Click the mouse.**

   A blank column is inserted in the worksheet, and the Formula dialog box, shown in Figure 17-4, appears.

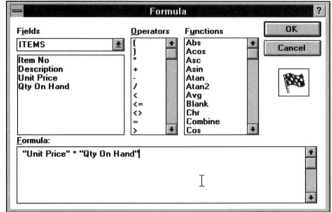

Figure 17-4:
The Formula
dialog box.

3. **Build a formula for the column by clicking the various pieces that you want to include in the formula or by typing the formula in the Formula text box.**

   For more information about creating formulas, see Chapter 13.

4. **Click OK.**

   The results of the formula appear in each cell of the new column.

Note: You can change the formula for a formula column by double-clicking any cell in the column. This action calls forth the Formula dialog box, wherein you can edit to your heart's content.

Removing a column from a worksheet

To remove a column, click the column heading and press the Delete key. The column is removed from the worksheet. (Don't worry. The data is not actually deleted from the database. It's just removed from the worksheet view.)

Rearranging columns

You can change the order of columns in a worksheet by clicking the heading for the column that you want to move. The mouse pointer quickly changes to a grabbing hand. Then you can drag the column to its new location.

Be careful when you drag the column heading. If you drag it beyond the left or top border of the worksheet, a crosstab will be created, jumbling up your worksheet possibly beyond repair. If that happens, your best bet is to delete the worksheet and create a new one.

Printing a worksheet

Printing an Approach worksheet is just like printing any other view, except that you may need to set certain printing options before you begin. To set the printing options, follow this procedure:

1. **Switch to the worksheet view and press Ctrl+E, click the Info icon, or choose Worksheet⇨Style and Properties while no worksheet cell is selected.**

   The InfoBox appears.

2. **Click the Printing tab.**

   The printing options come forward, as shown in Figure 17-5.

Figure 17-5: The InfoBox printing options for a worksheet.

Settings for: Worksheet: Worksheet 1

Basics \ Macros \ Printing \

☑ Print title: Monthly Sales
☑ Print date
☑ Print page number

3. **Select the printing options that you want to use.**

   Print title: Check this option if you want a title printed at the top of the worksheet and then type the title that you want.

   Print date: Check this option if you want the date included in the printout.

   Print page number: Check this option if you want to print page numbers.

4. **Double-click the control box in the upper-left corner of the InfoBox to dismiss the InfoBox.**

Now you can use Approach's normal printing techniques to print the worksheet:

   ✔ Choose File⇨Print.

   ✔ Press Ctrl+P.

 ✔ Click the Print icon.

Cursing at Crosstabs

A *crosstab* is similar to a worksheet, but instead of displaying each database record in a separate row, each crosstab row represents summary values for a group of related records.

For example, consider a database for a mythical professional chess league in which each record contains the following information about a chess player: the team name, the player's first name and last name, and the player's salary. Figure 17-6 shows a simple crosstab that shows the total player salaries for each team. Each row in the crosstab displays the total of all the salary fields for a given team. The values shown in the row headings correspond to the different values that appear in the Team field in the database.

The crosstab in Figure 17-6 is simple — as crosstabs should be. You can create crosstabs that summarize data based on several fields, and you can summarize not only rows but columns as well. For example, you can use a sales database to create a crosstab that summarizes sales by product within sales district for each salesman. The columns can summarize the products and sales districts, and the rows can summarize sales by individual sales reps. Such complex crosstabs can easily get out of control, so you can leave them to the computer nerds to figure out. In the rest of this chapter, you learn how to work with simple crosstabs.

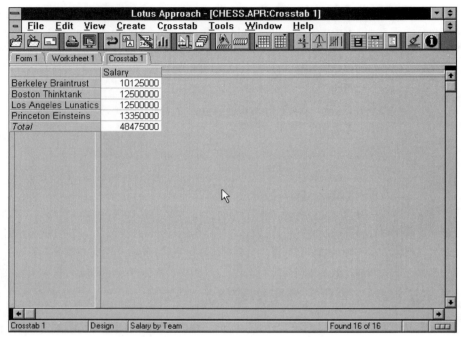

Figure 17-6:
A simple
crosstab.

Creating a simple crosstab

To create a simple crosstab, such as the one shown in Figure 17-6, use the
Crosstab Assistant. Here's the procedure:

1. Decide which field's data you want to summarize.

This step is the most important one in creating a crosstab. Fields that you
use to summarize crosstab data should be fields that contain repeating
data that can be used to categorize the records. For example, in the chess
database, player records can be categorized by the Team field, but the
First Name or Last Name fields would be inappropriate for categorizing
records.

For more complex crosstabs, you can categorize records based on two or
more fields at once.

2. Choose Create➪Crosstab.

This command summons the Crosstab Assistant, which handles most of
the dirty work of creating crosstabs for you.

Figure 17-7 shows the Crosstab Assistant. Like most Approach Assistants, the Crosstab Assistant breaks the task of creating crosstabs into simple steps. The first step is to tell Approach which fields you want to use in summarizing the rows. If you decide that you need to return to a step to correct a mistake, you can click the Back button or click the tab for the step you want to return to.

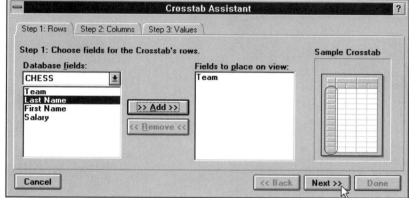

Figure 17-7:
The Rows
settings of
the Crosstab
Assistant.

3. **Click the field that you want to use in summarizing the rows and then click Add.**

   The field appears in the Fields to place on view list. Although you can select more than one field, simple crosstabs require only a single field to summarize rows.

4. **Click Next.**

   The Columns settings for the Crosstab Assistant are displayed, as shown in Figure 17-8.

5. **Skip the Columns settings for simple crosstabs.**

   If you want to summarize data that is grouped by more than one field, select the additional fields here. Otherwise, do not select additional fields.

6. **Click Next.**

   The Values settings for the Crosstab Assistant are displayed, as shown in Figure 17-9.

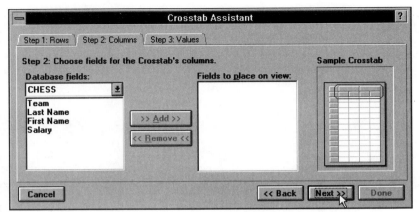

Figure 17-8:
The Columns settings of the Crosstab Assistant.

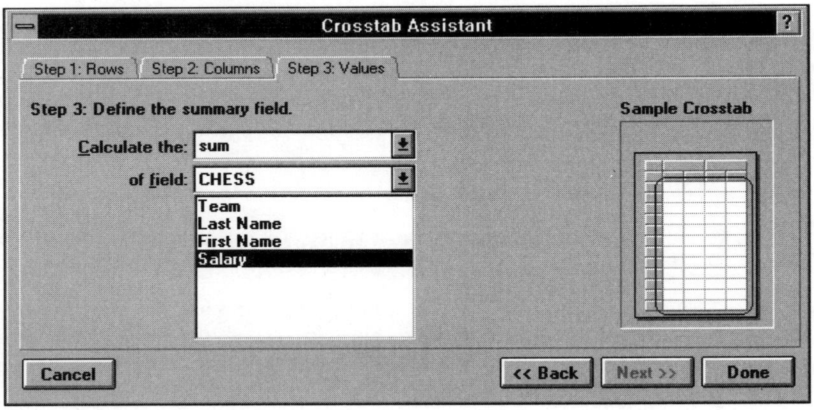

Figure 17-9:
The Values settings of the Crosstab Assistant.

7. **Select the type of calculation that you want Approach to perform and the database field that you want Approach to perform it on.**

   This step is where you tell Approach which database field you want summarized in the body of the crosstab. In Figure 17-9, I told Approach to calculate the sum of the Salary fields for each group of records.

8. **Click Done.**

   The Assistant dutifully prepares the crosstab for you.

Creating crosstabs looks easy, but messing up the task is easy too. Here are some thoughts that may alleviate your suffering:

✔ If you mess up a crosstab by telling the Assistant to group by the wrong fields or by using the wrong formula for the calculation, deleting the view and starting over is usually easier than trying to correct the crosstab. To delete a crosstab, switch to Design mood (*mode,* if you prefer) and choose Edit⇨Delete crosstab.

✔ Notice that the Crosstab Assistant inserts a Total row at the bottom of the crosstab, summarizing totals for the entire database. If you don't want this row, click the Total row heading and press Delete or choose Edit⇨Cut.

✔ Another way to create a crosstab is to call up a worksheet view and then drag one of the column headings over to the row heading area. The field you drag will be used to group summary data for rows, and the remaining worksheet columns will be converted to Sum or Count formulas.

Adding more columns to a crosstab

You can add more columns to the crosstab after you have created the crosstab. For example, in a simple crosstab of a Sales database that summarizes Sales Amount grouped by Sales Rep, you also may want to see a summary of the Sales Commission field so that you know how much commission each sales rep has earned. For the additional summary, you just create a new column that sums the Sales Commission field.

Or you may want to see a count of how many players are on each team in the chess database. You simply create a new column that contains a count of any field in the database. It doesn't really matter which field you use, so long as the field contains a value for each player's record. The Last Name field will work as well as any.

Here is the procedure for adding a new summary column to a crosstab:

1. **Call up the Add Field dialog box by choosing Crosstab⇨Add field.**

   Or click the Add Field icon in the toolbar or the Tools palette. The Add Field dialog box appears, listing all of the fields in the database.

2. **Drag the field that you want to add into the body of the crosstab at the location where you want to insert the new column.**

   The new column is added. If the field is a text field, the Count function is used to indicate how many records in each grouping have a value for that field. For numeric fields, a Sum function is used. For instructions on changing the function, see the section, "Changing a crosstab formula," later in this chapter.

3. **That's all!**

   You're done.

Be careful not to drag the field into the column heading area! If you do, Approach regroups the crosstab, using the field you added as a category field. If that happens, quickly use the Edit⇨Undo command to remove the field.

Changing a crosstab formula

If you want to change the formula used to calculate the summary values that appear in a crosstab column, follow this procedure:

1. **Click the heading of the column whose function you want to change.**

2. **Press Ctrl+E or click the Info button to bring up the InfoBox for the column.**

3. **Click the Formula tab to call up the column's formula.**

    See Figure 17-10.

Figure 17-10:
The InfoBox
shows the
crosstab
formula.

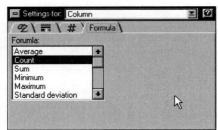

4. **Click the formula that you want to use to calculate the summary values.**

    Table 17-1 lists the formulas you can use to calculate summary values.

5. **Double-click the InfoBox's control box in the upper-left corner of the dialog box.**

    The InfoBox disappears; you're done.

Table 17-1   Summary Formulas for Crosstab Calculations

Formula	What It Does
Average	Adds up the total value of the fields and then divides the result by the number of records in the summary group that have a value for the field. (Note that a value of zero is different from no value at all. Zero is considered to be a value, but Average ignores records for which the field has no value.)
Count	Counts the number of records in the summary group that have a value for the field.
Sum	Adds up the values of the field for all records in the summary group.
Minimum	The smallest value for the field from all records in the summary group.
Maximum	The largest value for the field from all records in the summary group.
Standard deviation	The standard deviation of the field values for all records in the group.
Variance	The variance of the field values for all records in the group.

Chapter 18

Charting Your Course

● ●

In This Chapter

▶ Understanding charts

▶ Creating a chart by using the Chart Assistant

▶ Changing to a different chart type

▶ Making your chart look better

▶ Changing chart text

● ●

*N*umbers, numbers, numbers. If a database has too many numbers, pretty soon all the numbers start to look the same. When you can't tell one number from the next, the time has come to put the numbers into a chart. Charts turn numbers into pictures, which have been the preferred mode of communication ever since Ross Perot ran for president.

Figure 18-1 shows a chart created by Lotus Approach. This chart was created from a database that tracks fouls committed by players in a mythical professional chess league. The chart summarizes the occurrences of the various kinds of fouls committed by the four teams in the league.

Note: Approach charts are actually drawn by a thingamabob called Lotus Chart, which works the same way with other Lotus programs such as 1-2-3, Ami Pro, and Freelance Graphics. The charting features may look a bit different in those programs, but all of them are based on Lotus Chart. If you're already familiar with creating charts in any of those programs, this chapter will be a piece of cake.

Understanding Charts

If you've never worked with a charting program, creating a chart can be a daunting task. Lotus Chart takes a series of numbers from a database and renders them as a graph. Many different kinds of charts are possible, from simple bar charts, to pie charts, to exotic high-low-open-close charts and scatter charts. Very cool, but a little confusing to the uninitiated.

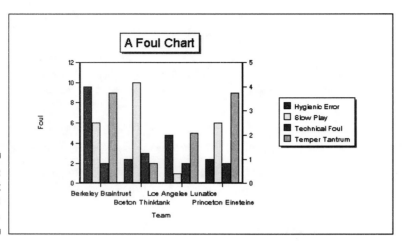

Figure 18-1:
A chart
created with
Approach.

This list shows some of the jargon that you have to contend with when you're working with charts:

Chart or graph: Same thing. These terms are used interchangeably. A chart or graph is nothing more than a bunch of numbers turned into a picture. After all, a picture is worth a thousand numbers.

Chart type: Lotus Chart supports several different chart types: bar charts, area charts, pie charts, line charts, and others. Different kinds of charts are better suited to displaying different kinds of data.

3-D chart: Some charts have a 3-dimensional effect that gives them a jazzier look. Nothing special here; the effect is mostly cosmetic. (Rumor has it that Lotus has hired world-renowned physicist Stephen Hawking to create 4-D charts in an effort to stay one dimension ahead of Microsoft.)

Data window: If you use Lotus Chart from Ami Pro or Freelance Graphics, you use a special data window to enter the values to be plotted on the chart. The data window isn't used in Approach; I just threw it in here in case you are an Ami Pro or Freelance Graphics user and you're stumped because you can't find it. In Approach, the data comes directly from the database, so the data window isn't necessary.

Series: A collection of related numbers to be plotted. Simple charts use only one series, in which each value is usually plotted along the x-axis. More complicated charts, such as the chart in Figure 18-1, can use more than one series. Lotus Chart enables you to use up to 23 series, which is more than anyone other than the Rainman can comprehend.

Axis: This term has nothing to do with the bad guys in World War II. The x-axis is the line along the bottom of a chart; the y-axis is the line along the left edge of a chart. The x-axis usually indicates categories. Actual data values are plotted along the y-axis. Lotus Chart automatically provides labels for the x-axis and the y-axis, but you can change them.

Legend: A box in which the various series plotted on the chart are identified. Lotus Chart creates a legend automatically.

Lotus Chart has its own extensive on-line help. In fact, the Approach *User's Guide* contains very little about charting. To learn more about Lotus Chart, call up the Help⇨Contents command and then click the Charting icon.

Creating a Chart

Creating a chart of your database data is a pretty straightforward matter as soon as you realize that Approach comes with a Chart Assistant that does all the work for you. All you have to do is tell the Assistant what to do, and it will gladly oblige. You don't even have to leave a tip.

To create a chart, just follow these steps:

1. **Open the database for which you want to create a new chart.**

    Choose File⇨Open, click the Open icon, or select the file from the Welcome to Approach dialog box.

2. **Choose Create⇨Chart.**

   You see the first page of the Chart Assistant (shown in Figure 18-2), in which the Assistant asks some basic questions about the chart.

3. **If the suggested name bores you, you can type something else in the View name & title text box.**

4. **From the SmartMaster style list, select 2D Charts or 3D Charts.**

   For a sensible look, stick with 2D charts. For that trying-hard-to-impress look, go with 3D charts.

5. **Pick a chart type from the SmartMaster layout list.**

   The Sample Chart box shows a sample of the selected chart type to help you decide. (Note that the tabs on the Chart Assistant vary depending on the chart type you pick.)

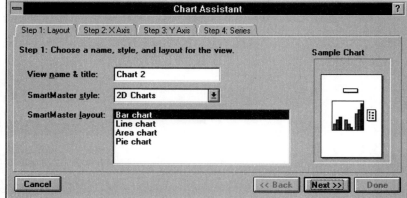

Figure 18-2:
The Chart
Assistant
asks some
basic
questions
about the
chart.

6. Click Next.

The second page of the Chart Assistant appears, in which the Assistant becomes more stern as it asks you what field to use for the x-axis. See Figure 18-3.

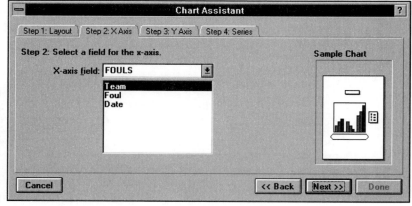

Figure 18-3:
The Chart
Assistant
sternly asks
about the
x-axis.

7. Click the field that you want to use for the x-axis.

The x-axis is the field that you want to use to group data along the horizontal border of the chart. For the chart shown in Figure 18-1, the x-axis is the Team field.

8. Click Next.

The Chart Assistant now has the nerve to ask about the y-axis, as shown in Figure 18-4.

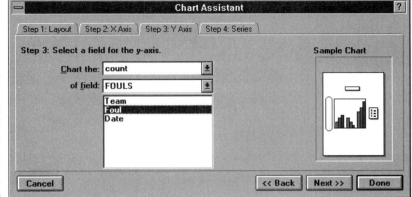

Figure 18-4:
The Chart
Assistant
boldly asks
what field to
use for the
y-axis.

9. **Click the field that you want to use for the y-axis and click the type of calculation that you want to perform on the field.**

   The y-axis represents the field whose value you want to have plotted on the chart. Approach groups all of the records that have the same value for the x-axis field, and then it performs the calculation you choose here to determine what value to plot on the y-axis.

   Table 18-1, later in this section, lists the calculations that you can use for the y-axis. For the team fouls chart in Figure 18-1, the y-axis is the Count calculation for the Foul field.

10. **Click Next.**

    The Chart Assistant demands to know whether you want to use an additional series to plot the data, as you can see in Figure 18-5.

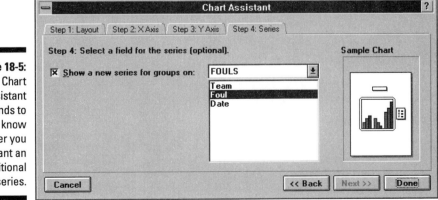

Figure 18-5:
The Chart
Assistant
demands to
know
whether you
want an
additional
series.

Use an extra series when you want to plot several sets of data for each value that appears on the x-axis. For example, looking back to Figure 18-1, you can see that on the x-axis four bars appear for each team, one bar for each type of foul. To create this chart, I used the Foul field to group an additional series.

To use an additional series, check the check box for Show a new series for groups on and then select the field by which you want to group the new series.

11. Click Done.

Stand back and watch Approach create the chart.

When the chart is finished, Approach displays it for you in Preview mood. If you don't like it, switch to Design mood and fiddle around with it until you like it, following the procedures presented in the following sections of this chapter.

Table 18-1 lists the calculations that you can use for the y-axis.

Table 18-1	Calculations You Can Use in Charts
Calculation	*What It Does*
Average	The average value of the field.
Count	The number of records that have a value for the field.
Sum	The sum of the field values for each record.
Smallest item	The smallest value for the field.
Largest item	The largest value for the field.
Standard deviation	The standard deviation of the field values.
Variance	The variance of the field values.

Here are some points to ponder before you get too carried away with creating charts.

✔ *Note:* If you want to change the database field used for the x-axis, the y-axis, or the series, choose Chart⇨Chart Data Source. This command calls up the Chart Data Source Assistant, which is identical to the Chart Assistant except that the first step, in which you identify the chart type, is omitted.

✔ Another way to create a chart is to first create a crosstab that summarizes the data that you want to chart. Then choose Crosstab⇨Chart Crosstab. A chart will be created automatically. For more information about crosstabs, see Chapter 17.

Changing the Chart Type

You can create 20 basic kinds of charts by using Lotus Chart. Each chart type conveys information that has a different emphasis. For example, sales data plotted in a column chart may emphasize the relative performance of different regions, whereas the same data plotted as a line chart may emphasize the increase or decrease of sales over time. The kind of chart that's best for your data depends on the nature of the data and on which aspects of it you want to emphasize.

Fortunately, Approach doesn't force you to decide on the final chart type up front. You can easily change the chart type at any time without changing the chart data. These steps explain how to change the chart type:

1. Double-click the chart to call up the InfoBox.

The chart InfoBox appears, as shown in Figure 18-6. If the InfoBox doesn't look quite like the one in Figure 18-6, some element of the chart, such as the legend or title, may been selected when you double-clicked. Click the button at the top of the InfoBox (labeled Title, Legend, X-axis, Y-axis, or whatever) and select Chart from the menu that appears.

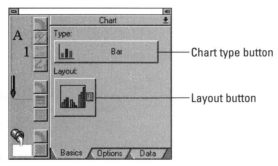

Chart type button

Layout button

Figure 18-6:
The Chart
InfoBox.

2. Click the chart type button to reveal a menu of available chart types.

Table 18-2, later in this section, lists the 20 chart types that are available from this menu. Figure 18-7 shows what the chart type menu looks like.

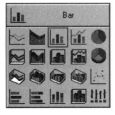

Figure 18-7:
The chart
type menu.

3. **Click the chart type that you want to use.**

4. **Click the Layout button and pick from one of the layouts that are available for the chart type that you picked in Step 3.**

   Each of the chart types has several layout variations to choose from. For example, Figure 18-8 shows the layout options for bar charts. Pick the one you like best.

Figure 18-8:
The layout
menu.

5. **Double-click the control box in the upper-left corner of the InfoBox to dismiss the InfoBox.**

   You're done!

Table 18-2	Chart Types
Icon	*Chart Type*
	Line chart
	Line chart with depth
	3-D line chart
	Area chart
	Area chart with depth
	3-D area chart
	Bar chart
	Bar chart with depth

Icon	Chart Type
	3-D bar chart
	Stacked bar chart
	Stacked bar chart with depth
	Horizontal bar chart
	Horizontal stacked bar chart
	Mixed bar and line chart
	Mixed bar and line chart with depth
	Mixed 3-D bar and line chart
	Scatter chart
	High-Low-Close-Open chart
	Pie chart
	3-D Pie chart

Improving a Chart's Appearance

Lotus Chart enables you to tweak a chart's appearance in many ways. In fact, you could probably spend the rest of the decade exploring the various bells and whistles that accompany charts.

You control chart ornamentation through the Chart InfoBox, which is similar to the InfoBox that you're used to seeing within Approach, yet different in several ways:

✔ In Chart, the InfoBox tabs, which you click to call up different controls, are on the bottom instead of on the top.

✔ The button at the very top of the Chart InfoBox activates a menu where you can select the chart element with which you want to fiddle. The regular Approach InfoBox doesn't have this button.

✔ A series of buttons down the left side of the Chart InfoBox causes additional controls to appear. You can use these controls to change the text color, font and style, line width, fill color, and so on. Figure 18-9 indicates the function of each button.

✔ Buttons in the middle of the Chart InfoBox often activate additional menus that offer choices. For example, when you click the Layout button that is shown in Figure 18-6, you see a menu of the layout options for bar charts.

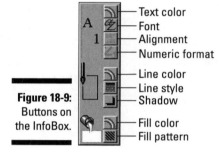

Text color
Font
Alignment
Numeric format
Line color
Line style
Shadow
Fill color
Fill pattern

Figure 18-9:
Buttons on
the InfoBox.

In short, the Chart InfoBox is decidedly different than the regular InfoBox. Feel free to experiment with it. After you get a feel for it, you'll have no trouble with any of the following procedures.

You can bring up the Chart InfoBox in several ways:

✔ Double-click the chart.

✔ Choose Chart⇨Style and Properties.

✔ Right-click the chart to bring up the quick menu and then choose the Style and Properties command.

✔ Press Ctrl+E.

After you activate the Chart InfoBox, you can adjust different chart elements by selecting the element that you want to adjust from the menu that appears when you click the button at the top of the InfoBox. Table 18-3 lists the various chart options that you can control from the Chart InfoBox.

Chart Element	Options You Can Set
Chart	Change the chart type and layout.
Title	Change the position of the title; add a subtitle; or change the text color, style, and font for the title text.
Legend	Change the position and text style for the legend.
X-axis	Add elements, such as tick marks and grid lines, to the x-axis; change the scale for the x-axis.
Y-axis	Add elements, such as tick marks and grid lines, to the y-axis; change the scale for the y-axis.
Series	Change the colors assigned to each series or hide series you don't want to see, such as a series that indicates a downward sales trend.
Series labels	Add value or percentage labels to each series.
Plot	Return the chart to its default position on the page.
Note	Add a note to the bottom of the chart.

Table 18-3   Chart Elements You Can Adjust from the Chart InfoBox

Many of the Chart InfoBox options include a check box labeled Visible. You use this check box to add or remove various chart elements. To add or remove a chart element, first select the element and then check or uncheck the Visible check box.

Adjusting Chart Text

Most charts have several text elements, such as titles and legends. You can edit any text element on a chart by following this procedure:

1. **Click the text that you want to edit.**

   The text element is selected; love handles appear as proof.

2. **Wait a moment.**

   Not long, just long enough for Windows to catch its breath. Try counting to three.

3. **Double-click the title text.**

   An insertion point should appear. If the InfoBox appears instead, you didn't wait long enough. Dismiss the InfoBox by double-clicking its control box (in the upper-left corner) and then try again.

4. **Edit the text.**

5. **Click outside the text when you're done.**

Part IV
Definitely Database Grad School Stuff

The 5th Wave   By Rich Tennant

"THE ENTIRE SYSTEM IS DOWN. THE COMPUTER PEOPLE BLAME THE MODEM PEOPLE WHO BLAME THE PHONE PEOPLE WHO BLAME IT ON OUR MOON BEING IN THE FIFTH HOUSE WITH VENUS ASCENDING."

In this part ...

This part is the one to turn to when you really want to impress your friends by showing them how much more you know about Approach than any normal person should need or want to know. You learn how to set up macros to automate routine chores, how to work with Approach on a network, how to fool around with Approach's preferences, and how to convert foreign data so Approach can use it.

You may want to grab your pocket protector and propeller cap before proceeding.

Chapter 19
Creating and Using Macros

• •

In This Chapter

▶ Creating a macro

▶ Macros that run automatically when you enter or exit a view

▶ Macro buttons

▶ Macros that are attached to fields

▶ Assigning a macro to a function key

• •

A macro is a sequence of commands that Approach records and makes available for you to play back whenever you want. Macros enable you to create customized shortcuts for things that you do over and over again. For example, perhaps at least 20 times a day you do a find to locate all your California customers and then you sort them into zip code sequence. A macro enables you to combine these two functions so that you don't have to perform them separately each time. You can add a button to one of your forms to invoke the macro. You also can create a separate view and attach the macro to it; then whenever you switch to this view, the macro runs automatically.

This chapter is a brief introduction to macros. It explains how to create simple macros, how to edit them if they don't do quite what you want, and the many ways to run a macro. Although macros are clearly an "advanced" Approach subject, this chapter isn't so advanced that pocket protectors are required.

Creating a Macro

To create a macro, follow these steps:

1. Try to talk yourself out of it.

Fiddling around with macros can be a bit of a time waster. Ask yourself whether you think that you will use the macro after you have gone to the trouble of creating it. If not, go directly to Step 10.

2. Choose Tools⇨Macros.

You also can call up the InfoBox, switch to the Macros tab, and click the Define Macro button. Either way, you are greeted by the Macros dialog box, which is shown in Figure 19-1. This dialog box is rather boring initially, but it gets more interesting after you create a few macros.

Figure 19-1:
The Macros
dialog box.

3. Click the New button.

Yet another dialog box appears, this one called Define Macro. See Figure 19-2.

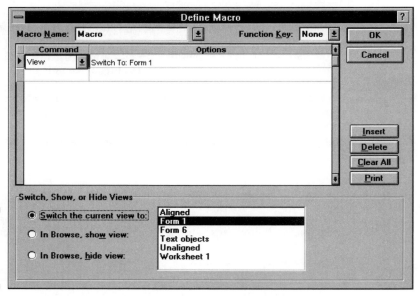

Figure 19-2:
The Define
Macro
dialog box.

4. **Type something more creative than "Macro" in the Macro Name text box.**

   Think of a descriptive name for the macro to help you remember what it does.

5. **Add the command that you want the macro to carry out.**

   The command area of the Define Macro dialog box is kind of like a spreadsheet. Each row contains a command to be carried out. The first column contains the name of the command, and the second column records any options that go along with the command, such as the name of the view that a View command should switch to or the search criteria for a Find command.

   New macros are automatically set up to carry out a View command. To change the View command to some other command, or to add additional commands, click a cell in the Command column and then click the cell again or click the down-arrow for the drop-down list to reveal a menu that lists all the commands you can use in a macro. Then click the command that you want to use.

6. **Set the options for the command that you picked in Step 5.**

   When you select a command, the bottom part of the Define Macro box changes to reflect the various options that are available for the command. Play with these options any way you want.

7. **Repeat Steps 5 and 6 to add additional commands to the macro.**

8. **After you add all the commands that you want, click OK.**

   The name of the new macro appears in the Macros dialog box.

9. **Click Done to dismiss the Macros dialog box.**

   The macro is finished.

10. **You're done.**

Table 19-1 lists the function carried out by each of the 27 macro commands that you can use.

Table 19-1   What All Those Macro Commands Do

Command	What It Does
Browse	Switches to Browse mood.
Close	Closes the database.
Delete	Deletes the current record, found set, or a file.
Dial	Dials the phone number in the selected field.
Edit	Copies, cuts, or pastes data to or from the Clipboard.
Enter	Accepts edits to the current record.
Exit	Exits Approach.
Export	Copies data from an Approach database to a foreign file format.
Find	Finds database records. The macro can supply the search criteria, or you can have the user supply the criteria.
Find Special	Finds duplicate or unique records.
Import	Copies data from a foreign file format into an Approach database.
Mail	Electronically sends data to another computer user. An e-mail system has to be in place for this command to work.
Menu Switch	Switches to a custom menu.
Message	Displays a message on the screen.
Open	Opens a file.
Preview	Switches to Preview mood.
Print	Prints the current view.
Records	Goes to a particular record, hides a record, or creates a new record.
Replicate	Copies a Lotus Notes database.
Run	Runs another macro. You can include a condition test.
Save	Saves the Approach file.
Set	Sets the value of a field.
Sort	Sorts database records.
Spell Check	Runs the spelling checker.
Tab	Tabs to the next field on the view or backwards to the previous field.
View	Switches to a different view.
Zoom	Changes the zoom factor.

Here are some key points to consider when you create macros:

- ✔ Macros are stored in the Approach files along with your views. Thus, each macro that you create is available only when the Approach file that contains the macro is open.

- ✔ To delete a macro, choose Tools⇨Macros, select the macro you want to delete, and click the Delete button.

- ✔ To edit a macro, choose Tools⇨Macros, select the macro you want to edit, and click the Edit button.

- ✔ You can delete a command from a macro by calling up the Define Macro dialog box, clicking the command that you want to delete, and clicking the Delete button.

- ✔ To insert a command in the middle of a macro, click the command before which you want to insert the new command and then click the Insert button.

- ✔ You can print the commands in a macro from the Define Macro dialog box by clicking the Print button.

The following sections explain the various methods of running a macro.

The many ways to include a Find in a macro

You can include five distinct kinds of Find commands in macros. To select the type of Find command that you want to use, just check one of the following options for the Find command in the Define Macro dialog box:

Perform stored find when macro is run: This option stores the find criteria along with the macro and automatically runs the Find when the macro is run. After you click the New Find button to set the criteria for the Find, you go to a variation of Find mood (*mode,* for you purists) where you can type find criteria in each database field. When you are finished, click OK to return to the Define Macro dialog box. After you set the criteria for a stored Find, you can change it by clicking the Edit Find button.

Go to find and wait for input: This option switches to Find mood when the macro is run and then waits for the user to enter the criteria for the query. After the user clicks OK, the macro continues.

Find again and wait for input: Switches to Find mood and enables the user to repeat the preceding Find.

Show all records: Shows all records in the database.

Refresh found set: Refreshes the Find. This option is useful in network settings in which another user may have added or deleted records since the Find was first run.

The Many Ways to Run a Macro

After you create a macro, you can choose from several methods to run it. You can run it from the Macros dialog box, you can choose Tools⇨Run Macro (or call up the InfoBox, switch to the Macros tab, and click the Define Macro button), or you can attach the macro to a view (or to an object on a view), button, field, or function key.

Running a macro from the Macros dialog box

You can run any macro from the Macros dialog box by following this procedure:

1. **Choose Tools⇨Macros.**

   You also can call up the InfoBox, switch to the Macros tab, and click the Define Macro button. Either way, the Macros dialog box appears.

2. **Click the macro you want to run.**

3. **Click the Run button.**

Attaching a macro to a view

If you attach a macro to a view, the macro runs automatically whenever you switch to that view. You can use this feature to perform a Find or a Sort (or both) whenever a view is displayed.

You also can attach a macro that runs whenever you switch away from a view. Such a macro can, for example, use a Find command to show all database records.

To attach a macro to a view, follow these steps:

1. **Switch to the view to which you want to attach the macro.**

2. **Choose View⇨Design, press Ctrl+D, or click the Design icon to switch to Design mood.**

3. **Call up the view's InfoBox by clicking the Info button or pressing Ctrl+E.**

   The InfoBox appears.

4. **Click the Macro tab to display the macro options.**

   See Figure 19-3.

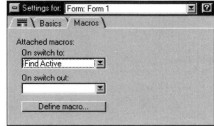

Figure 19-3:
The
InfoBox's
macro
options for
a view.

5. **If you want to run a macro whenever you switch to a view, select the macro name from the On switch to drop-down list.**

6. **If you want to run a macro whenever you switch away from a view, select the macro name from the On switch out drop-down list.**

7. **Double-click the InfoBox's control box (in the upper-left corner) when you're finished.**

From then on, an On switch to macro will be run when you switch to the view, and an On switch out macro will be run when you switch from the view to any other view.

Creating a macro button

Another way to run a macro is to attach the macro to a button on a form or other view. Then the macro is run whenever you click the button.

To create a macro button, follow these steps:

1. **Switch to the view on which you want the button to appear.**

 2. **Choose View⬧Design, press Ctrl+D, or click the Design icon to switch to Design mood.**

3. **If the Tools palette is not visible, activate it by pressing Ctrl+L or by choosing View⬧>Show Drawing Tools.**

    Figure 19-4 shows the Tools palette.

 4. **Click the Macro Button icon in the Tools palette.**

    The cursor changes to a crosshair.

Figure 19-4:
The Tools
palette.

5. Draw the button on the form.

Point the crosshair cursor where you want one corner of the button to appear and then press and hold the left mouse button while dragging the mouse diagonally to where you want the opposite corner of the button to be. When you release the mouse, the button will be added, and the InfoBox shown in Figure 19-5 will appear.

Figure 19-5:
The InfoBox
macro
options for a
button.

6. Select the macro that you want to run when the user clicks the button by selecting the macro name in the On clicked list.

You also can specify a macro to run when the user tabs into or out of the button. This method is useful for fields that require unusual default values or fields that have complicated validation requirements that can't be handled by Approach's normal default and validation options.

If you haven't yet created the macro, you can click the Define Macro button to call up the Define Macro dialog box.

7. Click the Basics tab in the InfoBox.

The Basics InfoBox options appear, as shown in Figure 19-6.

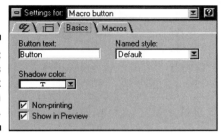

Figure 19-6:
The Basics
InfoBox
options for a
button.

8. **Type a meaningful name for the button in the Button text box.**

The text that you type is what appears on the button; "Button" just isn't quite descriptive enough.

9. **Double-click the InfoBox's control box (in the upper-left corner) when you're finished.**

Some people like to create a separate form that acts as a menu of macro commands. To create a menu form, choose Create➪Form to create a blank form. Then add a button for each macro that you want to be accessible from the form.

Attaching a macro to a field

You also can attach a macro to any field on a view so that the macro is run whenever the user tabs into or out of the field or changes the contents of the field. You can use this feature to verify that correct data was entered into the field in cases where Approach's data validation features aren't adequate. You can use it to supply a default value for a field that you can't supply simply by specifying a default value in Field Definition.

To attach a macro to a field, switch to Design mood, double-click the field, and call up its InfoBox. Then click the Macros tab and set the macro options.

Assigning a macro to a function key

You can assign a macro to any of the 12 function keys that live near the top of the keyboard. Then you can run the macro at any time simply by pressing the function key.

To assign a macro to a function key, follow these steps:

1. **Choose Tools⇨Macros.**

   You also can call up the InfoBox, switch to the Macros tab, and click the Define Macro button. Either way, the familiar Macros dialog box appears

2. **Click the macro that you want to assign to a function key.**

3. **Click Edit.**

   The Define Macro dialog box appears.

4. **Select the function key to which you want to assign the macro from the Function Key list.**

5. **Click OK.**

   You are returned to the Macros dialog box.

6. **Click Done.**

   The Macros dialog box is whisked away.

Here are a few important caveats concerning function key assignments:

- ✔ Avoid assigning a macro to F1. Most Windows users expect F1 to call up the Help facility. If you assign a macro to F1, you can no longer use F1 to call up Help. Plus, you'll probably end up accidentally running the macro when you want to call up Help. Then you'll really need help!

- ✔ Function key assignments are always available, no matter what view is displayed.

- ✔ You may want to include somewhere a text object that lists the function keys to which you've assigned macros. Otherwise, innocent users won't have any clue about which function keys to press.

A Real-World Example

To put the information in this chapter into perspective, Figure 19-7 shows an example of the type of macro that you can create to make a real-life Approach application easier to use. This macro automates the steps that the user takes to display and print a report in a video rental store database. The report lists all customers who have video tapes checked out. These customers are listed in alphabetical order by name.

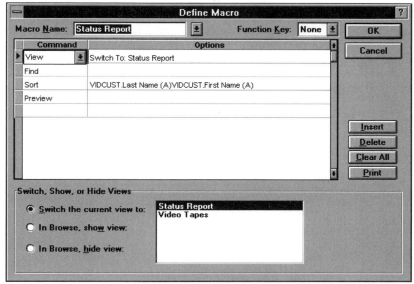

Figure 19-7:
A macro
that
prepares a
report for
printing.

The macro has four commands:

View: The first macro command switches to the view named Status Report, which contains the report to be printed. I created the report as a simple Columnar report by using the Report Assistant.

Find: The next macro command executes a find. This Find command runs a find that I defined and saved when I created the macro. It selects only those records that have a nonblank value in the VIDEO Title field, indicating that the customer currently has a video rented out. The effect of this command is to exclude from the report any customers who don't have tapes rented.

Sort: The third macro command sorts the records into order by Last Name and then by First Name.

Preview: The last macro command switches to Preview mood so that the user can see what the report will look like when it is printed. To actually print the report, the user needs to click the Print button in the SmartIcon bar.

This macro is designed so that it can be attached to a button that appears on the main form or attached to the Status Report view itself so that it runs whenever the user switches to the view.

Chapter 20

Using Approach on a Network

In This Chapter

▶ Understanding networks

▶ Accessing a network database

▶ Opening a network database in single-user mode

▶ Setting Approach preferences for network sharing

*J*ust a few years ago, computer networks were exotic beasts found only in large companies and science fiction movies. Nowadays, though, networks can be found everywhere. Even companies that have only two computers have discovered that it's worth the $200 or so that it costs to network them together. So odds are your computer is connected to a network.

This chapter is a brief introduction to what happens when you use Approach on a computer that is connected to a network; there are no detailed instructions for setting up a network, or even for configuring Approach to operate on a network. That kind of task is best handled by stiff-lipped professionals with pocket protectors, who are known as *Network Administrators.* Instead, this chapter assumes that Approach has been properly installed on a network and thus simply touches on the ways a network can complicate the way you use Approach.

Remember that it is illegal to purchase a single copy of Approach and put it on a network so that everyone on the network can use it. If you have a network, you need to purchase one copy of Approach for each computer on which this program will be used.

What Is a Network?

A *network* is nothing more than two or more computers that are connected by a cable so that they can exchange information.

You can, of course, use other methods to exchange information between computers. Most of us have used what computer nerds call the *Sneakernet*. This method involves copying a file to a floppy disk and carrying the disk to someone else's computer. (The term *Sneakernet* is typical of computer nerds' attempts at humor.)

The whole problem with the *Sneakernet* is that it's slow, plus it wears a trail in your carpet. One day some penny-pinching computer geeks discovered that connecting computers with cables was actually cheaper than replacing the carpet every six months. Thus, the modern computer network was born.

With a computer network, you hook all the computers in your office together with cables, install a special *network adapter card* (an electronic circuit card that goes inside the computer) in each computer so you'll have a place to plug in the cable, set up and configure special network software to make the network work, and voilà, you have a working network. That's all there is to it.

Here are a few important tidbits to remember about networks:

- Networks are often called LANs. *LAN* is an acronym that stands for *Local Area Network*. Local area networks are networks in which all of the computers are within walking distance of one another, usually within the same building.

- Every computer connected to the network is said to be *on the network*. The technical term (which you can forget) for a computer that is on the network is a *node*.

- A network computer that contains disk drives, a printer, or other resources that are shared with other network computers is called a *server*. Server computers are usually the most powerful and expensive computers on the network. They often have huge disk drives and tons of memory.

- A network computer that isn't a *server* is called a *workstation*. Workstations are the computers that users use to get work done. The computer that's sitting on your desk is (I hope) a workstation.

- Sometimes the term *client* is used instead of *workstation*. Don't you love computer jargon?

- In some networks the server computers can do nothing but be a server. In these networks, the servers are called *dedicated servers* in recognition of their dedication to a single task. In other networks, any computer can be a server, and a computer can be a server and a workstation at the same time. These networks are called *peer-to-peer networks*.

✔ The most popular type of dedicated server network is Netware from a company called Novell. Several types of peer-to-peer networks are in use, the most popular being Windows for Workgroups from Microsoft and LANTastic from Artisoft.

✔ Disk drives, printers, and other resources that are connected directly to your own computer are called *local resources.* Disk drives, printers, and other resources that are on a server computer are called *network resources.*

✔ To use a network, you have to *log in* by supplying a user-ID and a password. Then you can access the disk drives and printers on the network servers. The ideal setup is for your computer to log on the network automatically when you start the computer, and for the server disks and printers to be automatically accessed.

✔ Aren't there a lot of bullets here? I could go on for another four or five pages on the subject of networks. The point is that there is a great deal to learn about using networks. Ask your network administrator about any procedures that you need to follow when you access the network. And pick up a copy of my book, *Networking For Dummies.*

Accessing a Network Database

When you use Approach on a network, the most sensible thing to do is to store all of your databases on one of the network server's disk drives so that other network users can share the database. Then everyone will have access to the most current data.

You access network disk drives the same way you access local disk drives: by using a drive letter. Most computers have a local disk drive named drive C. Other drive letters are assigned to network drives. For example, if J is assigned to a disk drive on a network server, you access files on the server drive by using J for the drive letter. Your network administrator will tell you which drive letters to use for network drives.

 To open a database that's stored on a network server, follow the same procedure that you use to open a database on a local disk drive: choose File⇨Open, click the Open icon, or select Existing File from the Welcome dialog box. The only difference is that when you specify the location of the file in the Open dialog box, you specify a network disk rather than your local disk.

If the database is password protected (network databases frequently are), you'll be asked to enter the password to access the database.

What happens if two people try to open the same database at the same time? Approach enables both of them to open it, but it takes precautions to prevent both users from updating the same record simultaneously. Otherwise, both users can freely access the data.

Opening a File in Single-User Mode

Although allowing several users to access a database simultaneously is great, on some occasions you may not want to permit simultaneous access. For example, if you want to change the design of a database by adding or removing fields, you shouldn't allow others to access the database while you work. Or if you want to print a critical report, you may need to lock out other users while the report prints.

One way to prevent other users from accessing a database is to punch 99 on your telephone, or whatever number activates the office-wide intercom, and say something such as, "Hey everybody! Don't touch the customer database for ten minutes, or I'll break your face!"

A more effective way is to follow this procedure:

1. **Choose File⇨Open or click the Open icon.**

   The Open dialog box appears.

2. **Select dBASE or Paradox as the file type in the List files of type field.**

3. **Click the Connect button.**

   For dBASE files, the dialog box in Figure 20-1 appears. For Paradox files, the dialog box in Figure 20-2 appears.

4. **For dBASE files, uncheck the Database sharing field.**

Figure 20-1:
The Connect dialog box for dBASE files.

```
┌─────────────────── dBASE Network Connection ──────────── ? ┐
│                                                            │
│  ☐ Database sharing                    ┌──────────┐        │
│  ☐ Local databases are shared          │    OK    │        │
│                                        └──────────┘        │
│  ☐ Sharing data only with other Approach users ┌────────┐  │
│                                        │ Cancel │         │
│                                        └────────┘         │
└────────────────────────────────────────────────────────────┘
```

Figure 20-2:
The Connect dialog box for Paradox files.

```
┌─────────────────── Paradox Network Connection ──────────── ? ┐
│  ○ Use Paradox 3.5 networking          ┌──────────┐          │
│  ● Use Paradox 4.x networking          │    OK    │          │
│                                        └──────────┘          │
│                                        ┌──────────┐          │
│                                        │  Cancel  │          │
│              User name: [          ]   └──────────┘          │
│   Network control file path: [                    ]         │
└────────────────────────────────────────────────────────────┘
```

5. **For Paradox files, erase the contents of the U̲ser name and N̲etwork control file path fields.**

   Be sure to write down the contents of these fields before you delete them; to restore shared access, you have to restore the contents of these fields!

6. **Click OK.**

   You return to the Open dialog box.

7. **Select the file that you want to open and click OK.**

   The file is opened for single-user access.

To enable other users to share the database, click the C̲onnect button and check the D̲atabase sharing check box (dBASE files), or restore the U̲ser name and N̲etwork control file path text boxes to their previous contents (Paradox).

Setting Approach Preferences for Network Sharing

Chapter 21 explains all about setting Approach's preferences by using the Tools⇨Preferences command. Two of these preference options affect the way Approach works with a network:

D̲ownload data before previewing: This option causes Approach to copy all of a database to your hard disk whenever you enter Preview mode. It shields you from database updates made by other users so you can be sure that the data you see is the data that will be printed.

Lock records using o̲ptimistic record locking: This option enables several users to edit the same record at the same time. However, if both users try to save their changes, only the first user's changes are saved. The second user receives an error message indicating that someone else has already changed the record. This locking method is faster than the more conservative method, which prevents users from editing the same records at the same time.

For more information about setting these preferences and other Approach preferences, see Chapter 21.

Chapter 21

Playing with Preferences

● ●

In This Chapter

▶ Understanding Approach preferences

▶ Setting display preferences

▶ Setting database order preferences

▶ Setting password preferences

▶ Setting the general preferences

● ●

*Y*ou use the Tools⇨Preferences command to set the myriad preference options that affect the way Approach works. Of course, you can't use this command to pick your real preferences, such as playing golf instead of toiling with your computer. But you can do stuff that's almost as much fun, such as displaying a ruler or setting the default sort order for your favorite databases.

You should read this chapter when you finally decide to give in to the Tools⇨Preferences command and you want to know what all of those options do. This chapter describes the most useful preferences, but, what's more important, it tells you which preferences you can safely ignore so that you (unlike some people I know — me, for example) can catch up on your golf.

Note: I am aware, of course, that for many people, golf is a more frustrating pastime than playing with Approach. And for some, golf is more boring that reading Approach's on-line help. If you're one of those poor, unenlightened souls, feel free to substitute your favorite nongolf pastime.

What's with All the Options?

When you call up the Tools⇨Preferences command, you are presented with a killer dialog box that has tabs out the wazoo (whatever a *wazoo* is). Each of the tabs has its own set of options controls. To switch from one tab to another, just click the tab label at the top of the dialog box.

Here's the lowdown on the seven tabs that appear in the Preferences dialog box:

Display: Contains options that control the appearance of the Approach window.

Order: Sets the default sort order for databases.

Password: Sets passwords for Approach files.

Dialer: Configures the modem so that Approach can instruct it to dial phone numbers.

Database: Sets some general options for databases.

Index: Enables you to use dBASE, FoxPro, or Paradox indexes that have already been created by those programs.

General: Contains a hodgepodge of miscellaneous options that Approach's programmers couldn't squeeze in anywhere else.

To set preferences for Approach, follow these steps:

1. **Choose Tools⇨Preferences.**

   The Preferences dialog box appears.

2. **Click the tab that contains a preference that you want to set.**

   If you're not sure which tab to click, cycle through them all until you find what you're looking for.

3. **Set the preferences however you want.**

   Most of the preferences are simple check boxes that you click to check or uncheck. Some require that you select a choice from a drop-down list, and some have the audacity to require that you actually type something as proof of your keyboard proficiency.

4. Repeat Step 3 until you've exhausted your options or you've exhausted yourself.

You can set more than one preference with a single use of the Tools➪Preferences command.

5. Click OK.

You're done!

Dealing with Display Preferences

You can use the options on the Display tab, shown in Figure 21-1, to customize the appearance of Approach's humble display. You can see that the options are arranged into four groups: Show, Show in Design, Default Style, and Grid.

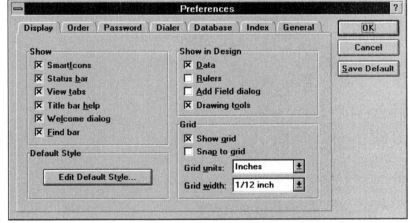

Figure 21-1:
The Display
preferences
tab.

This list summarizes the functions of the Show preferences:

SmartIcons: This option displays or hides the SmartIcon bar. Uncheck it if you don't like the SmartIcons and you want to free up the screen real estate so you can see more of your database views.

Status bar: This option displays or hides the Status Bar at the bottom of the screen. If you'd rather have the extra space to see more data, uncheck this one too.

View tabs: This option displays or hides those tabs that enable you to switch quickly from one view to another. If you uncheck this option, you can see more of your data, but you have to use the View menu to switch among views.

Title bar help: Ever notice that when you point to a menu command, a brief description of the command or icon appears in the title bar? If having to see that description bugs you, uncheck this option.

Welcome dialog: Uncheck this option to get rid of the Welcome to Lotus Approach dialog box. When this option is unchecked, you have to choose File⇨Open or click the Open icon to open database files.

Find bar: Whenever you switch to Find mood (*mode* for you computer nerd purists), the Find Bar is displayed, offering you several buttons to assist your searches. If you don't like it, uncheck this option.

The Show in Design options apply only when you are working in Design mood:

Data: Mr. Data from "Star Trek: The Next Generation" appears on the screen. Okay, not really. Check this option if you want to see actual data in database fields rather than the field names.

Rulers: Displays a list of every U.S. President since George Washington. Okay, just kidding again. Check this option to display vertical and horizontal rulers to help align objects that you place on a view.

Add Field dialog: Check this option if you want the Add Field dialog box to automatically appear whenever you switch to Design mood.

Drawing tools: Check this option if you want the floating Tools palette to appear automatically whenever you switch to Design mood.

The Default Style box contains a single button that is labeled Edit Default Style. If you click this button, another dialog box appears where you can set the formatting options that you want to apply to objects that you create in Design.

You use the Grid settings to control the grid, which helps align Design objects:

Show grid: Check this option if you want the grid displayed automatically.

Snap to grid: Check this option if you want objects to stick to the grid.

Grid units: Use this option to change the unit of measure used for the next option (Inches or Centimeters).

Grid width: Use this option to change the spacing of the grid.

Ogling Order Preferences

You use the Order tab, shown in Figure 21-2, to establish a default sort order for a database. If you do not establish a default sort order, records are maintained in the order in which you enter them.

To set the sort order for a database, follow these steps:

1. **Open the database.**

2. **Choose Tools⇨Preferences.**

3. **Click the Order tab.**

4. **Select the database whose sort order you want to set in the Maintain default sort for box.**

5. **Click the field on which you want the database sorted in the Database fields list.**

6. **Click Ascending or Descending to specify ascending or descending order for the field.**

7. **Click Add.**

8. **Repeat Steps 5 – 7 if you want the database sorted on more than one field.**

9. **Click OK.**

If you make a mistake, you can use the Remove button to remove a sort field, or you can use the Clear All button to remove all sort fields and start over.

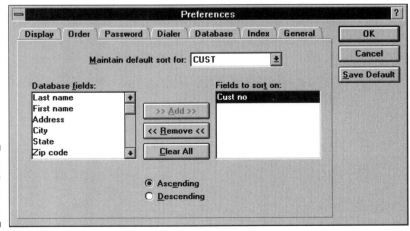

Figure 21-2:
The Order preferences tab.

Playing with Password Preferences

You use the Passwords tab, shown in Figure 21-3, to set a password for a database or an Approach file. A database can have two kinds of passwords: a read/write password and a read-only password. The read/write password enables you to update database records, whereas the read-only password enables you to read but not update database records. If you assign either type of password to a database, Approach requires you to enter the password when you open the file.

This capability enables you to let some users access the database with full read-write privileges and others view, but not update, data in the database. All you have to do is provide the read/write password only to those users who need to update the database and share the read-only password with all other users.

Because you cannot assign a read-only password without first assigning a read/write password, the Read-only password field is grayed-out in Figure 21-3.

If you create a password for an Approach file, Approach requires you to enter the password whenever you switch to Design mood. You can use this password to ensure that no one changes your views.

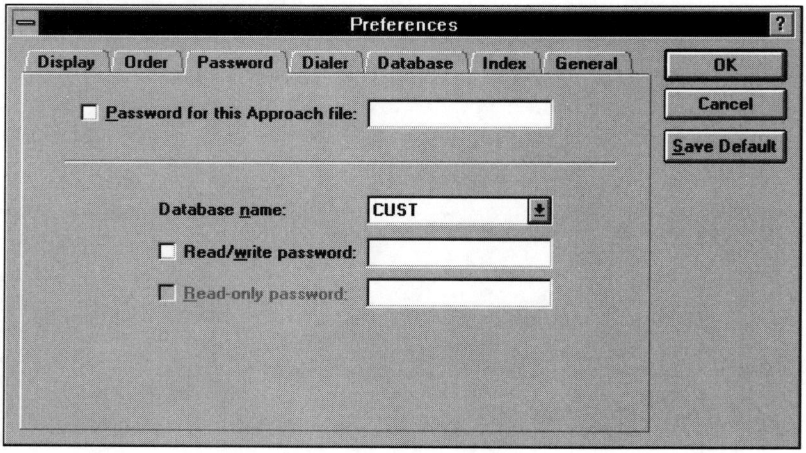

Figure 21-3:
Setting the
Password
preferences.

To assign a password to a file, follow these steps:

1. **Open the database.**

2. **Choose Tools⇨Preferences.**

3. **Click the Password tab.**

4. **To assign an Approach password, type a password into the Password for this Approach file text box.**

5. **To assign a database password, select the database from the Database name list and then type a password for the Read/write password box or the Read-only password box.**

6. **When Approach asks you to type the password again, type it again.**

   Having you retype the password is Approach's way of making sure that you didn't type the password incorrectly. Notice that the password that you type doesn't display on the screen as you type it. Instead, any password that you type is displayed as asterisks. The asterisks keep the bad guys from reading your password when they peer over your shoulder. But if the bad guys can't see your password, then neither can you. So how can you be sure that you didn't make a typo while you were entering the password? By typing it again. If you don't type the password exactly the same both times, Approach makes you start over again from the beginning.

7. **Write the password down!**

   If you forget it, you won't be able to access the database.

8. **Click OK.**

If you want to change the password later, all you have to do is open the database and type the password when prompted. Then repeat the preceding procedure, typing the new password in place of the old one.

Saluting the General Preferences

Back in the days of Approach 1.0, the preferences on the General tab were lowly Private Preferences. But they re-upped for version 2 and eventually decided to make a career of it. Now, in version 3.0, they've made it all the way to the rank of General. You'd better snap-to whenever you call up these preferences (see Figure 21-4).

This list enumerates what the General preferences do:

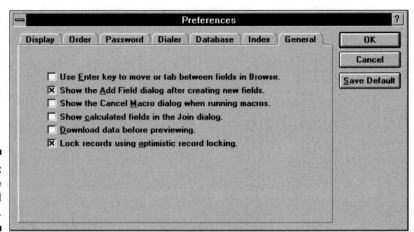

Figure 21-4:
Setting the
General
preferences.

Use Enter key to move or tab between fields in Browse: When this preference is checked, the Enter key works just like the Tab key. If you uncheck this preference, pressing the Enter key enters data that you've typed in a field but doesn't move the cursor to the next field on the view.

Show the Add Field dialog after creating new fields: With this preference checked, the Add Field dialog box is automatically displayed whenever you create a new database field.

Show the Cancel Macro dialog when running macros: If you want to be able to cancel a macro while it is running, check this preference.

Show calculated fields in the Join dialog: Check this option if you want to join databases based on a calculated field.

Download data before previewing: If this option is checked, database data that lives on a network drive is copied to the local drive when you enter Preview mood. Then, when you print the data, it appears exactly as it does in Preview.

Lock records using optimistic record locking: This preference enables several users to edit a record simultaneously, but only the first user can save changes. Subsequent attempts to save changes to the record cause the display of a warning indicating that data may be lost. This method is faster, but not quite as reliable, as pessimistic record locking, which prohibits users from editing a record that is being edited by another user.

Chapter 22
Conversion Experiences

● ●

In This Chapter

▶ Converting spreadsheet files
▶ Converting delimited text files
▶ Converting fixed-length text files
▶ Importing foreign data into an Approach database
▶ Exporting Approach data

● ●

*I*n the spirit of NAFTA, this chapter explains how to exchange data with files created by other programs. Sure, building a brick-walled protectionist fortress around your files and never even acknowledging the existence of other programs would be nice, but that strategy wouldn't be — as a former president would say — *prudent.* Other programs are here to stay, so you need to learn to get along with your neighbors.

Actually, Approach is a bit peculiar when it comes to working with data created by other programs. Most programs have their own unique, proprietary file formats that they and they alone can utilize. Recognizing the need for cooperation in the computer world, most programs also can convert data that's stored in other, similar file formats. For example, most word processing programs can open documents created by other word processing programs and automatically convert the file format as they open the documents.

Not so with Approach. Approach doesn't have it's own database file format. Instead, it utilizes the database file formats used by several popular competing database programs — most notably dBASE (III and IV), Paradox, and FoxPro. Approach can open these database files without the need for any kind of conversion processes whatsoever. So if you turned to this chapter for information about converting dBASE, Paradox, or FoxPro data to Approach, you can stop right now. You already know how to convert them: just open the file.

This chapter focuses on converting data into an Approach database when the data isn't already in a format that Approach can use. For example, perhaps you have a list of 100 names and addresses in a Lotus 1-2-3 spreadsheet, a

WordPerfect secondary mail-merge file, or a shareware database program called CheaperBase. This chapter explains how to deal with oddball files such as these.

Opening a Foreign File

Approach enables you to open files that are stored in various foreign formats. You can open Lotus 1-2-3 or Excel spreadsheet files to convert spreadsheet data to an Approach database. Or you can open one of two types of DOS text files: delimited files or fixed-length files. These special text file formats are often used to convert files created by word processors or other programs to Approach.

When you open a file that has a foreign format, Approach automatically converts the file to an Approach database, normally using dBASE as the database file format (you can tell Approach to use the Paradox or FoxPro formats instead of dBASE). Approach also creates default form and worksheet views for the converted database.

Opening a spreadsheet file

Approach enables you to open Lotus 1-2-3 or Microsoft Excel spreadsheet files, and it automatically converts them to database files. Each row is converted to a database record, and the spreadsheet columns represent database fields.

To convert a spreadsheet to a database, follow these steps:

1. **Call up the Open dialog box by choosing File⇨Open, clicking on the Open icon, or selecting Open an Existing File from the Welcome to Lotus Approach dialog box.**

2. **In the List files of type field, select Excel (*.XLS) or Lotus 1-2-3 (*.WK*) for the file type.**

3. **Click the spreadsheet file that you want to open.**

   You may have to rummage about the hard disk to find the file.

4. **Click OK.**

   The Field Names dialog box appears, as shown in Figure 22-1.

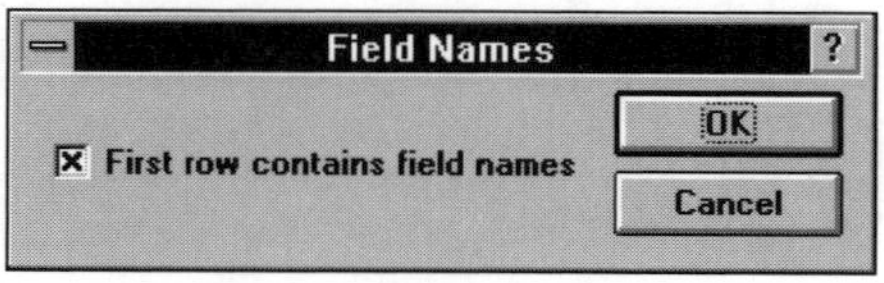

Figure 22-1:
The Field
Names
dialog box.

Field Names

[X] First row contains field names

OK

Cancel

5. **If the first row of the spreadsheet contains labels that can be used as field names, check the First row contains field names check box.**

   If the first row of the spreadsheet does not contain usable field names, uncheck this field. Approach then uses the column headings for the field names (A, B, C, and so on).

6. **Click OK.**

   The Convert To dialog box appears, as shown in Figure 22-2.

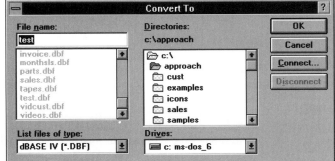

Figure 22-2:
The Convert
To dialog
box.

7. **Click OK to accept the name and file format for the new database.**

   If you want to use a different name or file type, change the fields accordingly before you click OK.

8. **You're done!**

   The spreadsheet is converted.

Opening a delimited text file

A *delimited text file* is a special type of DOS text file in which each database record appears on a separate line and database fields are separated from each other with a *delimiter,* which is nothing more than a computer geek term for a comma. Usually, fields are also contained within quotation marks.

Delimited text files are often used to convert data from another program, such as a word processing program or a database program that Approach doesn't recognize. Such programs don't routinely store their data in delimited text files, but they usually provide a command that you can use to convert their files to delimited text files. After you convert a file to a delimited text file, you can open the delimited file in Approach and convert it to an Approach database.

Here is an example of a delimited text file that contains but two records:

```
"Johnson","Mary","234 Oakdale","Tohoma","CA","93844"
"Henry","Patrick","345 3rd Street","Orangedale","CA","93748"
```

If you open this type of delimited text file in Approach, Approach assigns field names such as Field1, Field2, and so on, for each database field.

Some delimited text files contain field names in the first file record:

```
"Last Name","First Name","Address","City","State","Zip Code"
"Johnson","Mary","234 Oakdale","Tohoma","CA","93844"
"Henry","Patrick","345 3rd Street","Orangedale","CA","93748"
```

When you open this type of file, you can tell Approach that the first record contains field names. Approach then uses the field names contained in the file.

To convert data to Approach via a delimited text file, follow these steps:

1. Create a delimited text file that you can import into Approach.

You have to check the foreign program's documentation to find out how to create a delimited text file. Usually, you just use an Export command, but sometimes you have to use a separate conversion program to create the delimited text file.

Make sure that you use TXT for the file extension of the converted file. Otherwise, you won't be able to locate the file when you try to open it from Approach.

2. In Approach, call up the Open dialog box by choosing File⇨Open, clicking the Open icon, or selecting Open an Existing File from the Welcome to Lotus Approach dialog box.

3. In the List files of type field, select Text – Delimited (*.TXT) for the file type.

4. Click the text file that you want to open.

You may have to rummage about the hard disk to find the file.

5. Click OK.

The Text File Options dialog box, shown in Figure 22-3, appears.

6. Change the settings on the Text File Options dialog box if you must.

Most delimited text files use commas to separate the fields, but you can select Semicolons, Spaces, Tabs, or any Other character to use for the delimiter. If you select the Other option, be sure to type the character that you want to use for the delimiter in the box provided.

Figure 22-3:
The Text File
Options
dialog box.

You also can specify whether the file uses the standard Windows character-ter set or the DOS or OS/2 character set. (This option usually doesn't matter, so you can safely ignore it.)

Finally, you can tell Approach that the database contains field names by checking the First row contains field names check box.

7. Click OK.

When you click OK, the Convert To dialog box appears.

8. Click OK to accept the name and file format for the new database.

If you want to use a different name or file type, change the fields accordingly before you click OK.

9. You're done!

The spreadsheet is converted.

Opening a fixed-length text file

A *fixed-length text file* is a special type of DOS text file in which each field occupies a fixed number of character positions. For example, the first 20 characters of each record in a customer file may contain the customer's Last Name. The next 20 characters may contain the First Name, and so on.

Some foreign programs store their data files in fixed-length format, so you can convert them directly to Approach. Very few programs document the structure of their data files, though, so you have to examine the files yourself and count the number of character positions allotted to each field. This work is definitely the kind of task that you should bribe a computer guru to do for you. Offer the guru a six pack of Jolt Cola, a Twinkie, and a thick stack of napkins.

The procedure for opening a fixed-length text file is nearly the same as the procedure for opening delimited text files, with the following exceptions:

- When you call up the Open dialog box, specify Text – Fixed-Length (*.TXT) in the List files of type field.

- Instead of seeing the Text File Options dialog box, you see the Fixed Length Text File Setup dialog box shown in Figure 22-4. Use this dialog box to tell Approach the name, starting position, data type (text or numeric), and width of each field in the database. Or, better yet, offer your guru a jelly donut to do this task for you.

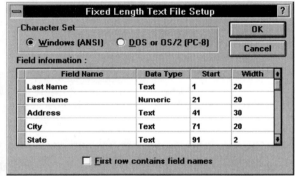

Figure 22-4:
The Fixed-
Length Text
File Setup
dialog box.

Field Name	Data Type	Start	Width
Last Name	Text	1	20
First Name	Numeric	21	20
Address	Text	41	30
City	Text	71	20
State	Text	91	2

Fixed Length Text File Setup

Character Set
● Windows (ANSI)   ○ DOS or OS/2 (PC-8)

Field information :

□ First row contains field names

OK   Cancel

Importing Foreign Data

When you *import* data into Approach, data is copied into an existing database. You can use the File⇨Import Data command to merge two Approach databases or to add records from a foreign database to an Approach database.

Here is the procedure:

1. **Open the database into which you want to import the data.**

   For example, if you have an existing customer database and you want to add records from a delimited text file into it, open the customer database.

2. **Choose File⇨Import Data.**

   The Import dialog box appears, which looks so much like the Open dialog box that I won't waste paper repeating it here. Thus, I'll sleep well tonight, knowing that I am doing my share to save the rain forest.

3. **In the List files of type list, select the type of file that you want to import, and then click the file that you want to import.**

   You may have to rummage about the hard disk to find the file.

4. **Click OK.**

   Depending on the file type you selected, you may see the Text File Options or Fixed Length Text File Setup dialog box. Do whatever it says.

5. **When the Import Setup dialog box appears, stare at it for a moment.**

   Figure 22-5 shows the Import Setup dialog box. It's a bit bewildering at first, until you figure out that it's simply asking you to match up fields in the file you're importing with fields in the Approach database. After a field on the left is matched up with a field on the right, the field on the left is grayed out. In Figure 22-5, the fields were automatically matched up because the fields in the input file use the same names as the fields in the Cust database.

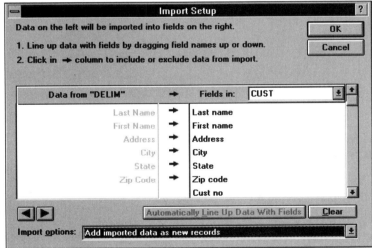

Figure 22-5:
The Import Setup dialog box.

6. **Line up fields from the data file with fields in the database.**

   If the fields aren't lined up correctly, drag the database fields up and down until they line up with the corresponding fields. Then click in the column between the field names to add an arrow indicating that a field should be included when data is imported. Notice that when you click the arrow to match up a field, the field name on the left is grayed out. (To exclude a field, click the arrow to make it go away.)

7. **Select an Import option.**

   You have three options to choose from:

   Add imported data as new records: Each record in the imported file is copied into the database as a new record.

   Use imported data to update existing records: Uses data in the import file to update existing records in the database. Any records in the import file that don't have corresponding records in the database are ignored.

   Use imported data to update & add to existing records: Uses data in the import file to update existing records in the database. Any records in the import file that don't have corresponding records in the database are added as new records.

   If you pick the second or third option, an additional column appears in the Fields portion of the Import Setup dialog box. In this column, click next to the fields that you want Approach to use to determine whether a record in the import file matches a record in the database. For example, in a customer database, you may click the Customer Number field or the Last Name and First Name fields.

8. **Click OK.**

   The data is imported.

You're done!

Exporting Approach Data

In Approach, you save database data in foreign formats by using the File➪Export Data command. Here's the procedure:

1. **Choose File➪Export Data.**

   The Export Dialog box appears, as shown in Figure 22-6.

2. **Choose the file format in the List files of type list.**

3. **Specify the database fields that you want to include in the export file by clicking each field and then clicking the Add button.**

4. **Select the All records option to export the entire database, or select the Found set only option to export only those records found by a Find command.**

5. **Type a filename in the File name text box.**

6. **Click OK.**

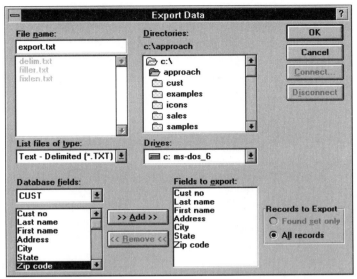

Figure 22-6:
The Export
dialog box.

7. **If you selected a text file type, the Text File Options or Fixed Length Text File Setup dialog box appears. Fill out its options and then click OK.**

8. **That's all!**

   You're done.

Part V
The Part of Tens

In this part ...

1f you keep this book in the bathroom, the chapters in this part are the ones that people will read most. Each of these chapters consists of ten (more or less, but who's counting?) things that are worth knowing about various aspects of using Approach. Without further ado, here they are, direct from the home office in sunny Fresno, California.

Chapter 23
Ten Database Commandments

In This Chapter

▶ Thou shalt carefully planneth the layout of thy data

▶ Thou shalt avoideth redundancy, repetition, and reiteration

▶ Thou shalt frequently saveth thy design changes

▶ Thou shalt not hoggeth a network database

▶ Thou shalt backeth up thy hard disk religiously

▶ Thou shalt storeth each file in its proper directory

▶ Thou shalt not abuseth Approach's design features

▶ Thou shalt not violateth thy Approach license

▶ Thou shalt not fondleth thy APPROACH.INI file or any other INI file

▶ Remember thy computer gurus, to keep them happy

> Fear not! For I bring you glad tidings of great joy.
> For behold, a program shall conceive and bear a new version,
> And the name of the program shall be Approach!
> And it shall be a database unto you.
> *— Relationals 1:1*

And so it came to pass that these Ten Database Commandments were handed down from generation to generation, to be worn as frontlets between the computer nerds eyes (where their glasses are taped). Obey these commandments, and all shall go well with you, with your children, and with your children's children.

I. Thou Shalt Carefully Planneth the Layout of Thy Data

The moment that you get the urge to fire up Approach and begin defining the fields for a new database, stop yourself. Take a deep breath, count to ten, and then go have an Eskimo Pie. When you've wiped the last bit of ice cream from your chin, pull out a pad of paper and begin sketching out what fields the database will contain. Think about whether everything should go into a single database file or whether you should create several files that can be joined. In short, plan ahead. Correcting a bad database design is much easier before you load 1,000 records into it.

II. Thou Shalt Avoideth Redundancy, Repetition, and Reiteration

If you were a computer guru with no outside life, you'd probably study the technique of relational database design known as *normalization*. But you're not, so keep the basic principle of normalization in the back of your mind as you design databases: try not to repeat yourself. For example, if you have two databases that require a customer's name and address, don't put the name and address fields in both databases. Instead, put the name and address fields in a separate database and join the other two databases to it. Then, if the customer moves, you have to update the address in only one place.

III. Thou Shalt Frequently Saveth Thy Design Changes

Remember that although Approach immediately saves database changes to the database files, design changes are stored in the Approach file and are not saved until you save them. Whenever you work in Design mood, press Ctrl+S every few minutes or click the Save icon to save your work. Saving files takes only a second, and you never know when an errant Scud may drop in your backyard.

IV. Thou Shalt Not Hoggeth a Network Database

Although it is possible to open a network database in such a way that other network users are prevented from accessing the database, doing so is not a good way to make friends.

V. Thou Shalt Backeth Up Thy Hard Disk Religiously

Prayer is a wonderful thing, but when you lose an important database file, nothing beats a good backup disk or tape.

VI. Thou Shalt Storeth Each File in Its Proper Directory

Whenever you create a database or Approach file, double-check the directory in which you're saving the file. Saving the file in the wrong directory is all too easy, and then you have to spend hours searching for the file later.

VII. Thou Shalt Not Abuseth Approach's Design Features

Yes, you can display every database field in a different font, use 92 colors on a single form, and fill every last pixel of empty space with pictures. If you want your forms to look like ransom notes, this is the way to do it. Otherwise, keep your forms simple.

VIII. Thou Shalt Not Violateth Thy Approach License

How would you like it if Inspector Clouseau barged into your office, looked over your shoulder as you ran Approach from a network server, and asked, "Do you have a liesaunce?"

"A *liesaunce?*" you reply, puzzled.

"Yes, of course, liesaunce. That is what I said. The law specifically prohibits the playing of a computer program on a network without a proper liesaunce."

You don't want Clouseau on your case, do you?

IX. Thou Shalt Not Fondleth Thy APPROACH.INI File or Any Other INI File

These files are off limits. If you break this commandment, you'd better keep the next one.

X. Remember Thy Computer Gurus, to Keep Them Happy

Throw them an occasional donut. Treat them like human beings, no matter how ridiculous that idea seems. You want them to be your friends.

Chapter 24
Ten Approach Shortcuts

*J*ust about anything that can be done in Approach can be done via the menus or SmartIcons. But a few shortcuts are worth knowing about.

Keyboard Shortcuts to Change Moods

To change Approach moods (well, *modes* to uptight computer nerds), remember the following keyboard shortcuts:

Mood	Keyboard Shortcut
Design	Ctrl+D
Browse	Ctrl+B
Preview	Ctrl+Shift+B
Find	Ctrl+F

Design Clicks

When you work in Design mood, keep the following mouse-click tricks in mind:

- ✔ Right-click any object in Design mood to bring up a quick menu that lists things that you can do to the object.
- ✔ Double-click any object in Design mood to bring up the InfoBox for the object.
- ✔ Shift-click objects to gang select them.

Ctrl+X, Ctrl+C, and Ctrl+V to Cut, Copy, and Paste

Just about all Windows programs respond to these keyboard shortcuts:

Shortcut	*Action*
Ctrl+X	Cut the selection to the Clipboard.
Ctrl+C	Copy the selection to the Clipboard.
Ctrl+V	Insert the contents of the Clipboard.

Note: Before you use Ctrl+X or Ctrl+C, select the object that you want to cut or copy.

Ctrl+Z: the Steve Urkel Key

Oops! Did I do that? Press Ctrl+Z, and maybe it will go away.

Note: This trick works mainly in Design mood; you can't undo most changes in Browse mood.

Helpful Design Shortcuts

Here are some valuable keyboard shortcuts to use when you are working in Design mood:

Shortcut	Action
Ctrl+E	Call up the InfoBox.
Ctrl+L	Reveal the floating Tools palette.
Ctrl+M	Fast format.
Ctrl+J	Show the ruler.
Ctrl+Y	Snap to the grid.
Ctrl+G	Group.
Ctrl+U	Ungroup.
Ctrl+I	Align.

Useful Browse Mood Shortcuts

These keyboard shortcuts work when you are working in Browse mood:

Shortcut	Action
Ctrl+Home	Go to the first record.
Ctrl+End	Go to the last record.
Ctrl+W	Go to a specific record.
Ctrl+N	Create a new record.
Ctrl+H	Hide the record.
Ctrl+Delete	Delete the record.
Ctrl+P	Print the current view.

Shortcuts to Other Programs

These shortcuts aren't only Approach shortcuts; you can use them with any Windows programs. To switch to another program, use one of these combinations:

Shortcut	*Action*
Alt+Esc	Switch to the next program in line.
Alt+Tab	Display the name of the next program in line. While holding down the Alt key, keep pressing Tab until the name of the program to which you want to switch appears. Release both keys to switch to that program.
Ctrl+Esc	See a list of all active programs. Double-click the one to which you want to switch.

F1: the Panic Button

Stuck? Press F1 to activate Approach's Help. With luck, you can find enough information to get going again. The help is *context sensitive,* which means that it tries to figure out what you were doing when you pressed F1 and give you specific help for that task.

Chapter 25
Ten Things That Often Go Wrong

● ●

In This Chapter

▶ You lose your file

▶ You run out of memory

▶ You run out of disk space

▶ You can't find Approach

▶ You can't find a record

▶ You accidentally delete a file

▶ You accidentally delete a record

▶ Your printer can't handle it

▶ Your car blows up

● ●

*P*robably more like 10,000 things can go wrong, but this chapter describes some of the things that go wrong most often.

I Can't Find My File!

You spent hours polishing the most beautiful forms ever seen, and now you can't find the file. You know that you saved it, but it's not there! The problem is probably one of two things: either you saved the file in a directory other than the one you think you saved it in, or you used a different name to save it than you intended.

The solution? Start looking. Look in other directories besides the one you think you stored the file in. Look for filenames that are similar to the one you intended to use.

If you're adventurous, pop over to File Manager and activate the File⇨Search command. It can help you search for missing files. For help with File Manager, refer to Appendix B.

I've Run Out of Memory!

Many computers that have only 4MB of internal memory are running Windows these days. Although 4MB may be enough to load Windows and Approach, before long you see messages about running short on memory. Instead of purchasing more computer memory (which isn't a bad idea if you have only 4MB), avoid running more than one Windows program at a time. Also, try removing fonts that you don't need. The more fonts you have installed on the computer, the less memory you have free for other programs. (To remove fonts, fire up the Control Panel and click the Fonts icon. Choose the fonts you don't need and then click the Remove button.)

I've Run Out of Disk Space!

Nothing is more frustrating than running out of disk space when you are trying to save a file. What to do? Press Alt+Tab to move over to Program Manager and then launch File Manager and rummage through the hard disk, looking for files that you don't need. Delete enough files to free up a few megabytes and then press Alt+Tab to move back to Approach and save the file.

If the hard disk is full and you can't find more than a few files to delete, you may consider activating the DOS 6 disk-doubling program, DoubleSpace, or the DOS 6.22 equivalent, DriveSpace. Check out *More DOS For Dummies* by Dan Gookin (IDG Books Worldwide — who else?) for information about using DoubleSpace and DriveSpace.

Approach Has Vanished!

You're working at your computer, minding your own business, when all of a sudden — Whoosh! — Approach disappears. What happened? Most likely, you clicked some area outside of the Approach window or you pressed Alt+Esc or Alt+Tab, which whisks you away to another program. To get Approach back, press Ctrl+Esc. A list of all the active programs pops up; double-click Approach to return to Approach.

Note: Approach also can vanish into thin air if you use a screen saver program. Try jiggling the mouse to see whether Approach reappears.

I Can't Find a Record!

Before you panic, try clicking the Show All icon. The record may have been temporarily hidden from view by Find.

I Accidentally Deleted a File!

Just learned how to delete files and couldn't stop yourself, eh? Relax. It happens to the best of us. Odds are that you can get that deleted file back if you act quickly. Conjure up File Manager and use the File⇨Undelete command, or launch the Undelete program from the Microsoft Tools group. They can help you get your file back. (Undelete is available only if you have DOS 6 or a later version.) Refer to Appendix B for help on using File Manager.

I Accidentally Deleted a Record!

Funny thing, you can get a whole file back if you accidentally delete it, but if you accidentally delete the wrong record, you're out of luck. It's very aggravating to accidentally delete a record and then call up the Edit menu only to notice that the Undo command is grayed out, unavailable for use. You can't undo a delete. The best you can do is retype the record's fields, or fall back to a backup copy of the database.

If you accidentally delete a whole bunch of records, such as a found set or an entire database, the best thing to do is revert to a backup. This is the reason why backing up your files every day is important.

My Printer Won't Print!

What a bother. Your printer may not print for all sorts of reasons. Here are a few things to check:

 ✔ Make sure that the printer's power cord is plugged in and that the printer is turned on.

- ✔ The printer cable must be connected to both the printer and the computer's printer port. If the cable has come loose, turn off both the computer and the printer, reattach the cable, and then restart the computer and the printer. (You know better, of course, than to turn off the computer without first saving any work in progress, exiting from any active application programs, and shutting down Windows. So I won't say anything about it. Not even a little parenthetical reminder at the end of this paragraph.)

- ✔ If your printer has a switch labeled On-line or Select, press it until the corresponding light comes on.

- ✔ Make sure that the printer has plenty of paper.

- ✔ If you're using a dot-matrix printer, make sure that the ribbon is okay. For a laser printer, make sure that the toner cartridge has plenty of life left.

- ✔ Summon the File⇨Print Setup command and make sure that you've selected the correct printer.

- ✔ If you're printing on a network printer, holler at the network administrator until he or she fixes the problem.

My Car Blew Up!

Sorry, I can't help you with this one. You should have changed the oil more often and maybe checked the coolant level.

Chapter 26

Ten New Features of Approach 3.0

● ●

In This Chapter

▶ Improved appearances

▶ New features

▶ Better help

▶ Easier to use macros

● ●

*I*f you're an experienced Approach 2.1 user who is just upgrading to Approach 3.0, you probably turned to this chapter first. It lists the most important new features of Approach 3.0.

Consistency with SmartSuite Applications

If you already know how to do something in Lotus 1-2-3, Ami Pro, or Freelance Graphics, try it in Approach. Chances are better than even that it will work. Wherever possible, Approach has borrowed the techniques used in the other SmartSuite programs.

Notetabs

Throughout Approach, you see dialog boxes and windows that have notebook-style tab dividers at the top (and occasionally at the bottom). These tabs enable Approach programmers to cram more controls into a single dialog box than would otherwise be possible. For example, Figure 26-1 shows the Preferences dialog box, which you can see by choosing Tools⇨Preferences. Notice how the top of the dialog box consists of a row of notebook tabs. You can click on any of these tabs to bring forth a different set of dialog box controls.

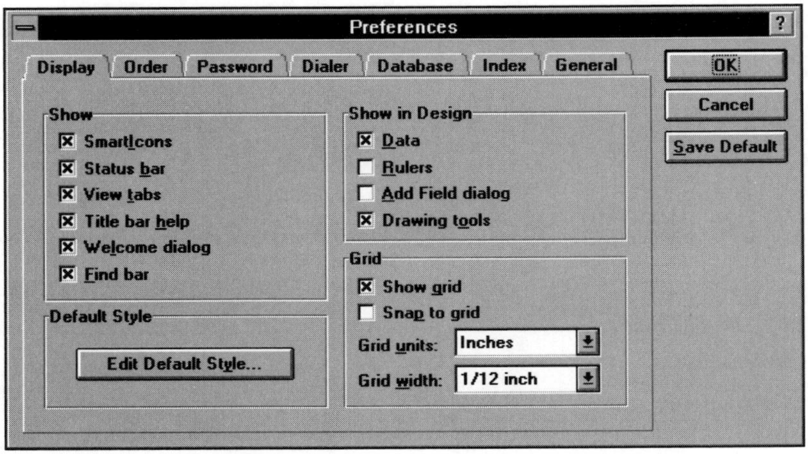

Figure 26-1:
Approach's
new
notebook-
style
interface.

Assistants

Approach comes with several built-in Assistants, which are specially designed dialog boxes that step you through complex procedures. For example, Figure 26-2 shows the Report Assistant, which walks you through the steps necessary to create reports. The Assistants use a separate notebook tab for each step, so you can backtrack, if necessary.

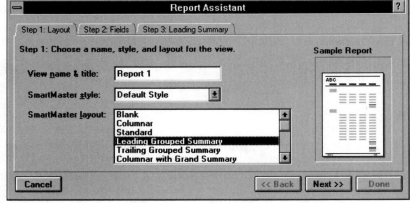

Figure 26-2:
Approach's
new
Assistants
help you
with
complex
procedures.

The InfoBox

The InfoBox is a single, consolidated control center for formatting design objects. By calling up the InfoBox for an object, you can set the object's text style, font, line width, color, background color, border style, and who knows what else. See Figure 26-3.

Figure 26-3:
Approach's new InfoBox provides a single point of control for all aspects of a design object's format.

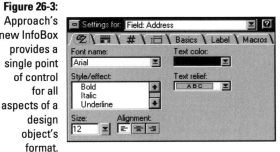

Templates

Approach now comes with 52 predesigned database templates for common business and home applications, plus sample applications. Why reinvent the wheel when Approach comes with everything from wagon wheels to snow tires?

On-Line Tutorials

You can now turn to an on-line tutorial to learn how to use the basic features of Approach. Getting the computer to teach you how to use the computer can be a satisfying form of revenge.

Improved Macros

Macros are greatly improved in Approach 3.0. Lotus has added 27 new macro commands and a thoroughly revamped macro facility that makes creating macros easier than ever. You can attach a macro to a view, to a button, or to a database field. And best of all, you don't have to learn a complicated programming language to create sophisticated macros, as you do in another database program that shall remain nameless (but you spell it *A-c-c-e-s-s*).

Fast Format

The Fast Format command is one of my favorite new features in Approach. It enables you to spend all of your effort getting one design object (a field, button, geometric shape, or whatever) to look precisely the way you want it to look. When you finally get it just right, you can call up the Fast Format command to suck up the object's format and then spit it out on other objects to make them look the same instantly. It's a real time-saver.

SmartMasters

If you've become bored with Approach 2.1's plain-looking forms and reports, you'll love the new SmartMasters. SmartMasters control the basic layout and appearance of forms, reports, and other views. For example, when you create a new form, you can select one of three different SmartMaster layouts (Blank, Columnar, and Standard) and any of 13 different SmartMaster styles (such as the two 3-D look styles and two Chisel styles). Another big time-saver.

Chapter 27

Ten Topics to Discuss
When Your Host Is Verklempt

*O*h dear, I'm starting to get verklempt. I've got gespilkus in my connectizoid. Talk among yourselves. Here are some topics:

The Relational Database Model Is neither Relational nor a Model. Discuss.

What's all this nonsense about the relational database model? If relational databases are so good at relationships, how come Lotus and Microsoft are always fighting about whose database program is the best?

And then they want us to think it's a model. If it's a model, where are all the little plastic parts? Where's the little tube of glue and all those little bottles of paint, especially Battleship Gray, Flat Black, and my personal favorite, Olive Drab?

Actually, the assertion that the relational database model is not really relational, at least not in the sense that most people think, has some truth to it. Most people believe that the term *relational* means that relational databases enable you to define the relationships between database files. The term really comes from the mathematical set theory on which relational databases are based. Fortunately, only people with slide rules in their pocket protectors need care about such things.

The Normalization Process Is neither Normal nor a Process. Discuss.

Normalization is the process of transforming okay database designs into really great database designs. The basic idea is to eliminate information that is repeated within database records or in several databases. For example, when you first design an Invoice database, you may be tempted to include the customer's name and address, because the name and address are printed on the invoices. However, you'll quickly discover that other databases need the customer's name and address, too. The solution is to place the customer's name and address in a separate Customer database and then include only the Customer Number field in the Invoice database and in other databases that need this name and address information.

Another goal of normalization is eliminating dependencies between database fields. As an example, suppose that you included a Sales Tax Rate field in the Invoice database. But wait — doesn't the sales tax depend on what state the customer lives in? Technically, you've created a dependency between the Sales Tax Rate field in the Invoice database and the State field in the Customer database. To normalize this database design, you should create yet another database with a name such as TaxRates, containing two fields: State and Sales Tax Rate. You can then join the Invoice database to the Customer database by using Customer Number and join the Customer database to the TaxRates database by using the State field. What a bother.

The founders of relational database theory specified something like 98 degrees of normality, known as the *normal forms.* Now, if you want to spend an extra two weeks normalizing all your databases, you just may arrive at the Fourth Normal Form, the Nirvana of the Relational Database religion. Truth is, though, the only normal person who really cares is someone who's designing the nationwide database for American Express or something. So nothing is *normal* about it.

To be honest, I've studied this normalization stuff, and believe me, there is no step-by-step procedure that works every time. It's an art, not a scientific process. Even if you decide to study it (which isn't normal, remember), you'll discover that many tradeoffs are involved in normalizing a database. For example, moving the Sales Tax Rate field to a separate database will probably slow Approach down by forcing it to read the TaxRates database every time it retrieves an Invoice record. Because of such performance hits, database junkies sometimes knowingly create Abby Normal designs that are more efficient than completely normalized designs.

SmartIcons Are neither Smart nor Icons. Discuss.

If they were smart, you could tell them to sit, and they'd drop to the bottom of the screen. Tell them to heel, and they'd follow the mouse around the screen. Tell them to roll over, and they'd flip upside down. But all they do is sit there asleep half the time.

And they're not really *icons,* they're *buttons.* Everybody else except Lotus calls them *buttons.*

Structured Query Language Is neither a Language nor Is It Just for Queries. Discuss.

When database jockeys invented SQL, it was supposed to be a friendly, English-like language that nonprogrammers could quickly learn. Sure. Consider this example of an SQL query:

```
select fname,lname from cust temptbl where not exists
(select * from invoice where invoice.custno = temptbl.custno)
```

This "simple and easy to understand" query finds all customers who don't have any invoice records.

If SQL is a language, it's not like any language I've ever spoken.

Oh, and it's not just a query language, either. You can use SQL to insert and delete database records and even to define new databases. Here's an example of an SQL statement that has nothing to do with a query:

```
create table mktg.cust
  (custno char(6)   not null,
    fname  char(20)  not null,
    lname  char(20)  not null,
    addr   char(30)  not null,
    city   char(20)  not null,
    state  char(2)   not null,
    zip    char(10)  not null)
in database acct
```

The preceding statement is the SQL equivalent of Approach's Field Definition dialog box.

Aren't you glad Approach doesn't make you use SQL?

(By the way, there is a raging debate about how to pronounce *SQL*. Some say it should be spelled out, as in *Es Que El*. Others say it should be pronounced *sequel*. Relational database zealots argue about these deep issues late at night at their local espresso shops.)

E. F. Codd and C. J. Date Are neither Fish nor Are They Nuts. Discuss.

E. F. Codd and C. J. Date are the fellows you can either thank or blame for the current state of affairs where database programs are concerned. They are the fathers of the relational database model. Back in the 1970s, when most of us were watching "Three's Company" and trying on leisure suits, these guys were hammering out the details of the relational database model. Three cheers!

There is an unwritten rule that says if you make a contribution to computer technology as important as these guys have, you can't have a real name, just initials. No one knows their real names, just as no one knows the real name of B. J. from *M*A*S*H*.

Sincerely,

D. A. Lowe

Chapter 28

Ten Types of Form Fields

In This Chapter

▶ Adding field boxes

▶ Using drop-down lists and field box and list fields

▶ Presenting fields as check boxes

▶ Showing fields as radio buttons

*H*ere are ten (well, four actually, but who's counting?) different ways that you can display database fields on your forms. For more information about creating forms, see Chapter 9.

Field Boxes

When you use the Form Assistant to create a form, database fields are added to the form as field boxes such as the one shown in Figure 28-1.

Figure 28-1:
A field
displayed as
a field box.

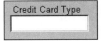

Field boxes are the best way to display most types of database fields, such as name and address fields and numeric fields. They enable the user to type any value into the field. If you want to limit the values that the user can enter into a field, you should consider using one of the other methods of displaying form fields.

Drop-Down Lists, and Field Box and List Fields

Approach has two types of view fields that enable the user to pick values from a predefined list of values: drop-down list fields, and field box and list fields. If you use a drop-down list, the user can't type data into the field. Instead, the user picks one of several values from a list that drops down when the user clicks the drop-down arrow that appears in the field. Figure 28-2 shows an example of a drop-down list field, both before and after the user clicks the drop-down arrow.

Figure 28-2:
A field displayed as a drop-down list.

A field box and list field is the same as a drop-down list field, except that the user can type a value into the field if all of the values in the list are appropriate.

To display a field as a drop-down list or a field-box and list field, follow this procedure:

1. **In Design Mood, double-click the field that you want to make a drop-down list.**

   Its InfoBox appears.

2. **Select Drop-down list or Field box list for the Data entry type field.**

   The difference is that a drop-down list forces the user to pick one of the values in the list, whereas a field box list enables the user to pick one of the list values or type a value in the field.

   Whichever you choose, the Drop-Down List dialog box pops up, as shown in Figure 28-3.

3. **Type the allowable values in the List boxes.**

   In Figure 28-3, I typed three values: **VISA**, **Master Card**, and **Am Ex.**

   You can insert or remove items from the middle of the list by clicking the Insert or Delete buttons.

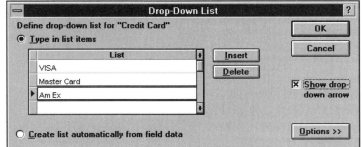

4. **Check the S̲how drop-down arrow check box to ensure that the drop-down arrow is displayed on the form.**

5. **Click OK.**

You're done! The field is displayed as a drop-down list. Here are a couple of bonus points to consider:

✔ When the C̲reate list automatically from field data button is selected, Approach scans the contents of the field in all records in the database and creates a list of all the unique values. This option is useful if the database already contains records.

✔ If you click the O̲ptions button, you see a bunch of extra options for creating the list from field data. You can use these options to create the list from a different database field (or even a field in a different database) or to create a filter so that only certain records are used to create the list.

Check Boxes

Check boxes are another way to enable the user to select one of several preset values. Having a small number of values to choose from (three or four at most) is best.

Figure 28-4 shows an example of a database field presented in check box format. As you can see, each possible value is assigned a separate check box.

To show a field as check boxes, follow these steps:

1. **In Design Mood, double-click the field that you want to show as check boxes.**

   Its InfoBox appears.

2. **Select Checkboxes for the Data entry type field.**

   The Define Checkbox dialog box pops up, as shown in Figure 28-5.

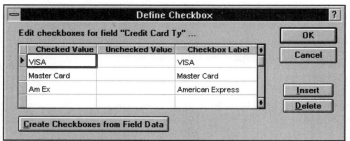

Figure 28-5:
The Define
Checkbox
dialog box.

3. **For each check box that you want to display for the field, type the value to be entered into the field if the user checks the box in the Checked Value column; type the value to be entered if the user unchecks the box in the Unchecked value column; and type the label for the check box in the Checkbox label column.**

   In Figure 28-5, I created three check boxes for VISA, Master Card, and Am Ex. For each check box, I left the Unchecked Value cell blank: if the user unchecks a check box, the field will be set to blanks.

   You can insert or remove items from the middle of the list of check boxes by clicking the Insert or Delete buttons.

4. **Click OK.**

That's all there is. Here are some points to keep in mind:

✔ A database field can have only one value at a time. As a result, only one of the check boxes for a field can be selected at a time. When the user clicks a check box, any other selected check box is automatically unchecked.

✔ For a boolean database field, use a single check box and set the Checked Value to Yes and the Unchecked Value to No.

✔ When the Create Check boxes from Field Data button is selected, Approach scans the contents of the field in all records in the database and creates check boxes for each unique value.

Radio Buttons

Radio buttons are similar to check boxes except for an important difference: You can click a check box to uncheck it, so that none of the check boxes is selected, but one of the radio buttons is always selected.

Figure 28-6 shows an example of a database field displayed as radio buttons. Notice that I added an option for None — just in case the customer pays in cash or by check, as people still do on occasion.

Figure 28-6:
A field
displayed as
radio
buttons.

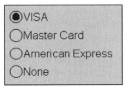

To show a database field as radio buttons, follow these steps:

1. **In Design Mood, double-click the field that you want to show as radio buttons.**

   Its InfoBox appears.

2. **Select Radio buttons for the Data entry type field.**

   The Define Radio Buttons dialog box pops up, as shown in Figure 28-7.

Figure 28-7:
The Define
Radio
Buttons
dialog box.

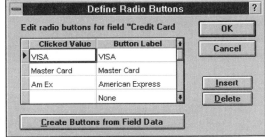

3. **For each radio button that you want to display for the field, type the value to be entered into the field if the user clicks the button in the Clicked Value column and the label for the button in the Button Label column.**

In Figure 28-7, I created four radio buttons for VISA, Master Card, American Express, and None.

You can insert or remove items from the middle of the list of buttons by clicking the Insert or Delete buttons.

4. Click OK.

You're done. Keep these points in mind:

✔ For a boolean database field, use two radio buttons, one that assigns the value Yes, the other that assigns the value No.

✔ You can check the Create Buttons from Field Data button to cause Approach to scan the contents of the field in all records in the database and create radio buttons for each unique value.

Part VI
Appendixes

The 5th Wave   **By Rich Tennant**

After spending hours trying to get the system up and running, Carl discovers that everything had been plugged into a "Clapper" light socket when he tries to kill a mosquito.

In this part ...

These appendixes contain some handy information that can help you impress your local computer guru or help you figure out some things for yourself when your guru isn't around. One appendix explains how to install Approach; another one helps you make your way through the Windows File Manager. The Glossary is here so you can look up the words your guru throws at you — or figure out what to call that thing that isn't working. (Just be careful that you don't start talking to your guru about Approach's moods and love handles. Most gurus are such propellerheads that they won't know what you're talking about.)

Appendix A
Installing Lotus Approach

● ●

*T*hroughout this book, I assumed that Approach already lives on your computer. If you're not so lucky, this appendix guides you through the tedious process known as *installation,* a form of torture devised by sadistic programmers way back in the earliest days of programming history.

If you're faced with the prospect of installing Approach on a computer, you have two choices:

 ✔ Do it yourself.

 ✔ Bribe your friendly neighborhood computer guru to do it for you.

A one-pound bag of M&Ms and a six-pack of Jolt Cola are usually sufficient to persuade a computer guru to do the installation job for you. You can probably pull it off yourself, though. It's tedious but not overly complicated.

System Requirements

To run Approach, you need four things:

 ✔ A computer that runs Windows 3.1

 ✔ About 23MB (megabytes) of hard disk space

 ✔ At least 4MB (megabytes) of RAM (but you'll be a happier Approach camper if you have 6MB or more)

 ✔ A mouse, track ball or other pointing device (your index finger alone isn't sufficient)

Yes, I said 23MB of disk space. Approach consumes that much disk space if you install all of its options. (If you're tight on disk space, you can instruct Approach to leave out some of its lesser-used features so that it can fit in as little as 10MB of disk space.)

Installing Approach

To install Approach, follow these steps:

1. **Cancel all appointments.**

   Actually installing Approach takes only about 20 minutes — but you'll want to play with your new toy, too. Set aside the better part of an afternoon to indulge yourself.

2. **Find the Approach installation disks.**

   I assume that you have your own copy of the disks. If you are "borrowing" someone else's copy of Approach, shame on you! That's stealing, it's against the law, and it just isn't nice. Put this book down right now and march straight over to your neighborhood computer shop to buy your own copy of Approach.

3. **Start your computer and Windows.**

   If your computer doesn't automatically launch right into Windows, type **WIN** at the DOS command prompt.

4. **Find the Program Manager.**

   It's probably right there on top, but if you can't see it, press Ctrl+Esc (hold down Ctrl and press Esc once) to pop up the Task List. Look through the list until you find Program Manager and then double-click it.

5. **Stick the Approach disk 1 in the disk drive.**

   If you have just one floppy drive, it's called drive A. If you have two floppy drives, one atop the other, usually the one on top is drive A, and the one on the bottom is drive B. If you have two floppy drives side by side, usually the one on the left is drive A and the one on the right is drive B.

6. **Choose File⇨Run.**

   This step calls forth the Run dialog box, in which you can run a command. The command that you want to run is INSTALL, on either drive A or drive B, depending on which drive you inserted the disk into. For drive A, type the following line in the Command Line field:

   ```
   A:INSTALL
   ```

   For drive B, type this line:

   ```
   B:INSTALL
   ```

   No spaces and no period at the end. Just press A or B, type a colon, and type **INSTALL.** Figure A-1 shows the Run dialog box with the correct command for drive B.

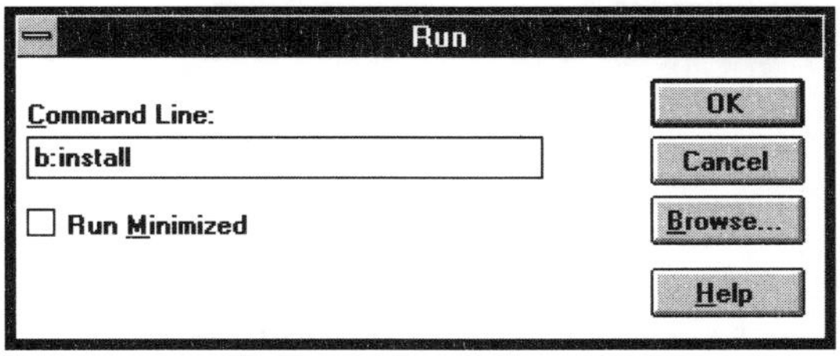

Figure A-1:
The Run
dialog box.

7. Press the Enter key.

You hear the floppy drive churn back and forth for an unbearably long
time. Finally, just when you're about to give up, the Approach Installation
dialog box appears, as shown in Figure A-2. From this point on, just follow
the instructions on the screen.

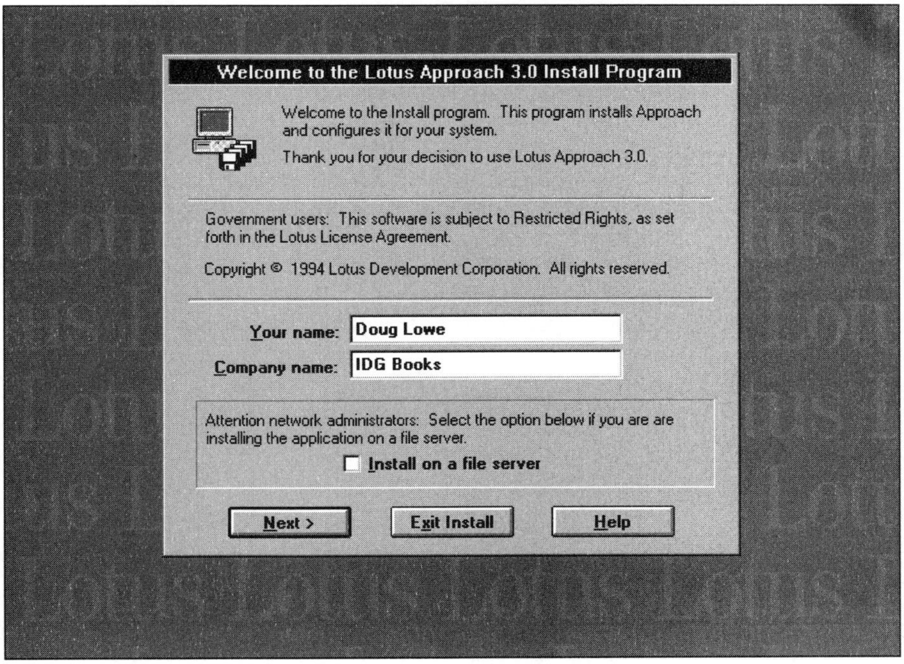

Figure A-2:
The
Installation
dialog box.
Welcome to
Approach
Installation!

These pointers can help you get through the day:

- ✔ Read and follow all on-screen instructions carefully.

- ✔ Type your name and company name carefully and double-check them.

- ✔ When the program asks you to choose which type of installation to perform, pick All features. This selection installs everything, including the Ginsu knives, cheese shredder, and optional rotisserie attachment. It requires about 23MB of disk space. If you don't have that much disk space, opt for the Minimum features installation or pick the Customize features option and then select which components of Approach to leave out.

- ✔ Install asks you for the drive and directory in which to install the Approach program files. You can change the drive if you have more than one hard disk on the computer, but you best leave the directory at the default (\approach).

- ✔ When Approach asks which Program Manager group to use, choose the default setting (Lotus Applications).

- ✔ When Install says to swap disks, take the old disk out of the drive and place it face down on top of the discard pile. Then draw a new disk from the top of the kitty, insert it into the drive, and press Enter. Remember that you cannot lead a point card until hearts have been broken.

- ✔ Watch the pretty display as Approach installs.

- ✔ Now is a good time to fill out the registration card.

- ✔ When you're done, don't forget to remove the last disk from the floppy drive. Gather up your spent installation disks and store them someplace safe. You never know when you may need them again.

Appendix B
Surviving File Manager

● ●

*F*ile Manager is what separates normal people from computer nerds. Computer nerds love File Manager. They think it's cool, and there's nothing they'd rather do than point and click their way through dense tree-structured directories, electronic machete in hand. Hack! Hack!

Normal people like you and me dread File Manager. We turn to it only when we must, and then with resentment and spite. The bad news is that we need File Manager all too often. We need it to do routine file management chores such as copying files, creating directories, renaming and deleting files, and formatting floppy disks. You can't do most of these chores from within the familiar confines of Approach, so you're forced to venture into the world of File Manager. Harumph!

This appendix covers File Manager with a Special Forces mentality. It shows you how to get in, get the job done, and get out quickly.

Note: File Manager is not a part of Approach, but it's available on every Windows system because it's a part of Windows.

Starting File Manager

Follow this procedure to fire up File Manager:

1. Switch to Program Manager.

Press Alt-Tab repeatedly until Program Manager appears or press Ctrl-Esc and double-click Program Manager in the task list.

File Manager

2. Find the File Manager icon.

If the File Manager icon is not on the screen, look for a Program Manager group icon named Main and double-click it. File Manager usually hangs out in this Main group.

3. Double-click the File Manager icon.

File Manager springs to life. Hide your children. Don't let them look at Figure B-1.

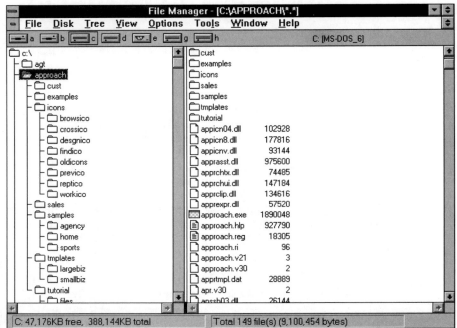

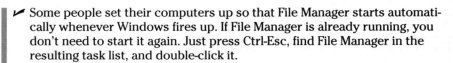

Figure B-1:
The File
Manager.

✔ Some people set their computers up so that File Manager starts automatically whenever Windows fires up. If File Manager is already running, you don't need to start it again. Just press Ctrl-Esc, find File Manager in the resulting task list, and double-click it.

✔ When File Manager fires itself up, it may not take over the entire screen. If it doesn't, the first thing to do is click the maximize button in the upper-right corner of the File Manager window.

Finding Files and Directories

The most basic File Manager chore is rifling through the directories on your disks to find and select files. Here is a summary of how to do the most important file-finding tasks:

Looking at a different drive: To change File Manager's display to a different drive, click that drive's icon.

Peering into a specific directory: To display the files that reside in a particular directory, click that directory's folder icon.

Finding directories that aren't shown: You can expand the directory tree so that all directories are shown by choosing Tree➪Expand All. Depending on how many directories you have, you also may have to scroll the directory tree to find a directory.

Selecting files: To select a file, click it. To select several files, hold down the Ctrl key while you click the files. To select a block of files, click the first file that you want to select and then hold down the Shift key and click the last file in the block. The two files that you clicked, plus all the files in between, will be selected.

Selecting all the files in a directory: Choose File➪Select Files, to pop up the dialog box shown in Figure B-2. Click the Select button and then click Close. (After you click Select, the Cancel button that you see in Figure B-2 changes to a Close button.)

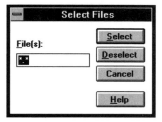

Figure B-2:
The Select
Files dialog
box.

✔ Avoid the natural urge to double-click the drive icons, which opens up a separate window for the drive. Keep double-clicking them, and pretty soon you'll have dozens of little drive windows cluttering up the screen. Although these little drive windows have a purpose, only advanced File Manager junkies know how to use them.

✔ If you double-click an Approach file, File Manager launches Approach and opens the file.

✔ After you select a file, you can unselect it by clicking it again.

Doing Stuff to Files

File Manager comes fully equipped with all of the file management features you need. You can use it to copy or move files, change a file's name, and delete files. Table B-1 lists the menu commands and keyboard shortcuts that you use to perform these routine file-handling chores.

Table B-1	Routine File Handling Chores	
File Handling Chore	*Menu Command*	*Keyboard Shortcut*
Copy a file or files	File⇨Copy	F8
Move a file or files	File⇨Move	F7
Delete a file or files	File⇨Delete	Delete
Undelete deleted files	File⇨Undelete	(none)
Rename a file	File⇨Rename	(none)
Create a directory	File⇨Create Directory	(none)

Copying and moving files

Copying a file means making a duplicate of it in another directory (perhaps on another drive) or in the same directory but with a different name. *Moving* a file is similar, except that, after the duplicate is made, the original file is deleted.

To copy or move files, follow these steps:

1. **Select the file or files that you want to copy or move.**

2. **Drag the files to the directory to which you want them copied or moved.**

    The hard part is knowing whether to hold down the Ctrl key or the Shift key while you drag the files. Four possibilities exist:

    Copying a file to a different directory on the same drive: Hold down the Ctrl key while you drag the files to the new directory.

    Moving a file to a different directory on the same drive: Don't hold down any key. Just drag the files to the new directory.

    Copying a file to a different drive: Don't hold down any key. Just drag the files to one of the drive icons.

    Moving a file to a different drive: Hold down the Shift key while you drag the files to one of the drive icons.

3. **If File Manager confronts you with an annoying question about whether you really want to copy the files, answer Yes — unless you were just kidding.**

4. **If File Manager confronts you with a scary question about overwriting an existing file, think about it before you click Yes.**

- ✔ Confused about when to hold down the Ctrl or Alt keys? So am I. The guy who made up these rules is now selling hot dogs at the King Dome.

- ✔ You also can copy and move files by choosing File⇨Copy or File⇨Move. This method spares you the mental anguish of remembering whether to use the Ctrl or Shift keys, but it replaces one form of punishment with another: you have to remember how to type a DOS path. See Figure B-3. You just can't win the File Manager game.

- ✔ If you want to make a duplicate of a file in the same directory but use a different name, choose File⇨Copy and type the new filename when the Copy dialog box appears.

Figure B-3:
The Copy
dialog box.

```
┌─────────────────────────────────────────────────┐
│ ▭                      Copy                        │
├─────────────────────────────────────────────────┤
│ Current Directory: C:\APPROACH\SALES    ┌────────┐│
│ From:    ┌──────────────────────────┐   │   OK   ││
│          │ CUST.DBF                 │   └────────┘│
│ To:   ◉  ┌──────────────────────────┐   ┌────────┐│
│          │                          │   │ Cancel ││
│          └──────────────────────────┘   └────────┘│
│       ○ Copy to Clipboard               ┌────────┐│
│                                         │  Help  ││
│                                         └────────┘│
└─────────────────────────────────────────────────┘
```

Renaming files

To change the name of a file, follow these steps:

1. **Select the file that you want to rename.**

2. **Choose File⇨Rename.**

3. **Type the new name for the file.**

4. **Click OK.**

That's all there is to it.

- ✔ If you attempt to change a file's name to the name of some other file, File Manager will complain bitterly. Don't be offended. File Manager is just trying to keep you out of trouble.

- ✔ You can rename more than one file at a time, but only if you're a whiz with wild cards. If you're a mere mortal, rename files one at a time.

Deleting files

Deleting files is the only thing that's easy to do with File Manager. Follow this simple, two-step procedure:

1. **Select the file or files that you want to delete.**

   See how easy this is?

2. **Press the Delete key.**

   I told you this was easy.

- ✔ File Manager may ask whether you're sure you know what you're doing. Feel your forehead and click Yes if it's not too hot.
- ✔ To delete a whole directory, click the directory folder icon and press Delete.
- ✔ If you like to do things the hard way, you can delete files by using the File➪Delete command.

- ✔ If you delete a file by mistake, quickly run the File➪Undelete command to get the file back. But don't delay. Every time you save another file to disk, you reduce the odds of getting your file back by undeleting it. (The Undelete command is available only if you're using DOS 6.0 or later.)

Creating a new directory

To create a new directory, follow this procedure:

1. **Click the directory in which you want the new directory to live.**

2. **Choose File➪Create Directory.**

   The Create Directory dialog box appears as shown in Figure B-4.

3. **Type the name of the directory that you want to create.**

   In the example in Figure B-4, I typed **junk**.

4. **Click OK.**

   You're done.

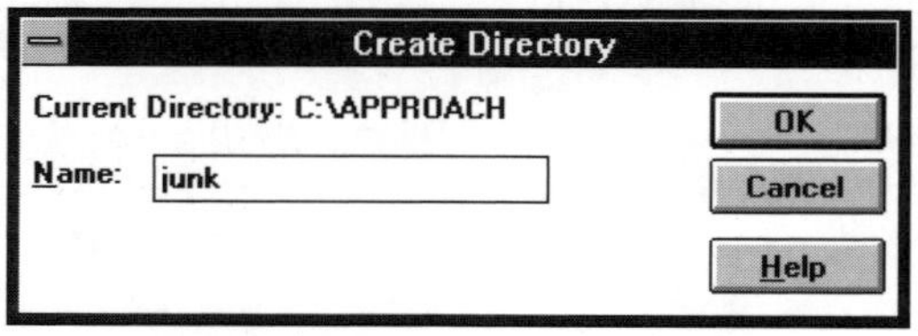

Figure B-4:
The Create Directory dialog box.

Create Directory	
Current Directory: C:\APPROACH	OK
Name: junk	Cancel
	Help

TECHNICAL STUFF

Using directories wisely

The biggest file-management mistake that most beginners make is dumping all of their files into one directory. Having only one directory is the electronic equivalent of storing all of your tax records in a shoe box. Sure, all the files are there, but finding anything is next to impossible. Show the shoe box to your accountant on April 14, and you'll be lucky if the accountant stops laughing long enough to show you how to file for an extension.

Use directories to organize your files. Don't just dump all your files into one directory. Instead, create a separate directory for each project and dump all of the files for each project into its directory. Although each directory may have several Approach files and database files in it, you won't have any trouble distinguishing your inventory database from your PTA mailing list database if you keep them in separate directories.

✔ Store as few files as possible in the root directory. The root directory is kind of like a fire lane which should be kept free for emergency vehicles at all times.

✔ Don't store Approach databases in the \APPROACH directory. The \APPROACH directory is where all of Approach's program files belong. You don't want your own files mingling with them.

✔ Nothing keeps you from storing files that belong to different application programs in the same directory. Each file's extension identifies the program that created the file. No need to segregate.

✔ Don't forget to clean out your directories periodically by deleting files you no longer need.

✔ The number of files that you can store in a directory is not limited, nor is the number of directories that you can create. The only exception to this rule is that the root directory can have no more than 254 files and subdirectories. For that reason, you should keep the root directory free of unnecessary files.

Formatting Floppy Disks

One common computer chore that users often do in File Manager is formatting floppy disks. File Manager's Disk➪Format Disk command is a welcome alternative to the bare-bones DOS Format command.

To format a floppy disk, follow these steps:

1. **Buy some floppy disks.**

2. **Fire up File Manager.**

   Double-click the File Manager icon in Program Manager's Main group or press Ctrl-Esc to pop up the task list and see whether File Manager is already running.

3. Choose File⊅Format Disk.

This command calls forth the friendly Format Disk dialog box, which is shown in Figure B-5.

Figure B-5:
The Format Disk dialog box.

Format Disk		
Disk In:	Drive A:	OK
Capacity:	1.2 MB	Cancel
Options		Help
Label:		
☐ Make System Disk		
☐ Quick Format		

4. If you have two floppy disk drives, pick the one that you want to use from the Disk In drop-down list.

The Disk In field is initially set to format disks in drive A. You have to change it if you want to format disks in drive B.

5. Insert a blank floppy disk into the drive and press OK.

6. When File Manager asks whether you really mean it, click Yes.

7. Wait while File Manager formats the disk.

After File Manager finishes formatting the disk, it asks whether you want to format another floppy disk, which makes formatting a batch of floppy disks easy.

8. Click Yes and repeat Steps 4 – 7 if you need to format more disks, or click No if you're finished.

✓ You can type a name for the floppy disk in the Label box if you want, but little purpose is served. I usually ignore the label.

✓ I hate formatting disks. I usually spend the extra buck or two to buy disks that are already formatted. So I hardly ever get to use this command. Sniff.

✓ When I buy floppy disks, I always look for special offers, such as "Free Game On Eleventh Disk." I've collected a couple of good games in recent years, including a great submarine simulation and a couple of pretty good card games. (Any day now I expect to see OS/2 offered free with a box of disks.)

✓ Formatting a disk wipes out any files that are stored on the disk. Unless you're formatting brand new disks right out of the box, always check the disk first to make sure that it doesn't contain any important files.

Backing Up Your Files

When was the last time you changed the oil in your car, took your dog for a walk, or backed up the files on your hard disk? The neglect of any of these three responsibilities can have disastrous consequences. This appendix isn't the time or place for a stern lecture about the importance of backing up, though, so I'll spare the soapbox.

The best way to back up your files is to use an Official Backup Program. If you have DOS 6.0 or 6.2, you're lucky: you already own a pretty decent backup program called Microsoft Backup. You should be able to find it buried somewhere in Program Manager, probably in a group named Microsoft Tools.

✔ Remember what I said about this not being the time or place for a lecture? Well, I lied. Back up your files every day. You never know when a stray asteroid will strike your city, possibly wiping out all human life and erasing your files too! Look what happened to Jupiter! Don't put it off. Back up *today*.

✔ Always have plenty of disks on hand for backups.

✔ You don't have to back up every file on your hard disk every day. Just back up the files that you changed that day. Microsoft Backup has a slick feature called *incremental backup* that does precisely that, and it does it automatically so that you don't even have to think about it.

✔ If you want to learn how to put Microsoft Backup to good use, check out Chapter 6 in *More Windows For Dummies* by Andy Rathbone.

Glossary

- -

Access
A database program made by Microsoft. Similar in many ways to Approach but a bit more complicated to use.

Ami Pro
A word processing program made by Lotus and included in SmartSuite.

Approach
Only the best database program ever.

Approach file
A file that contains the views, macros, and other Approach goodies needed to play with a database. Everything except the actual database data is stored in the Approach file; the data itself is stored in a separate *database file.*

Arithmetic expression
An expression that produces a numeric result.

Assistant
A special type of dialog box in Approach that guides you through a tedious process, such as creating a report or form letter.

axis
Not the bad guys in WWII, but the horizontal and vertical lines against which chart data is plotted. See *x-axis* and *y-axis.*

back up
What you ought to do to your files right now.

boolean field
A database field that can have only one of two possible values: Yes or No.

Browse mode
One of four basic modes that Approach works in. Browse mode enables you to examine and modify database records by using forms, reports, worksheets, and other views.

byte
A single character of information, such as a letter or numeral.

calculated field
A database field whose value is calculated based on a formula. The formula can refer to other fields. For example, a Sales Tax field may be calculated by multiplying the contents of a Subtotal field by a fixed tax rate.

chart
A type of database view in which database data is graphically represented as a line, bar, pie, or other type of graph.

Chart Assistant

An Assistant dialog box for creating new charts. See *Assistant.*

client

See *workstation.*

Clipboard

A magic place where snippets of data can be temporarily stored. To *copy* something to the Clipboard, select it and press Ctrl+C. To *cut* something to the Clipboard, select it and press Ctrl+X. To insert the contents of the Clipboard, place the cursor where you want the Clipboard contents inserted and press Ctrl+V.

Clouseau

The most dangerous man in all of France. Some people say he only plays the fool.

column

In relational database terminology, a *field.*

columnar report

A report layout in which database fields are arranged in columns and each database record is printed on a separate line. Field labels are printed in the report heading at the top of each page.

columnar with grand summary report

A report layout in which data is presented as in a columnar report, with the addition of a summary line at the end of the report.

comparison expression

An expression that produces a Yes or No result by comparing two values.

crosstab

An Approach database view in which groups of records are summarized and presented in worksheet format.

Crosstab Assistant

An Assistant dialog box for creating new crosstabs. See *Assistant.*

database

A collection of information, such as an address book, shoe box full of tax records, and so on. A *computer database* is what you get when you store this kind of information on your computer.

database file

A file used to store database data. Approach doesn't have its own special type of database file. Instead, it uses and creates database files in dBASE, Paradox, or FoxPro format.

date field

A database field that holds date values.

DB2

A humongous database program that is used mostly on mainframe computers. Approach can access data stored in a DB2 database but only when the appropriate voodoo incantations are spoken.

dBASE

The granddaddy of PC database programs. Many folks still use dBASE, even though better programs are available nowadays.

dedicated server

A computer used exclusively as a network server. See *server.*

default value
A value supplied for a field if the user does not enter a value.

delimited text file
A file in which each database record appears on a separate line and database fields are separated from one another by a *delimiter character,* usually a comma.

delimiter
The special character used to separate fields in a delimited text file, usually a comma.

Design mode
One of four basic modes in which Approach works. Design mode enables you to modify or create new forms, reports, worksheets, or other views.

Design object
Something you've added to a form or report, such as a database field, a bit of text, or a geometric object such as a circle or rectangle.

directory
A repository for files on a hard disk. If all of the files on a hard disk were stored in a single location, you'd never be able to organize and track them. Directories enable you to apply the concept of "divide and conquer" to your hard disk. Each directory has a name that can be up to eight characters in length.

disk
A device that stores information magnetically on a disk. A *hard disk* is permanently sealed in an enclosure and has a capacity usually measured in hundreds of megabytes. A *floppy disk* is removable and can have a capacity of 360K, 720K, 1.2MB, 1.44MB, or 2.88MB.

DOS
Disk Operating System, the most popular operating system for IBM and IBM-compatible computers.

DoubleSpace
A feature of MS-DOS 6.0 and 6.2 that compresses data so that it requires less disk space. DoubleSpace increases the effective capacity of the disk, often by a factor of 2:1 or more. Microsoft ran into some legal difficulties regarding DoubleSpace, so it replaced DoubleSpace with a similar compression program called DriveSpace in MS-DOS 6.22.

DriveSpace
A feature of MS-DOS 6.22 that compresses data so that it requires less disk space. DriveSpace increases the effective capacity of the disk, often by a factor of 2:1 or more. DriveSpace was Microsoft's response to legal problems it encountered with DoubleSpace.

duplicate record
A record that is identical to some other record in the database. According to true relational database theory, having identical records is not allowed. However, Approach allows duplicate records, turning its nose up at the Relational Zealots.

dynaset
In Microsoft Access, the result of a query. The same thing in Approach is called a *found set,* which is a much more sensible term. Dynasets don't have anything to do with Approach, but I included the term here to give you ammunition to use against people who think Access is easier to use than Approach.

export

Saving data from an Approach database in another format.

expression

A combination of operators and operands that yields a calculated result. See *formula*.

Fast Format

An Approach feature that enables you to apply the format of one object to another object.

field

One snippet of information, such as a customer's name, address, phone number, or zip code.

field object

A design object that shows the contents of a database field.

File Manager

A necessary but unpleasant part of Windows that enables you to copy, rename, and delete files as well as to create new directories and perform countless other boring file management chores.

filename

A name assigned to a file in DOS. The name can consist of up to eight letters and numbers, plus an optional three-letter *extension* that identifies the file type. The extension is separated from the rest of the filename with a period, and it usually serves to identify the type of file (for example, to distinguish a word processing file from a spreadsheet file).

Find mode

One of four basic modes that Approach works in. Find mode enables you to set up search criteria to initiate a find. When Approach has found the records that match the search criteria, it flips back to Browse mode so you can examine and modify the *found set.*

fixed-length text file

A file in which each database record appears on a separate line and each field occupies a fixed number of character positions.

foreign key

The term used by database zealots to refer to a field that corresponds to the primary key field of a different database. For example, the Customer Number field in an Invoice database is a foreign key (assuming that Customer Number is the primary key for the Customer Database).

form

A database view that presents database records in a manner that resembles a printed form, with just one database record shown on the screen at a time. Half the fun of using Approach is creating good-looking forms.

Form Assistant

An Assistant dialog box for creating new forms. See *Assistant.*

form letter

Junk mail you can send to people whose names and addresses are stored in an Approach database.

Form Letter Assistant

An Assistant dialog box for creating new
form letters. See *Assistant.*

formula

How the value for a calculated field is
determined. For example, the formula
`SubTotal * 0.065` can be used to calculate the value for a Sales Tax field.

found set

A table that consists of all the records that
match a search criteria.

FoxPro

Yet another database program sold by
Microsoft. Why so many Microsoft database
programs? Ask Bill Gates next time you see
him on the ferry.

Freelance Graphics

A desktop presentation program made by
Lotus and included in SmartSuite.

function

An Approach routine that you can include in
formulas to perform complex calculations,
such as calculating loan payments.

GB

Gigabyte, roughly one billion bytes (1024MB
to be precise). See *K, MB, TB,* and *byte.*

Golden Retriever

Definitely one of the less intelligent canine
varieties, one of which just dug up a plant in
my backyard.

graph

See *Chart.*

grid

A pattern of evenly spaced dots that can be
used to align objects while you are working
in Design mode.

group

Design objects that have been combined so
that they act as a single object.

guru

Anyone who knows more about computers
than you do.

icon bar

A row of icon buttons that serve as special
command shortcuts for Approach. The icon
bar is just below the menu bar.

import

Merging data from another source into an
existing Approach database.

InfoBox

A multitab dialog box that enables you to
control all formatting settings for a design
object.

Internet

A humongous network of networks that
spans the globe and gives you access to just
about anything you could ever hope for,
provided you can figure out how to work it.
This book has absolutely nothing to do with
Internet, but my editor said that Internet is a
hot buzzword in publishing these days and
that I should try to squeeze in something
about the Internet if I could. So here it is.

join

A way of connecting two databases that have a common field, such as a customer number or inventory part number. For example, a Customer database may be joined to an Invoice database so that all of the invoices for a particular customer can be seen. See *one-to-one join, one-to-many join, many-to-one join,* and *many-to-many join.*

join field

The field used to relate two databases involved in a join.

K

Kilobytes, roughly one thousand bytes (1024 to be precise). See *GB, MB, TB,* and *byte.*

LAN

Local area network, a network of computers that are relatively close to one another, generally in the same building. See *WAN.*

LANtastic

A popular peer-to-peer networking system. See *peer-to-peer network.*

layer

The position of a design object relative to other design objects, which is used to determine what happens when objects overlap. If two objects overlap, the object at the higher layer obscures the object at the lower layer.

leading grouped summary report

A report layout in which database records are grouped based on a database field and summary information is printed before and after each group of records.

lingua franca

A type of pasta consumed in mass quantities by Relational Database Zealots.

local resource

A disk drive, printer, or other device that is attached to a computer rather than accessed via the network. See *network resource.*

log in

What you have to do to access the network. Logging in identifies you to the network and grants you access to network resources.

logical expression

An expression that produces a Yes or No result, usually by combining two or more comparison expressions.

Lotus 1-2-3

A spreadsheet program made by Lotus and included in SmartSuite.

Lotus Chart

The charting mechanism used in all programs in Lotus SmartSuite (1-2-3, Ami Pro, Approach, and Freelance Graphics).

Lotus Organizer

An address book and calendar program made by Lotus and included in SmartSuite.

macro

A sequence of Approach operations that are carried out together. You can attach a macro to a macro button, to a view, or to a field.

macro button

A design object that looks like a dialog box button. The user can click the button to invoke a macro.

mailing label

Approach enables you to print mailing labels by using addresses stored in a database.

Mailing Label Assistant

An Assistant dialog box for creating new mailing labels. See *Assistant*.

mainframe computer

A huge computer housed in a glass house on raised floors. The cable that connects the disk drives to the CPU weighs more than most PCs. Approach has the ability to access data stored on a mainframe computer, but only after your friendly neighborhood mainframe computer programmers have figured out a way to make the connection to the mainframe work.

many-to-many join

A join in which records in one database can be related to many records in another database, and vice-versa. In Approach, you can't create many-to-many joins directly, but you can create them by creating an intermediate database that contains one record for each relationship between the two databases. For example, a Parts database that contains one record for each inventory item can have a many-to-many relationship with a Suppliers database that has one record for each supplier. In other words, each part may be supplied by more than one supplier, and each supplier can supply more than one part. An intermediate Part-Supplier database can be created that contains one record for each part-supplier combination.

many-to-one join

A join in which more than one record in one database can be related to a single record in another database. An example would be an Invoice database joined to a Customer database, where several invoice records can be related to a single customer record.

MB

Megabyte, roughly one million bytes (1024K to be precise). See *GB, K, TB,* and *byte*.

Media Player

The program needed to play video clips embedded in a database. The Media Player that comes with Windows 3.1 can't handle video, so you have to get an updated version by purchasing Microsoft Video for Windows. (You also can download a scaled-back version of Media Player from CompuServe.)

memo field

A database field that holds more text than a text field can accommodate.

menu bar

The row of menu choices that reclines atop most Windows application programs, including Approach.

metaphor

A literary construction suitable for Shakespeare and Steinbeck but a bit overused by computer book writers. Writers are supposed to yell "Phor!" before they use a metaphor.

Mood

Approach works in four distinct modes, which I call *moods:* Browse, Design, Find, and Preview. See *Browse mode, Design mode, Find mode,* and *Preview mode*.

NetWare

The chief priest of networks, the proud child of Novell Inc. NetWare requires at least one computer on the network to be set aside as a dedicated server.

network

A bunch of computers that are connected so that they can share information.

network resource

A disk drive, printer, or other device that is located in a server computer and accessed via the network, in contrast to a *local resource,* which is attached to a user's computer.

normalization

The process of eliminating unnecessarily duplicated database fields from a database design.

notetabs

Those tab divider things that appear at the top of many Approach dialog boxes and enable you to switch between various sets of dialog box controls.

numeric field

A database field that holds numbers.

object-oriented database

The latest in database religions. Its proponents believe that relational database is the root of all evil.

OLE

Object Linking and Embedding, a fancy feature of Windows 3.1 that you can use to include data that was created by one program in a file created by another program. OLE is the way to put sound bites and video clips in a database.

OLE object

A bit o' something that belongs to another program and is inserted into a database.

one-to-many join

A join in which each record in one database is related to one or more records in another database. An example is a Customer database joined to an Invoice database, where each customer record can be related to more than one invoice record.

one-to-one join

A join in which each record in one database can be related to only one record in the other database. An example is a Sales database that contains one record for each customer joined to a Credit database that also contains one record for each customer. In this example, each customer record in the Sales database is related to one customer record in the Credit database.

operand

A value that is used in an expression. An operand can be a number, a bit of text enclosed in quotes, or a database field.

operator

A symbol used in an expression to perform a mathematical operation, such as addition (+), subtraction (-), multiplication (*), or division (/).

optimistic record locking

A record locking technique in which Approach doesn't prevent multiple users from accessing records at the same time. However, Approach issues a warning if a user attempts to modify a record and Approach discovers that another user has snuck in and modified the same record while the first user wasn't looking.

panel

A portion of a report that contains a particular type of information, such as the report heading, fields for individual records, summary fields, and so on.

Paradox

A database program made by Borland. Definitely more difficult to use than Approach.

password

A secret code that enables you to access something on the computer. Approach enables you to protect databases by creating _read-write_ or _read-only_ passwords. Computer networks also use passwords so that only authorized users can access the network.

peer-to-peer network

A network in which any computer can be a server if it wants to be. Kind of like the network version of the Great American Dream. LANtastic and Windows for Workgroups are two popular peer-to-peer networking systems.

pessimistic record locking

A record locking technique, originally developed by the donkey Eeyore, in which Approach assumes that whenever one user wants to update a database record, another user will try to update the same record at the same time. Pessimistic record locking goes to great lengths to prevent other users from accessing a record that is being updated.

picture object

A design object that places a picture on a view. The picture can be any of several popular graphics file formats.

PicturePlus field

A database field that holds pictures or OLE objects.

polygamy

The practice of enabling one database to join with more than one other database.

Preview mode

One of four basic modes that Approach works in. Preview mode shows how a form, report, or other view will appear when printed.

primary key

A field that uniquely identifies each record in a database. Not every database requires a primary key, but a primary key is useful when you want to include the database in a join.

Program Manager

An unfortunately necessary part of Windows that is used to start application programs.

query

Approach doesn't use this term, but it refers to setting up the search criteria when you are working in Find mood.

read-only password

A password that enables you to read the contents of an Approach database but not to add new records or modify existing records.

read-write password

A password that enables you to read and modify the contents of an Approach database.

record

All of the information gathered in a database for a particular thing such as a person, inventory item, and so on. For example, in a customer database, each customer has one record. Each record has one occurrence of each database *field*.

record locking

A technique Approach uses to ensure that network users don't mangle a database record by modifying it at the same time. See *optimistic record locking*.

relational database

A religion whose followers believe that salvation will be awarded only to those who create databases that follow the relational database model. Approach closely adheres to the relational database model.

relational database model

A style of database in which data is stored in tables that are made up of rows and columns and that can be manipulated only in strict adherence to the principles of mathematical set theory.

repeating panel

A portion of a database form or report that shows one or more records that are related to a database record via a join.

report

A database view in which database records are listed in various ways so that meaningful information can be shown. Reports usually end up being printed.

Report Assistant

An Assistant dialog box for creating new reports. See *Assistant*.

row

In relational database terminology, a *record*.

ruler

A representation of a ruler, above and to the right of the design area, that is used to align design objects. Pressing Ctrl+J summons the ruler.

serial number

A special type of default value for a database field, in which each new record is assigned a number that is one greater than the previous record.

series

A collection of related numbers to be plotted in a chart. Lotus Chart can plot up to 23 series.

server

A computer that is on the network and shares resources with other network users. The server may be dedicated, which means its sole purpose in life is to provide service for network users, or it may be used as a workstation as well. See *workstation*.

shape object

A design object that places an ellipse, circle, rectangle, square, or line on a view.

SmartIcon

The trademark name that Lotus uses for *button*. SmartIcons are shortcuts for Approach commands.

SmartMaster

A combination of format and layout options that guarantees that your database views will look mahvelous.

SmartSuite

A big package that includes Lotus 1-2-3, Ami Pro, Approach, Organizer, Freelance Graphics, a 24-piece ratchet set, 6 Ginsu Knives, and a bird feeder all for one low, low price.

sneakernet

An inexpensive form of computer networking in which data is shared by copying the files to floppy disks and walking them between computers.

Sound Recorder

The program needed to play sounds embedded in a database. Sound Recorder comes with Windows and is buried in the Accessories Program Manager group.

SQL

See *Structured Query Language.*

SQL Server

A database program made by Microsoft and Sybase that requires the use of Structured Query Language. SQL Server is used mostly on large networks.

standard report

A report layout in which each database record is shown in a separate panel, with field labels printed adjacent to each field.

status bar

A row of useful information displayed at the bottom of the Approach screen. The status bar is filled with surprises — try clicking on various parts of it to see what happens.

Structured Query Language (SQL)

A query language for relational databases that was invented by a couple of computer science PhDs and is best used by other computer science PhDs. Approach can work with database programs that require SQL, but Approach itself does not use or require SQL. (By the way, SQL is pronounced *sequel.*)

summary only report

A report layout similar to a trailing grouped summary report, except that individual records are not shown. Instead, only summary totals are shown.

table

In relational database terminology, a *database.*

TB

Terrazzo bytes, imported from Italy. Just kidding. Actually, TB stands for terabytes, approximately one trillion bytes (1024GB to be precise). See *GB, K, MB,* and *byte.*

template

A predefined database that you can use as a model for your own databases. Approach comes with billions and billions of templates already set up for you.

text field

A database field that is made up of text characters, such as a name, address, product description, and so on. In Approach, text fields can be up to 255 characters in length.

text file

A file that can be edited by the DOS EDIT command. See *delimited text file* and *fixed-length text file.*

text object
A design object that places text on a view.

time field
A database field that holds time values.

TLA
Three Letter Acronym, such as *FAT* (File Allocation Table), *DUM* (Dirty Upper Memory), and *HPY* (hierarchical programmatic yodel).

Tools palette
A collection of design icon buttons that floats freely so you can position it anywhere on the screen. You can summon the Tools palette by pressing Ctrl+L.

trailing grouped summary report
A report layout in which database records are grouped based on a database field and summary information is printed after each group of records.

tuple
An esoteric mathematical term that proves that the people who invented the relational database model need to get a life.

validation
A way of keeping bad data out of a database. Approach enables you to set the following validation options: Unique, which means that each record in a database must have a different value for the field; From/To, which means that any value entered into the field must fall within a specified range; Filled in, which means that the field cannot be left empty; One of, which means that the field's value must be one of a list of values supplied when you design the database; Formula is true, which supplies a formula

that must be true for the field value to be accepted; In field, which enables you to look up the value in another database to validate it.

variable field
A field whose value can be set and examined by a macro.

view
A portal through which database data can be seen and manipulated. Approach enables you to create several types of views: forms, reports, worksheets, crosstabs, form letters, mailing labels, and charts.

votive candles
Short stubby candles often used in religious services or when attempting troublesome computer feats.

WAN
Wide Area Network, a network that is spread all over the city, state, or continent, as opposed to a *Local Area Network,* which is usually contained in a single building.

Welcome to Lotus Approach dialog box
A dialog box that appears whenever you start Approach or close an Approach file. You use this dialog box to quickly open an existing file or create a new file.

Windows
An "operating environment" that supposedly makes DOS computers easier to use but whose main purpose is to require users to purchase more memory and bigger hard disks.

Windows for Workgroups

A special version of Windows designed to create peer-to-peer networks. See *peer-to-peer network*.

worksheet

A database view in which Approach data is shown as a spreadsheet, where each record is a row and each field is a column.

Worksheet Assistant

An Assistant dialog box for creating new worksheets. See *Assistant*.

workstation

A computer that is on the network and has access to network data and devices. Also called a *client*.

x-axis

The line along the bottom of a chart that categorizes chart data.

y-axis

The line along the edge of a chart that scales chart values.

Index

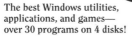

IDG BOOKS

Order Form

Order Center: (800) 762-2974 (8 a.m.-5 p.m., PST, weekdays) or (415) 312-0650

For Fastest Service: Photocopy This Order Form and FAX it to: (415) 358-1260

Quantity	ISBN	Title	Price	Total

Shipping & Handling Charges

Subtotal	U.S.	Canada & International	International Air Mail
Up to $20.00	Add $3.00	Add $4.00	Add $10.00
$20.01-40.00	$4.00	$5.00	$20.00
$40.01-60.00	$5.00	$6.00	$25.00
$60.01-80.00	$6.00	$8.00	$35.00
Over $80.00	$7.00	$10.00	$50.00

In U.S. and Canada, shipping is UPS ground or equivalent.
For Rush shipping call (800) 762-2974.

Subtotal _____
CA residents add applicable sales tax _____
IN and MA residents add 5% sales tax _____
IL residents add 6.25% sales tax _____
RI residents add 7% sales tax _____
Shipping _____
Total _____

Ship to:

Name _____

Company _____

Address _____

City/State/Zip _____

Daytime Phone _____

Payment: ❑ Check to IDG Books (US Funds Only)   ❑ Visa   ❑ Mastercard   ❑ American Express

Card# _____ Exp. _____ Signature _____

Please send this order form to: IDG Books, 155 Bovet Road, Suite 310, San Mateo, CA 94402.
Allow up to 3 weeks for delivery. Thank you!

IDG BOOKS WORLDWIDE REGISTRATION CARD

RETURN THIS REGISTRATION CARD FOR FREE CATALOG

Title of this book: Approach 3 For Windows For Dummies

My overall rating of this book: ❏ Very good [1] ❏ Good [2] ❏ Satisfactory [3] ❏ Fair [4] ❏ Poor [5]

How I first heard about this book:

❏ Found in bookstore; name: [6] _____ ❏ Book review: [7]

❏ Advertisement: [8] _____ ❏ Catalog: [9]

❏ Word of mouth; heard about book from friend, co-worker, etc.: [10] ❏ Other: [11]

What I liked most about this book:

_____
_____

What I would change, add, delete, etc., in future editions of this book:

_____
_____

Other comments: _____

Number of computer books I purchase in a year: ❏ 1 [12] ❏ 2-5 [13] ❏ 6-10 [14] ❏ More than 10 [15]

I would characterize my computer skills as: ❏ Beginner [16] ❏ Intermediate [17] ❏ Advanced [18] ❏ Professional [19]

I use ❏ DOS [20] ❏ Windows [21] ❏ OS/2 [22] ❏ Unix [23] ❏ Macintosh [24] ❏ Other: [25]_____

(please specify)

I would be interested in new books on the following subjects:
(please check all that apply, and use the spaces provided to identify specific software)

❏ Word processing: [26] _____ ❏ Spreadsheets: [27] _____

❏ Data bases: [28] _____ ❏ Desktop publishing: [29] _____

❏ File Utilities: [30] _____ ❏ Money management: [31] _____

❏ Networking: [32] _____ ❏ Programming languages: [33] _____

❏ Other: [34] _____

I use a PC at (please check all that apply): ❏ home [35] ❏ work [36] ❏ school [37] ❏ other: [38] _____

The disks I prefer to use are ❏ 5.25 [39] ❏ 3.5 [40] ❏ other: [41]_____

I have a CD ROM: ❏ yes [42] ❏ no [43]

I plan to buy or upgrade computer hardware this year: ❏ yes [44] ❏ no [45]

I plan to buy or upgrade computer software this year: ❏ yes [46] ❏ no [47]

Name: _____ Business title: [48] _____ Type of Business: [49] _____

Address (❏ home [50] ❏ work [51]/Company name: _____)

Street/Suite# _____

City [52]/State [53]/Zipcode [54]: _____ Country [55] _____

❏ **I liked this book!** You may quote me by name in future
IDG Books Worldwide promotional materials.

My daytime phone number is _____

IDG BOOKS

THE WORLD OF COMPUTER KNOWLEDGE

 **YES!**
Please keep me informed about IDG's World of Computer Knowledge.
Send me the latest IDG Books catalog.